THE ADVENTURE OF WILLIAM KILBURN MOSCROP
BOOK OF THE CRUISE

THE YOUNGER CHURCHMEN
LOOK AT THE CHURCH

THE MACMILLAN COMPANY
NEW YORK · BOSTON · CHICAGO · DALLAS
ATLANTA · SAN FRANCISCO

MACMILLAN & CO., Limited
LONDON · BOMBAY · CALCUTTA
MELBOURNE

THE MACMILLAN COMPANY
OF CANADA, Limited
TORONTO

THE
YOUNGER CHURCHMEN
LOOK AT THE CHURCH

EDITED BY

RALPH H. READ

Former President of the Conference of Younger Churchmen
Minister of the Hollis Avenue Congregational Church,
Bellaire, Long Island

WITH AN INTRODUCTION BY

KIRBY PAGE

NEW YORK

THE MACMILLAN COMPANY

1935

SET UP BY BROWN BROTHERS LINOTYPERS
PRINTED IN THE UNITED STATES OF AMERICA
BY THE FERRIS PRINTING COMPANY

PREFACE

It is not the purpose of this book to offer a new set of
destructive criticisms of the Christian Church. In a measure
the Church has already suffered from too many such attacks,
and from the fact that her own adherents have placed too
little faith in her. The people have lost their faith in the
value of the Church partly because the Church's own leaders
do not have such faith. In fact, the leaders have been altogether too persuasive in convincing others of the fact that
the Church is weak. This book will have failed in its mission, if it should come to be regarded primarily as an attack
upon the Church. To the degree that the book is polemic in
character it is such with but one end in view, namely, that
through the redemption of the Church it may be able to re-
deem society. As far as I know, every man who has contributed to this book is a firm believer in the Church.

The editor is of the personal conviction that, if the Church
is to contribute in a real way to the salvation of human society, a salvation which its own principles demand and imply,
it will require that men give the Church a new kind of loyalty and belief. Our generation has in a large way forgotten
how to be loyal. Men have come to regard the Church as a
helpful but not too necessary an adjunct to life. "A man can
be just as good a Christian outside the Church as inside it";
so men say. And the preacher has agreed that it is so. We
have failed to add that, if the statement is true it is because
the Church has set certain forces and principles to work in

society which have indirectly given us the benefits of religious effort without our present contribution to the continuance of religious principles in life. We may imagine that it is possible to live without the Church. But if we fail to make some contribution to its on-going in human society, future generations may not find it to be so.

Failing in all else the Christian Church dare not fail in its task of character creation, for the success of the good society will be determined in a great way by the character of the men who sustain it. The present moral and spiritual poverty of the Church can only be modified as men give their loyalty to her, making her what they want her to be. Without the finest loyalty of her members, the Church will not be able to muster sufficient strength to save either herself or the world in which she lives. And there are compensations in being loyal of which our generation knows little.

But character is both an influence upon and a victim of life. It is safe to say that that part of our world, which is of capitalistic domination and origin, is doing more to destroy character of the right sort than to create it. There have been those periods in human history when ideals were more determinative of the course of human events than economic facts. It is hardly so today. Our world is being driven by the relentless logic of economic circumstance, at least partly because our moral and spiritual ideals are powerless to resist this determinism. Christianity has always stood for the moral determination of history. It has challenged man to be the master of his fate rather than a poor pawn in the chess game of life. But man's contemporary ideals and moral standards have grown so perceptibly weak that he is as helpless before the tides of life as a rudderless ship that is tossed helplessly upon the tides of the sea.

Our character forming ideals have been fighting a losing battle in recent times because of the evils which have arisen out of a mechanical and industrial age. These evils have produced a paganism which destroys spiritual values faster than spiritual agencies can create them. As they are kicked about and disillusioned by the ruthlessness of the economic order, in which through awful struggle they seek to survive, men lose the hope and meaning which life should give to them. In turn the Church also falls prey to the disillusionment of this process. It has suffered correspondingly with the individual.

It would seem to be fair to assert that it is the general belief of the writers of this book that the Church will be able to save herself only as she struggles without surrender against those forces which menace her existence. The supremacy of spiritual ideals and belief in life's meaning can only be restored as men are able to reorganize their physical environment in such a way as to give character a chance. Paradoxically, as it may seem, character will also be needed in bringing this change to pass.

Disintegration and decay is taking place today within the whole of western civilization. As in the days of the corn doles of ancient Rome, which were but outward symbols of inner decay, so today, declining living standards, depreciated cultural possibilities, vast multitudes on public relief, and starvation are the outward manifestations of a disintegrating world. The failure of thousands to find meaning in the process is a by-product and not a cause.

It is the editor's conviction that the Church, while it may not become partisan in so doing, is the one institution which should, in the nature of things, become the strongest force in checking this disintegration. The disintegration itself is not inevitable. The future is entirely within the jurisdiction of man to mold. What the Church thinks about herself, her life, her mission in the world; what the Church leads society to think and to do, will become the deciding factor. The mighty uncontrolled inventions of man's mind have been released upon an unsuspecting life. We have created a huge monster which we have not yet learned to manage. Our future depends upon our learning this management. Without it society must needs slip into another dark ages, or at best into an untenable chaos. History has presented the Church with a kind of problem which she has never had to face before. This book is an attempt, small as it may be, to help the church discover herself in her new world. It is an attempt to guide the Church into a better day. If it seems extreme, it is because the writers are of the conviction that only an extreme solution will suffice to meet an extremely difficult problem.

The editor has also felt that there should be some value in approaching this problem from the particular viewpoint of the younger churchman; hence the title. Though conscious that youth is relatively more a matter of spirit than of years, nevertheless he has endeavored to make the voice of the younger man articulate. The venture will have to stand or fall upon its own merit. The editor wishes to acknowledge his great gratitude to the contributors for their faith, work and counsel, and also to the Conference of Younger Churchmen which has furnished inspiration for many of these pages.

RALPH H. READ.

March, 1935.

INTRODUCTION

THESE invigorating chapters constitute another link in the chain of evidence that a revolution in thought is sweeping through the ranks of clergymen in this nation. Wide contact with countless ministers in all sections of the country extending over the past fifteen years convinces me that there is a strong possibility of tearing away from support of the existing social order a substantial proportion of the professional leadership of the churches. At this moment there is probably more economic and political radicalism among younger ministers than can be found among the members of any other vocational or professional group in the United States.

Once more the fact is being demonstrated that religious institutions are not always opium for the people. It is true that with nauseating frequency the churches have attached themselves like barnacles to the hulk of iniquitous institutions and have sanctioned monstrous social customs and collective practices. Yet the churches throughout the centuries have given birth to innovators and insurgents. Too often the radicals nurtured by religion have been thrust out of the sacred precincts and compelled to face the fury of frightened conservatives. Jesus was crucified as a revolutionist, and of the early Christians it was said that "they who turn the world upside down have come here also." Some religionists in every generation have thrown off the shackles of vested interests through the compelling dynamic of a vision of the city of God and through an experience of glorious comradeship with the Eternal.

Some of the ablest and most zealous young radicals in America are to be found in ministerial circles. Literally hundreds of these gifted leaders I know personally and they cause me to be highly confident that during the critical days ahead a substantial section of the churches will throw its strength on the side of non-warlike revolution. It may well be that the churches hold the balance of power in the social struggle. The boundless significance of the middle class in the United States increases the responsibility of the churches, since religion is still a dominant force in the lives of millions of these people. One may say dogmatically that without the allegiance of vast numbers of middle-class men and women, there is no hope whatever that pacific revolution can be wrought in this country. If the middle class marches along solidly with vested interests in support of the status quo, then it is only a question of time until our liberties will be destroyed by a fascist dictatorship. If the American people drift blindly along without a clear realization of the alternatives before them and without resolute efforts to guide their own destinies, this continent will yet be visited with devastating civil war and unimaginable chaos.

That the churches will be torn asunder during the momentous days just ahead is altogether probable. Surely it is far more desirable to face a division, as painful as this will be, than to have the churches continue to support capitalism and war with all their intolerable evils. The successful revolutionist must combine depth of spiritual experience, warmth of affection for even those members of his congregation who oppose him, accuracy and fairness in the presentation of data, unswerving attachment to non-warlike methods of social change, high personal courage and sacrificial willingness to accept whatever consequences flow from resolute loyalty to his highest insights and deepest convictions. It is quite certain that the present generation will witness martyrdom not unlike that of earlier centuries. It is still true that genuine Christians are sent out as lambs among wolves and that the day will come when men will think that they are doing God a service by putting them to death.

Because many of the contributors to the present volume are in the forefront of the struggle for social justice, it is altogether likely that some of them will be compelled to drink the dregs of bitter persecution. As for myself, I glory in their insight and sanity and daring. They have been raised up for such a time as this. Let the reader, therefore, absorb the burning message of these chapters with far more than ordinary seriousness. Herein we are dealing with matters of life-and-death significance to our civilization.

KIRBY PAGE.

CONTENTS

CONTENTS

THE TRAGEDY OF THE CHRISTIAN CHURCH

RALPH H. READ

CHAPTER I

THE TRAGEDY OF THE CHRISTIAN CHURCH

THE Church stands before the judgment seat of the world. She is on trial before the ceaseless tides of human events and creatures. The new world which the Church is to build is not on trial, for it has not yet been created. Decision cannot be passed on what does not exist. But the Church, now centuries old, stands before the tribunal of the world acquitted or convicted, as the case may be. Her sins, which are many, are all of her own household, but they react upon the destiny of men and of nations. Her ideals, perennially powerful, are both discounted and marked down whenever they are outweighed by the evils within her walls. Serious introspection on occasions is therefore not out of place.

The world moves on. Only in a small way has the Church been able to keep pace with the revolutionary changes of its day and generation. The speed with which history moves makes watchfulness an imperative necessity. Little wonder the Church finds itself too often late! Its songs and theology are still bound in its dead though glorious past. Its prayers are still being said, and perhaps it is true as the old hymn has it, "A Thousand years the same." More serious even is the Church's inability to realistically interpret and understand the economic society in which it lives. Other non-religious groups have succeeded, in part at least, in such an understanding. However, the Church is only now beginning its

3

attempt to study in realistic fashion those forces and factors in the life of our economic society which do so much to predicate its well-being in one way or another. The Niebuhrs and the Wards have come none too soon to the Church's aid. In part they have saved us from complete sentimentality.

On the human side a hostile temper toward the Church is to be found among multitudes of serious and thoughtful people. The disappearance of Christendom is now an acknowledged fact. Its passing has been followed by a secular civilization which tends to put its sole trust in man. The consequent cynicism, arising out of humanistic endeavor that is separated from divine resource, reacts in turn to produce a disillusioned church. Disillusioned churches fail to inspire or render hopeful a despairing world. Again, the Church is no longer "the institution" in society but is counted as one among many. Many of these other institutions are doing effective work in building a better world. Some of them, indeed, may be doing more effective work than the Church.

These conditions are like connecting links in a chain which binds the whole institution to other regrettable situations. Good men whose desires and sympathies are Christian are thereby alienated from the Church's domains. It is not possible to estimate how many people, Christian at heart, are outside the Church today. Their number is great. These are also people whose hopes are united with those of religion. They are out because they feel that the Church is only little interested in dealing with the social sins which bid fair today of destroying all those cultural and spiritual values which the Church has prized.

In a sense, we have had nineteen centuries of Christian history but no Christianity. It is odd to speak of a Christian world or Christian nations. The mutual relations of the various peoples of all races have in them very little of the spirit of Jesus, the founder of Christianity. Our penal system still functions largely upon a principle of revenge. Many of our customs and laws are either vicious or immoral. Government still puts property above human rights. While millions of citizens live on a low physical and spiritual plane, and are denied the inalienable right of creative toil; and while children starve or suffer malnutrition from poor diet, the government designed for their welfare spends millions for mass butcheries to protect the investments of her privileged men of commerce. And the money is spent in the name of self-defense, which makes its spending the more ironical.

In a desperate attempt to discover a way out of this kind of an inhuman situation men take on revolutionary ideas of life. Such men within and without the Church are called "radicals" with no small amount of disdain attached to the use of the term. Within and without the Church they are regarded as a little outside of the pale of respectability. Hence their principles of life are discarded and they are persecuted in one way or another. Thinking ofttimes that they should find shelter and understanding in that institution which accepts Jesus as Master, they knock at the doors of the Church. But, as is its habit, the Church sees in them only unbelievers whom it needs to convert. It looks upon them as men of the world who are out to destroy.

Its own radical clergy is treated with little better veneration. The Church sees us as being uncertain. It regards us as being a shade off-color. We are possibly out of touch with God or unconcerned as to whether other men shall know

Him. The Church fails to realize that we believe in God no less because we desire the kind of world in which it may be possible for all men to believe in Him. As Carlyle once expressed it, if the lamp of the body is gone out how shall the soul be lighted. Men living in a society organized in opposition to eternal values are little apt to believe in them.

We, at least some of us, believe no less than all the others who waste many words in their talk of belief. Faith is love above all else. It is sympathy. It is concern for the last and least among the brethren. It is wonder and beauty and righteousness. It is not a mere passive standard or holy day. It is not simply a mechanically learned text or creed, but a way of life. It is not wearisome ritual nor the emotional exaltation of crosses and candles, lovely as these things may be. It is justice and mercy and compassion without which men never find God a reality. We want that Christ may have a chance at men's hearts. We do not desire to have his face hidden from the world by stocks and bonds and ruthless competition of man against man. Our golden calf is not the stockticker nor the counting board. Our ideal for men is not that their souls shall be ground down by the incessant rattle and grating of one cog upon another. We do not desire the snuffing out of their spirits in black mines, dark cellars or windowless factories wherein the light of day is seldom seen. Only sterile religion, ingrown, selfish, and compromised by wealth and softness does nothing about such things. The religion of Jesus must speak in terms audible and distinct.

In the Church there are literally multitudes of people who regard these interests as mundane or political, as being in no way a part of the gospel's concern. Between such persons, and those who know that to be interested is to be Christian, there is fixed a spiritual gulf which is as wide as the ocean. That gulf makes the highest kind of fellowship difficult if not impossible. No mingling of lovely ritual or sanctimonious stained glass will requite the soul of one who would find God in the difficult struggle for a better world.

There are children of modernity, victims of a pagan age and an irreligious temper, blinded by undigested scientific knowledge, who remain outside of the Church because of an understandable lack of sympathy for the good the Church would accomplish or appreciation of that for which it stands. The Church can scarcely be held responsible when it fails to enlist the support of these people. But what shall be able to save that church which drives thousands of kindred spirits, kindred of Christ, out into a lonely world to fellowship alone, without that spirit of life which the Church ought to provide? By turning in a reactionary way against the highest ethical implications of Jesus' gospel the Church loses many of its finest sons and daughters.

Theoretically, there is a certain amount of splendid interest. The depression and its glaring iniquities are raising up a new mood within the Church. Thousands are not as confident concerning the status quo and Christianity's relationship to it as they once were. A greater spirit of tolerance to radical ideas is prevalent. But the active interest is still confined to a minority group of leaders in the institution who are themselves too much tied to existing arrangements to be able to do much about it. The amount of following which these progressive leaders of the Church have among their own laity is questionable.

The rest either lack the required knowledge for interest

or are content with the rationalized dictum, "we will inspire people in the right way and our social problems will solve themselves." This reasoning of those who know conditions, and who yet choose not to be bothered, has in it more force than might at first be evident. A deeply inspired and spiritually illuminated body of people might feel driven to do many things in the direction of wiping out economic tyranny and injustice, and in building a better world than they are now doing. But aside from carrying on the usual methods of weekly worship, keeping open the traditional avenues of preaching, and the maintenance of the recreational features of institutionalized religion, there is slight evidence that the Church is even able to deeply inspire her members in their consciousness of God. Evidences of this failure find expression both in the peculiarities and strength of the Oxford Group Movement. The movement is a spontaneous answer to a spiritual need that has not been adequately provided. Such a movement, left to people of limited social vision, possesses a usefulness in the rebuilding of human society that is of doubtful value.

The springing up of heterogeneous movements in personal religion within the Church, unofficially launched, suggests the fact that the Church has not only failed in the creation of a Christian organization of society's life, but that it has also of late been unable to properly cultivate the spirit-life in its members. True religion and undefiled ought to minister to the widows and fatherless and to give spiritual sight to the morally blind. It should bring men into right relationships with themselves, with others, and with God. If the Christian religion is not to decay at its very roots, it will have to witness within its organization a rebirth of vital personal faith.

Personal religion minus social insight is no guarantee of the fruits of righteousness in society. Man's spirit-life must be augmented by the enlightenment of intelligent perception, and the sanity of clear mental sight into the ethical implications of the Christian gospel. Only thus will religious life be able to count in the battle for a better world. Having said this, the fact remains that the warm personal religion of the soul, out of which man develops his living experience of God and the love of God, constitutes the only soil rich enough in which to plant the seeds of a new society.

In saying this we do not mean that Christian people are the only people who are able to make a lasting contribution to a better world. Though the Communist may not describe his experience as we do, still he may live closer to the heart of God than does many a Christian. Who is this God who is so small and bigoted as to demand a label to be known? They know God who do his will.

All men experience God in some period in life to a greater or lesser extent. In the midst of the Areopagus in Athens Paul recognized the ignorant worship of the same God whom he himself worshiped in a more intelligent manner. The savage who bows down to wood and stone is conscious of the same spirit of life as are we. The spirit broods and men are conscious of its brooding. They cannot tell its going out or its coming in. The worship of the savage may be viewed only as more unenlightened. He may call his idol Buddha or something else, but it is still God. He feels the same God that we feel. Likewise, the hated radical may do the will of the righteous Marx; and Marx was more righteous than are many of us. The God of the radical may be the cosmic power of his deterministic ideal. But whenever the political radical comes into contact with reality and that reality is true, he is experiencing God. The label is not important. Only the degree of intelligence and right spirit is important and matters. God is truth. God is right. God is righteous reality obeyed in life. Our conceptions of God are not always right, not even our Christian conceptions. But the right that is in them is God's right.

Without doubt the Christian conception of God is the highest conception known to our world. It is the highest not because it is Christian, and with the genuine label of Christianity, but because it appears to have the most right in it. Whenever anyone, inside our faith or without it, lives better by that right than do we who profess the name, he is more Christian than are we though we may despise the label. Life and life's good count for more than labels. Persons are of greater worth than systems. The search for truth and goodness gives meaning to life. Truth makes men free whether it be the truth of Marx or of Jesus. And all truth is God's truth.

However, it is at the point of limited truth that religion and religious movements fail. Any religious movement which dogmatically limits the area of truth which may be explored is destined to a correspondingly limited existence. You cannot confine the approach to God and truth, for to do so is to refuse power which would otherwise be available. Religion cannot confine itself to a narrow area of the mind. It must likewise allow for differences in temperament. It must create a healthy physical environment in order to achieve a rich spiritual existence. Movements which would save men without saving their society are doomed before they begin. The answer that is given by a well-known contemporary movement in religion when confronted by the demands of social religion, "Oh, I see you are talking about economics. This is religion," demonstrates a handicapped spiritual vision. With such vision men are still left unregenerate. One may recognize these weaknesses in certain religious movements without altogether condemning them or failing to appreciate the good they accomplish. But the light shines greatest where widest truth permits God to touch the broadest area in man's soul and in its environment.

Those whose souls have been stirred and fanned by the breath of God into a living flame compose the soil in which may be nurtured the seeds of a reconstructed society. But the seeds are stifled by unrealistic interpretations of human society that are cultivated in the bland softness of economic privilege. The soul is also impoverished by selfish techniques and petty personal concerns which engross the individual in trivialities of guidance in those matters in which the person involved might well use his own mind. Tragically enough, men are starving while other men who lay claim to being good are naïvely assuming that the world will be made better when men are sufficiently Christian to mean well. A religious movement which is desirous of success will need a better understanding of the nature of progress. This understanding and its fruits in spiritual living await a better insight into the various aspects of the nature of life. The brutal as well as the good qualities of life must be appreciated, if a good society is to be created.

Personal salvation is as much a necessity as is social salvation, and the one cannot be had without the other. It is curiously significant that the Church was unable to effectively save the individual even in the days in which it was most zealous to do so. In part that failure was the result of an inadequate ideal of salvation. Because the churchman of yesterday did not know that Christian character is made difficult in an un-Christian social order, there was created within the Church a host of men economically materialistic; softened by the finer graces and amenities of life but a good bit less than Christian.

The phases of church life that have been narrated in this chapter constitute the tragedy of the Christian Church of which there is no greater. Together they form the reasons for the impotence of the Church. In the last chapter of this book I shall endeavor to outline a positive approach which the Church may take in a solution of these problems. It is a difficult order to plan for the salvation of the Church. However, it is a task which must be undertaken. Failure to begin the attempt can no longer be delayed. Therefore let us now consider the different aspects of the problem.

THE WORLD NEEDS THE CHURCH

JOHN COLEMAN BENNETT

CHAPTER II

THE WORLD NEEDS THE CHURCH

THE world's need of the Church (the existing organized Churches) is obscured both because the contributions of the Church are taken for granted and because the self-sufficient secularism which is characteristic of our time has created the illusion that the Church is unnecessary. Yet it is true that the modern world desperately needs the Church. It needs the Church to represent the things of God and to help people to lead the Christian life. It needs the Church as a protection against the encroachment of the Fascist state. It needs the Church to hold mankind together in the face of nationalism and the threat of war. It needs the Church to moderate the social struggle and turn the scale on the side of economic justice.

To say that the world needs the Church is to imply that there is some hope that the Church can meet that need at least in part. Before we set forth the need more fully it is necessary to consider briefly the present capacity of the Church to do its work in the world.

There is nothing which is easier to do than to write an indictment of the Church—the more so because the Church keeps alive in the world the standards by which it is judged.

NOTE.—Charles Scribner's Sons have kindly given us permission to repeat in Mr. Bennett's article some of the ideas used in his book, *Social Salvation*, which they are bringing out this Spring.—THE EDITOR.

We all know the bad side of the record: the persecutions which stain it red, the subservience of the Church to the nation, its support of economic privilege, its resistance to scientific truth, its futile divisions, its ecclesiastical pettiness, its compromises for the sake of power, the periods in which its clergy have been notorious for putting self-indulgence before the cure of souls. These things are in the record. Most of them are true in some degree in parts of the Church today. But they are known and condemned even more by sensitive churchmen than by outside critics of the Church.

The record has another side which is not so well known, partly because it is what one would expect to find. The Church has had its heroic periods, periods of spiritual devotion, intellectual power, and practical achievement. It has raised up many spirits who will always be a light to the world. In the days of its more spectacular faults the stream of spiritual life was never stopped and the truths which the Church represents were dimmed but never hidden. What is of more importance for our purpose is that today the Church is going through a period of reform along many lines which promise much for the future. It is adjusting itself in new ways to the needs of the world and to the loss of many of the props which in the past have given it artificial influence; such props as state support, respectability, a wide assumption of external authority, and the fear of hell.

Today the Church is coming to terms with modern knowledge, though it can never come to terms with many of the assumptions of modern culture. Its seminaries, with important exceptions, work on the assumption that there must be harmony between Christian faith and the assured results of science and historical criticism. The Church is in the act of purging itself of many of its ecclesiastical abuses. One evidence of this is that it is engaged in the most rigorous self-criticism. One would have to go far to find more drastic criticism of the Church than is to be found in religious weeklies. There have been surveys and surveys of the work of Church boards and educational institutions which indicate a wholesome spirit of self-criticism. A further evidence of this purging of abuses is the growth in interdenominational coöperation and the increase of Church mergers within the last two decades. The Church is learning to avail itself of the resources of science in the understanding and the healing of souls. Many efforts are being made to train ministers so that they will know enough psychology to give them insight into normal people for the prevention of mental sickness and the general guidance of life and to enable them to recognize cases which need expert psychiatric care. The Church is reexamining its relation to the nation. A surprising number of churchmen have repented of their part in the last war and intend, at all costs, to break completely with the war system. Finally the Church is beginning to realize that it has often been blind in its acceptance of the economic *status quo* and that there is a fundamental conflict between Christianity and capitalism as we have known it.

Obviously there are many exceptions to these general statements about the Church. Indeed if one were to judge the Church by counting heads of Christians in all parts of the world such statements would themselves represent the exceptions. There remain profound differences in the degree of adjustment to the world's needs between denominations and between different geographical sections. But all that is claimed here is that there are vital currents in the life of the

Church which are going in the directions suggested. They
are sufficiently representative of the leadership of the Church
to give not certainty but reasonable ground for hope that
the Church can go far in meeting the needs of the world
which are the subject of this chapter.[1]

1. *The World Needs the Church to Represent the Things of God and to Help People to Live the Christian Life*

There has never been a time when people needed more
than they need today the message, ministry, and worship of
the Church. Life has become so fragmentary and civilization
has destroyed for multitudes of people so many of the things
which protect the soul from disintegration—normal family
life, roots in the life of a community, creative work, contacts
with nature—that the things for which the Church stands are
the only things left to give wholeness to life. Moreover, if

---

[1] In the main the above statements are intended to apply to the Protestant Churches though there are encouraging signs also in the Catholic
Church, especially its growing concern for social justice and its resistance
to the Nazis in Germany. When the Church is mentioned in this chapter
the reference will be to the Protestant Churches unless the Catholic
Church is named. This is not the result of Protestant prejudice but of
the limits of space and of the writer's knowledge and of the fact that
Protestantism has a more strategic place than Catholicism in America.

The writer is aware that he is making statements which will appear
sweeping to those who are primarily critics of the Church without giving
evidence. He would point to the curriculum of many a theological
seminary which is an important prophecy for the future, to the work of
Church boards of education in modernizing and enriching the material
used in religious education, to such an agency as "The Council for
Clinical Training of Theological Students" which has made an important
start in giving seminary students training in mental hospitals, to the
kind of books which are chosen by the Religious Book of the Month
Club, to the influence of such a journal as the *Christian Century*, to the
social pronouncements of many official Church bodies and the social work
of Church boards and the Federal Council of Churches, and to the results
of the recent questionnaire sent to ministers on war and the economic
order. Those are all important straws. Put them together and they make
an impressive showing. They are ground not for complacency but for
hope.

the Christian faith in God is no illusion, then the world apart from the Church is a strange caricature of the real world. It has lost its true direction, its sense of proportion, and people live in a narrow segment of their real environment. To make these statements clearer it is important to set forth some of the things which are taken for granted which the Church does and which no other existing institution can take its place in doing.

The Church is the only institution in the world which stands for the revelation of God in Christ and mediates that truth and its implications to the individual at every stage in his life, day after day and year after year, at times of crisis and in life's routine. If it were not for that quiet and steady work of the Church where would the average individual come in contact with Christian truth or where, for that matter, would he come in contact with any coherent interpretation of life?

The Church is the only institution which deliberately offers people opportunity for public worship and seeks to train them in private worship.

The Church is the only institution which continually holds up the Christian ideal of life. Here its work does overlap with the work of other institutions such as schools, much secular literature, the law, and many organizations which seek the realization of specific ideals. But at its best the Church holds up an ideal which is higher and more inclusive.

The Church is the only institution which has the definite task of preserving within its life the influence of the faith of earlier generations and of undergirding the faith of the present with the faith of the past.

The Church, more than any other institution, provides in

most communities a spiritual fellowship which is essential to the higher and deeper life of most people. Where the local Church is inadequate, as it often is for more sophisticated Christians, the larger Church does throw up within its life groups and movements which in various ways supply this need of fellowship.

The Church is probably the only institution which stands for the whole of life in the modern community in a day in which every profession is specialized and education is secularized.

The Church counsels and befriends people in the hardest places of life.

The Church is a home for new agencies and movements before they have become self-supporting in the community. In this way it brings into many communities resources for adult education, recreation, clinical help which may be no part of the primary work of the Church but which are neglected by other more specialized agencies, and which belong to the work of the Church in so far as they meet human need which would not otherwise be met. One of the best illustrations of this work of the Church is the fact that ministers are taking a large part of the initiative in the neglected field of sex education and the preparing of people for marriage. Another is that the Church sometimes gives a meeting place to unpopular minorities. In giving a start to new attempts to lift the life of the community the Church is playing an old part which suggests the days when religion was the parent of the sciences and the arts which later achieved independence.

In these ways the Church helps people to live the Christian life. It could be put more broadly: the Church helps people to go on in the face of the problems of personal living. It is not claimed that the Church usually performs these functions well but rather that in the case of most of them there is no other institution whose business it is to perform them at all.

There is a common notion that the Church in the performance of these functions may be in time supplanted by psychiatrists and mental hygiene clinics. The psychiatrist often does give indispensable guidance for the individual. He may teach the Church much which it needs to learn. He may be the only one who can at certain points remove obstacles to the full Christian life. But there are limits to his work which time will not overcome. The relation of the psychiatrist to the things for which the Church stands is comparable to the relation of the physician to such indispensable means to health as fresh air, good food, and sanitation. It is no reflection upon the importance of the physician's work to say that he cannot take the place of these factors. So the Church provides the stuff out of which the healthy soul is made. It brings standards, goals, fellowship, an interpretation of life, and an experience of God which keep people spiritually well. It does much of the work of prevention and, if a cure is needed, the things which the Church represents help people to remain cured.

There is a fine statement of the relation between the work of the Church and that of the psychotherapist in C. G. Jung's *Modern Man in Search of a Soul,* especially the last chapter. Jung gives one interesting bit of testimony which is worth quoting: "Among all my patients in the second half of life— that is to say, over thirty-five—there has not been one whose problem in the last resort was not that of finding a religious outlook on life. It is safe to say that every one of them fell ill because he had lost that which the living religions of every age have given to their followers, and none of them has been really healed who did not regain his religious outlook. This of course has nothing whatever to do with a particular creed or membership of a Church." (Page 265.) It is only fair to say that Jung also shows how little confidence people who need help have in the Protestant clergy at present.

2. *The World Needs the Church as a Protection against the Encroachment of the Fascist State*

The growth of dictatorships with their claims to regiment the whole of life is one of the most alarming facts in the world. In too many countries all the values of responsible government, in the civil liberties of minorities have been thrown to the winds. When that happens, liberty disappears from most areas of life and truth goes with it. All that remains is the will of the strongest. Against that menace there is no more important protection than the Christian Church.

The mere existence of the Church is an obstacle to the complete regimentation of life, for the Church by its very nature claims a degree of spiritual freedom which cannot tolerate the claims of the totalitarian state. Even the state Churches of Germany, schooled since the time of Luther in subservience to the state, have been fighting bravely for their spiritual freedom and have not lost yet.

When the Church combines with this claim to spiritual freedom—which is what the German Protestant Churches are fighting for—the teaching of a social ethic which makes a frontal attack upon the policies of the state, the protection which the Church provides against the state is far greater. The fight against the application of the Aryan clause to the

Church is by implication a criticism of the state's anti-semitic policy—but the criticism remains implicit. The Church in America for a generation has done much sowing of the seed of a social ethic in the very field in which Fascist tares are most likely to grow—the middle classes. The habit of ethical criticism which such teaching does develop, combined with the Church's natural claim to spiritual freedom, may well be America's chief protection against Fascism. In comparison with it the liberalism of the universities will probably appear like a rope of sand. As for the labor movement and the radicals, the former in its opportunism is in danger of being swept in any direction, and the latter would be the first victims of, rather than obstacles to the success of Fascism. The strategic importance of the Church as a protection against Fascism is no ground for churchmen to become complacent. The American Churches are by no means ready for such a struggle and if the struggle comes it will try as by fire those minority groups within the Church which will bear the brunt of it. All that is claimed here is that the Church has within its life the resources for which to be thankful if the day of struggle comes.

3. The World Needs the Church to Hold Mankind Together in the Face of Nationalism and the Threat of War

The Church is one of the few international fellowships which can undercut the wild nationalism which is the order of the day. In the past its failure to do this has been tragic. The Catholic Church for all of its international power has preferred to allow its own people to go to war with each other without excommunication than run the risk of having a considerable number of them choose the nation against the

Church. Its attitude has been complicated by the persistence
within its social ethic of the idea of the divine ordination of
secular powers which makes it difficult for it to countenance
war resistance. This was one of the final obstacles which
Dr. W. E. Orchard had to overcome before he went over to
the Roman Church. He had been a pacifist even during the
last war and the Roman Church officially forbids pacifism.
He surmounted that difficulty by the reflection that in the
future the Roman Church should be one of the chief practical
obstacles to war and that in the case of any conceivable future
war he would be allowed to oppose it as an unjust war, if not
on grounds of general pacifism. It is to be hoped that he is
right. As for the Protestant Churches, they grow up with
modern nationalism and have regularly until the last decade
officially sanctioned the war system.

The cynic has ground for saying that the record of the
Church in this matter holds out little hope for the future.
But we can put beside that record the fact that the Church
has learned much from the war. The real repentance of many
of its leaders for their war record is most impressive. The
official attitudes of most of the denominations in England
and America go very far in breaking with the war system
and in subordinating the will of the nation to the will of
God. They fall just short of complete pacifism. The Anglican bishops at the last Lambeth conference—the bishops of a
state Church be it remembered—went on record to the effect
that the Church should not support the government in any
war unless first the government lives up to its obligations to
pacts and covenants and submits the matter in dispute to
arbitration or conciliation. Several of the largest American
denominations have declared that the Church should not sup-

port any war except to defend continental United States against actual invasion. These two kinds of reservation which bring the official attitudes of the Churches short of complete pacifism mark an enormous advance upon the assumption which has hitherto prevailed that a nation can count upon the support of the Church in carrying on a war anywhere in the defense of any national interest. This official qualified pacifism is supported, as far as it goes, and is constantly being pushed farther by a large minority of Christians who are absolute pacifists in their attitude towards international war. In the recent questionnaire answered by 20,870 American ministers, 12,904 replied that it was their present purpose "not to sanction any future war or participate as an armed combatant," and 13,997 said that the Church should now go on record as refusing to sanction or support any future war. These positions were taken by a larger percentage of theological students than by the ministers as a whole. How far this tendency towards pacifism within the Church will go, it is impossible to predict. The fact is that it has already gone unexpectedly far. Responsible churchmen are now beginning to count the cost of this break with the war system and to prepare for a future crisis.

If we are to be realistic we must face the fact that the influence of the pacifist churchmen is least in the countries which are closest to an actual war situation. In the nature of the case they could have no influence upon Japan and Russia. There are very few of them in Germany. German Lutheranism has never felt and does not feel that there is any conflict between the war system and Christianity although Luther and Melancthon had compunctions about the matter until the outbreak of the religious wars. In most of the other countries the issue rests with Catholicism. We have seen that in spite of its strategic position in the world for the prevention of war the Catholic Church is far from considering itself as a war-resisting institution. It makes concordats with the most militaristic states and it usually maintains its international position by being all things to all men.

These facts limit the scope of the work of the Church in preventing war at present but they do not render it unimportant. If it cannot prevent war everywhere, it can do much to keep America and Britain neutral in case of another war, and to do that would keep the war from being a world war. It can do much to moderate the policies of those two nations which, as the world's most powerful empires, have vast influence for war or peace. If war does come, the international Church (here the Catholic Church can be especially effective) will still be one of the few leverages for civilization in the world. After the war is over, it will be one of the first and greatest healers of the wounds of war. These seem small contributions when we compare them with the evil which the Church is not yet prepared to prevent, but even they are among the few rays of light which at present shine down on what seems to be a dark future. It is as we contemplate this situation that we see more clearly than ever the necessity of building a world-wide Christian Church.

There is an old letter, coming from the second century of the life of the Church, the *Epistle to Diognetus*. The unknown writer says of the Christians of his time that they hold the world together. That did not seem true then but when we see now how the Church did save the higher values in civilization during the Dark Ages it seems that the Christians did hold the world together in those centuries in which the Roman Empire was crumbling. In our day those words do not seem true, but it is not a rash prediction that from the perspective of a future beyond the present unstable and threatened civilization it will be seen that in very truth the Christians have held the world together. At least that is one of the contributions that is within their power.

4. *The World Needs the Church to Moderate the Social Struggle and to Turn the Scale in Favor of Economic Justice*

The Church has an indispensable part in the economic struggle in America. Conditions differ so much in different countries that no attempt will be made to discuss the place of the Church elsewhere. This emphasis upon the place of the Church in the economic struggle rests upon two assumptions. The first is that no social order is worth striving for which is not based upon the consent of a large majority of the people. The second is that in order to get such a majority behind any social revolution in America the classes which are under the influence of the Church must be won to varying degrees of acceptance of the new order. Each of these assumptions needs further discussion.

The first assumption means that, if there is not a clear prospect of winning seventy or eighty percent of the people to the acceptance of revolution after the event if not before, the new order will have to be maintained by the method of war. Perhaps the actual change can be brought about peacefully by a smaller majority and much of that majority may be passive, but the new order will not be stable unless most of the rest of the population is won by a "fait accompli." The bloody part of most revolutions, as George Soule has brought out, is not the actual revolutionary crisis but the consolidation of its results and the suppression of counter revolution. It is then that the terror begins. The inevitable result of the method of war in making and maintaining a revolution is that not only is much blood spilt and hate engendered but that also the highest values in democracy are lost.

There is no more pernicious error than the common notion among radicals that democracy is valuable only in so far as it serves the purposes of revolution. There are elements in the machinery of parliamentary government which may be considered as merely means to an end. But with democracy are bound up things which are as much ends in themselves as economic justice. The whole conception of government resting upon consent, the guarantees of civil liberties for minorities, the provisions for ordered change—change which will continue to be necessary after the revolution—these are the heart of democracy. Without them truth is violated in the interests of the strongest, law becomes the fiat of changing tyrants, persons become puppets, and further changes will always bring the danger of more violence and terror. It is in order to avoid such results as well as the destruction, bloodshed, and hate of civil war that it is so important to insist upon the persuasion of a large majority of the people to revolutionary change.

The second assumption follows that large sections of the constituency of the Church must be won to revolutionary change in order to get that majority. These people, most of them in the middle classes, will not usually be revolutionaries. It would be as much as can be expected if most of them are made understanding enough to be acquiescent after the event. If only the moral rationalizations of privilege are worn away by steady criticism from the Christian perspective, a real blow will have been struck at the props on which the present order rests. There will be many who will go much farther than this, for they will be brought to repentance under the influence of the Church to such an extent that they will welcome any change which promises more justice, even though they may take no initiative themselves. And there will be others, fewest of all in numbers but influential among the leaders of the Church, who will be active revolutionaries. There is a real chance that in these ways the Church can make just enough of a dent upon the middle classes to make the difference between the possibility and impossibility of peaceful revolution.

The Church has been at this task for a very short time, so short that it is impossible to predict, with assurance, the effect of its impact. In the past either its ethic has been irrelevant to the economic order or, if it has had a relevant ethic, it has been one of control of the *status quo* rather than one of social change. When the Church has really envisaged social change it has been change by act of God alone. Troeltsch in his massive history of the social teachings of the Churches sums up the situation in his discussion of Christian Socialism. He says:

Thus Christian Socialism alone has broken through these theories (theories of the nature of society characteristic of Patristic and Mediæval Christian ethics) and forced men to think out afresh the social ethic of Christianity and its relation to the actual changes of the social order. It has laid bare the worm eaten condition of the previous conventional Christian ethic, which at its best offered something for the ethics of the family or the individual, but which on the other hand, had no message for social ethics save that of acceptance of all existing institutions and conditions, much to the satisfaction of all in authority.

Even if we make allowance for some exaggeration in that statement it is near enough to the truth to make us realize the short history of the attempt of the Church to guide social change. Now that the crust of the conservatism of the Church has been broken through there is real ground for hope and dogmatisms based upon the past record of the Church are out of place.

These four tasks of the Church indicate its great significance for the modern world. In the performance of each one of these tasks it has a contribution to make which cannot be made by any other institution. It has roots within the very classes which must be prevented from becoming the tools of Fascism or the unyielding opponents of economic change. It has the leverage which comes from the common acceptance of the principles of the Christian ethic which further social insight can turn into the principles of revolution. The first function of the Church, the helping of people to live the Christian life is the central and persistent function. That will outlast all the others. But this is a time in history in which that function cannot be performed with much effect if the Church does not also take seriously the others. If it does not help to guide the social forces of our time, it will be refusing to remove many obstacles to abundant life for countless individuals; it will be rendered hollow by hypocrisy for allowing its own people to strain out the gnat of little sins and swallow the camel of world destroying evils, without repentance, in which their lives are involved.

There is always a temptation for those who share the perspective of this book to become so impatient with the existing Churches that, while admitting the importance of the functions of the Church outlined in this chapter, they contemplate breaking with the existing institutions and establishing a new religious movement uncompromisingly radical.

There are three reasons why that tempting policy is a mistake. The first is that a split with the Church on the basis of social radicalism is almost certain to involve a loss of great religious values in the older Churches. A new radical Church would probably be a one-sided institution which loses the support of tradition and which forgets the ultimate human problems which are common to every age and every social order. The second is that such a new Church would be one more sect. It would increase the divisions within the Christian forces. Though its purity of vision might justify such a break it does not take long for a new sect to get into a rut which makes its original excuse for existence a matter of history. The more exclusive it is at the start, the more pharasaical it will probably become with age. The third reason is that such a sect would lose contact with the very constituency which needs to be leavened by a radical social vision.

If we are impatient with the Church and still believe in the need for it, the most fruitful strategy is not to found a new sect but to create new movements and fellowships within the life of the Church which will witness to the prophetic Christian ideal for our time. They should die before they become vested interests and should not be allowed to become new sects. They should maintain contact with all the treasures which the Church has preserved from the past centuries of Christian faith. They should work within the Church, using at times its ecclesiastical machinery, seeking to draw along as far as they will come large sections of its constituency. The so-called "Oxford Groups" have used this method with important results and they have shown us all lessons in strategy. The many social movements within the Church, especially the Church of England, which have come and gone, but not without leaving a mark on the whole Church, show what is possible. The Fellowship of Reconciliation and the Fellowship of Socialist Christians are now attempting the same task. In ways of this kind the power of the Church may be released for the saving of souls and the healing of nations.

THE CHURCH AND THE WORLD
OF SOCIAL RELATIONSHIPS

CAMERON PARKER HALL

CHAPTER III

THE CHURCH AND THE WORLD OF SOCIAL RELATIONSHIPS

IN HIS contribution to a symposium some years ago, the Archbishop of York has written, "I am, I hope, a Christian Englishman; but I am also, I am afraid, an English Christian." The context reveals that this latter phrase is something more than a factual description; it is a confession that the total environment called "England" dilutes the quality of one's Christian witness. Just how "English" (or "American" or "German," for that matter) our Christianity is, may be seen in times of war when patriotism plays the tune for Christianity to dance.

The Archbishop's statement is an echo, expressed with penetrating insight into modern life, of Jesus' words, "Be ye in the world, but not of it." Modern Christians are conditioned by the world—economic, racial and national—in which they live. For this world is not static in reference to us who live in it; it is operative and dynamic in its influence since the day we were born. Every Christian lives in the confluence of two great streams of tradition—one the religious, having its source in Christ; the other the secular, having its springs in the material and the cultural. And the latter affects the flow and purity of the former. Our loyalties become rooted in our country; our attitudes toward the making of wealth and its distribution reflect our economic status; our prejudices indicate our racial classification. At every point, the Christian has to compete with the claims of family and class and nation and race. Our Christianity must always be described, because it is always qualified, by reference to the part of our environment that embodies the attitudes and loyalties and relationships of various social groups. This paper is concerned with the extent to which the Church analyzes this world, whose influence cannot be escaped, and whose effectiveness is in evidence in the present state of Christianity.

I

It will help us to set the problem in its true light if we understand that there is nothing in analysis that is uncongenial to the Christian mind. In fact, Christianity has been active in analysis, probing deeper and deeper into great areas of experience.

A. The Church has applied analysis to the inner life of man. Religion, in a large measure, is introspective, and through its insights the soul has been traced in its needs and aspirations, its weaknesses and capacities. To its task of bringing a cure for the soul, the Church has given relentless study and thought. It is true to say that the modern science of introspection—psychology—has given nothing new or original to the analysis of the depths of the inner life. Religion is the pioneer, and psychology has but enlarged, confirmed and illuminated what the man of religion has already dissected in the anatomy of the soul. The great doctrines of the Church—forgiveness, grace and redemption—testify to the able reading by the Church of the life that lies deep within.

B. The Church has ever engaged in an analysis of what

constitutes right individual conduct. The good life, and how human beings of all ages and conditions are to live in relation to other individuals has been a subject of robust thinking. The Church has been earnestly concerned with moral theology; in instances, it has vied with the Pharisees in laying a pattern of behavior that reaches down into the minutiæ of conduct.

C. The Church, of recent decades, has brought some of its best thought to bear upon various religious data. While geologists were laying bare the successive layers in the surface of the earth, religious scholars were tracing the historical process within the composition of the Bible. While biology was penetrating the secrets of life, historians of the Church were unfolding the intricacies of Biblical times. While anthropologists were bringing out the relationships within that complex whole which we call "mankind," the religious student was engrossed in the study of comparative religions. The analytical method, which is basic to science, has been a tool in the hands of the religious life, and religion would be seriously impoverished if it had been lacking.

D. And mention should, of course, be made of the great achievements in the field of theology. While religion apprehends reality more through the insights of the poet than the deliberations of the scholar, at the same time the Church has always been "thoughtful," in that it has challenged the best minds of every generation to maintain the grounds of faith. The Church has used the mental apparatus and the intellectual tools of the philosopher and the metaphysician. The creeds and confessions of the Church are as islands cast up by the ceaseless activity of the Christian mind upon the great realities within experience.

Traditionally, then, the Church has applied itself to the

analysis of the phenomena of experience; its atmosphere is congenial to the spirit that is both religious and enquiring.

There is one note, however, that must be sounded, and that is this: Analysis requires what we may term a certain cultural competence. Analysis does not spring forth full grown; it is nurtured in a cultural milieu. For one thing, like all creative effort, analysis requires an apparatus, or stock of tools. In this case, the tools consist of concepts, schools of thought, rationalizations of experience. In its theology, Christianity has made use of concepts gained outside the specifically Christian tradition, and yet powerful in their usefulness for Christian thought. The concept of the Logos was an intellectual tool which Christians discovered in another culture, and which was drafted to serve subsequent Christian thought. Just as much industrial activity is concerned with the making of tools by which goods may be fashioned, so considerable thought must be spent upon the shaping of the proper apparatus for analysis and other intellectual activity. So it was that there appeared certain concepts and generalizations in our culture before religion could launch out on the study of comparative religions.

And skill in the use of tools must go along with the appearance of the tools themselves; and this again is a matter of cultural development. The Soviets have found that it is one thing to place tractors upon farms; it is another matter to have them properly used. Mental tools, like physical instruments, need appropriate skills. A child cannot handle adequately the theme of God, because his mind has not lived long enough with the past experience of the race; if properly trained, his mind will show increasing facility in the use of this theme. In similar manner, a whole generation, a whole people, can be as a child in respect to worthwhile thought in any area of experience. The theological activity of Christian minds is more than the activity of the minds themselves; it is the product of minds played upon by a culture that has concerned itself with this theme.

And in addition to tools and skill, analysis also calls for freedom. If great thought is dependent upon the cultural stream of the past, it is likewise true that all great thought, of whatever kind, is a release from the past and is creative of a new and modified channel. If thought is to be more than the confirmation of our prejudices and the rationalization of our ignorance, it must be free to criticize and to accuse and to re-orient. The value which a cultural level grants to freedom of the mind is as important to analysis as are the achievements which that culture has attained in the particular subject at hand.

II

We are now ready to examine what the Church must do if it is to understand the world in which it lives, in order to transform it to the divine purpose revealed in the life of its Master.

A. Analysis of the world requires a basis of fact; it must have relevant and accurate data with which to deal. For example, how is one to analyze the merits of a strike (provided that he does) without knowing certain facts? In the thunder from the right and from the left, what are the real issues? What is the merit of labor's claim that its wages are not rising in relation to the cost of living, or that certain practices (such as the "stretch-out," for example) are militating against advantages supposedly accruing to labor?

Above the heat and passions of an industrial dispute, there is a body of factual data that is obtainable by research and sound reasoning.

Or take the very important question of taxation. In the present capitalistic system, where business is run for private profit, taxation is a vital factor in the distribution of wealth. What are the sources of wealth that may be tapped? What items of wealth are earned with the least ethical justification? What kinds of wealth can be taxed with least hardship to those who have little? What does careful thought reveal about a tax that levies the same amount upon an article when bought by a man earning the pay of an unskilled laborer, and when bought by a man drawing the salary of a high executive? Every tax bill has what philosophers are calling a "field," in respect to the distribution of wealth and to justice between social groups.

The elementary requirement for reaching the truth is soundness of data; and yet Church opinion has been invariably based upon little, if any, passion for the facts. And in this the Church shares the plight of the average citizen. It is a strange commentary on modern democracy that the source of news is so inadequate in establishing the facts. The average citizen is asked to make his decisions on premises that reflect a partisan point of view, and on data that is supplied to him to support the view of some major economic interest. Walter Lippmann, in his sound analysis of how public opinion is formed, has revealed what modifications facts undergo before they are passed on to the newspaper reader.

In the past, the Church has done most of its thinking on social issues by rearranging its prejudices, rather than by putting itself under the stern discipline of facts. There are signs that this situation is being remedied, if only partially. There are Foundations and Associations which bind themselves to ferret out data as relentlessly and impersonally as physicists trace down the composition of an atom. Research into statistics dealing with all phases of economic life is being pursued, and the picture of our social life that these findings give is being drawn for the understanding of the masses.

Steps have been taken by the churches themselves to build their thought about the world not upon any dream picture sketched by partisan authorities but by the facts that reward any honest and enquiring mind. The Steel Strike Report is a signal example of the Church doing its own research. There are church officials whose responsibilities are such that they can go from one storm center to another, seeing at first hand the conditions, studying it from all points of view, and then reporting back to their constituency their findings.

The Church is also seeking to disseminate the data that underlies the economic world. There are a few church publications that make a special point in doing this; the "Information Service" of the Federal Council of Churches is outstanding in this field. The effort in these papers is twofold: (1) To supply facts and information that do not appear in the press, but which are basic to any sound opinion; (2) To present impartially the claims of both sides in any controversy, as they present themselves to the open mind of a third party. Here the Church has available to it the findings gleaned by secular research bureaus, as well as its own contacts. Certainly, if there is to be any constructive dealing with the world around us, we will have to know it as it really is, and not as it is pictured by haphazard and prejudiced opinion.

B. Effective analysis calls for what we may term a "socio-logical sense." As Aristotle long ago pointed out, Man is a political animal. Man adopts traditions that were made for him long before, and he creates traditions that mold the life of generations to come. He organizes his social life upon certain generalizations and abstractions, such as the "law of supply and demand," and "national honor." He crystallizes his attitudes into institutions and laws that become, as it were, impersonal standards of action, which represent the level of conscience and intelligence to which the community must conform. For example, although opinion is in revolt against Child Labor today, the lack of conscience of an earlier day is solidified in political institutions, which still force Child Labor upon us until we go through the long process of constitutional amendment. Society is a fact, as much as the individuals who compose it are facts. It has its own reasons for being, its own strategy for surviving, its own pattern of behavior. Any analysis of the world must have a sociological sense—a feeling for the fact of society, and an interest in how men live together.

It is obvious that sociology has only recently risen upon the horizon of men's thinking. For centuries the arts held exclusive interest; a little over a hundred years ago the natural sciences forged ahead; and it is hardly a decade that the social sciences have received prominent attention, although they have been engaging the thought of students much longer. The world owes Karl Marx a debt of gratitude for precipitating its thought into a realistic study of what lies beneath the surface of society.

When one takes one's eyes from the superstructure of our economic life, which in some respects presents an imposing sight, to examine what lies beneath the street level and down in its foundations, one comes upon considerable shifting sand that can only spell disaster. For one thing, according to our present economic pattern, meeting the needs of people is incidental to the making of profits. Or, to put it the other way round, serving the needs of the public is rendered if and when it will bring private profit.

Stuart Chase has somewhere put this in graphic form by suggesting that any contractor will erect a building on the top of a mountain if a profit is assured, even if the building has no service value. While in a slum area, where human need cries out to heaven, that same contractor will not build homes for families because it does not pay (that is the reason, of course, why the government is having to enter the housing situation). The making of houses for people to live in is not the reason why houses are built; the end sought is profits.

It would be a superficial reading of the facts to single out the contractor for denunciation; he is to blame neither more nor less than we are; it is the structure of society that forces him to withhold his building skill from society unless there is profit for him personally. Fundamentally, society today is not organized to supply the needs of the many—it is organized to produce profits for the few.

Another illustration is suggested by the findings of the Milbank Foundation, which made a survey of the health of some 1,500 children in one of the poorer sections of New York City. The survey revealed that 40 per cent of the children were suffering from malnutrition. This is due basically to the fact that our food industries are organized to make money, and not to meet the elementary demands for food. A merchant will provide a rare delicacy to grace the table for a five-dollar meal; but he will not supply milk and meat to the children of impoverished families. Why? Because society is organized to provide profits for the meat packers and the milk distributors, and not food for children.

Again, wages, by which the mass of people can secure what they need, are not a first effort of society today, but come, if at all, only as a final outcome of a long process. The sequence is this: rising prices (or, to the same effect, decreasing costs) hold out the possibility of profit; this results in economic activity; this brings about the employment of workers; this means payment of wages, by which there will be a demand for goods, the buying of which will bring the profits anticipated in the beginning. The present basis for the hope of recovery lies in that chain, the significance of which for us is that the securing of profits for the few is the primary consideration, and the payment of wages comes only after a long series of steps has been taken.

The theory just outlined which is operative in the world in which the Church of today functions, is illustrated by the parable of Jesus, which told of Lazarus being fed by the crumbs falling from the table of Dives. Our economic life is run on the theory that the higher the table of the few is heaped with plenty, the more will be the crumbs that make up the meal of wage earners.

Here again, denunciation of this or that individual whose table drips crumbs is beside the point. The real point is that our society is organized as though that were the most humane and intelligent method.

C. Analysis on the part of the Church also calls for right ethical measurements. In every field of thoughtful endeavor, there must be a growing adequacy in the tools used. Astrophysics calls for enlarged scientific concepts to deal with the expanded phenomena of science; the Rosetta Stone has made insufficient earlier criteria in archeological research. Old measuring rods become outgrown as problems change.

The Church, like other cultural institutions, found itself catapulted into a dynamic industrial society with ethical weights and measures that were insufficient for the phenomena of this new order. For the ethic which the Church had developed, and around which it had cultivated strong emotions, dealt primarily with relationships within the home, relationships between the sexes and face-to-face relationships involving simple honesty.

The ethical scale upheld by the Church is revealed in sermons and Sunday School curricula. People were warned against dancing, but not against keeping in step with martial music. To work on Sunday was condemned, but little was said about the conduct of business on the other six days. Giving an honest day's work for a day's wage is always sound ethical teaching, but it needs to be paralleled with the paying of a living wage for an honest day's work. The Christian ethic in relation to the problems of imperialism, as noted in Professor Parker Moon's book, "Imperialism and World Politics," or to the problems of industry, as set forth in "Robber Barons," by Matthew Josephson, or to the problems of finance, as indicated in "Finance Speculation," by John T. Flynn—these remained out of the purview of the Christian conscience, and naturally so, for one cannot analyze with a measuring rod of inches problems that call for feet and yards.

There are two factors that account for the slowness of the

Church in laying strong hands upon the ethical problems raised by our modern world. It is perhaps more than coincidence that in America the modern missionary movement and the industrial revolution struck their full stride at about the same time. The missionary motive has always received major emphasis from the followers of Jesus, their incentive stemming from his own passion for men. And no praise can be too high for the sacrificial spirit and for the ability with which those in this movement have met difficult and dangerous problems.

But by this missionary emphasis, the eyes of the Church became fixed upon the paganism abroad and the ethical perversions of other lands. Experience reveals that it is hard, if not impossible, for human nature to maintain itself at high emotional tension about more than one absorbing theme at a time; and the great pressure of the missionary motive, as then construed, undoubtedly drained much ethical adventuring from our own problems.

Perhaps this may be better understood by a glance at the "home mission" enterprise. This latter phrase was not only used in connection with elements in our population who are not Christians, as the Indian and the Porto Rican; it was applied as well to work in sparsely settled communities and in underprivileged sections of large cities. But these objects of missionary solicitude were as truly Christian as those from whom came the wealth to carry on the work among them. The assumption seemed to be, however, that economic dependence placed one upon the spiritual level approximating the non-Christian abroad; while economic affluence lifted one above the need for "missionary" activity. This indicates that missionary zeal on the part of many was an effort to evade applying a more comprehensive ethical measurement to our changing economic life.

However, the human misery cast up by the angry tides of industry at the home base demanded action by the conscience. The dominant method followed was the way of charity. From those with wealth (no analysis was made of how these fortunes were accumulated) funds were raised to found hospitals and orphanages, to relieve homes ravaged by poverty, and to advance similar ameliorative measures. The strong giving their strength for the weak is, of course, an expression of the Christian spirit, and there will always be occasions for its operation; but as a solution of the ethical issues raised by industrial life, it is inadequate. For it analyzes the poor as objects of charity rather than as subjects of justice; it construes brotherhood in terms of giving out of one's accumulated plenty rather than in sharing economic power at the source of wealth. Charity takes conscience away from the real crux of the modern problem; it results in only a slight distribution of wealth, while it leaves unchanged the essential relationships of the groups within the economic pattern.

The Church will never bring ethical realism into the world in which it lives until its sense of sin is commensurate with the far-reaching implications of modern industry and nationalism. Halford Luccock, in his "Contemporary American Literature and Religion," has told that, at the death of the Shah of Persia, exception was taken by his government to the appointment of an American bank as executor for the Shah's American holdings on the ground that such a bank was a Christian institution, while the occasion called for one that was Mohammedan. The bank went to court and won its plea that it was entitled to be named executor because it was

not a Christian institution. That this verdict would characterize our social order cannot be doubted; and this is a direct
challenge to the moral earnestness of the Church.

The question whether evil is personified by the Devil is
secondary to the question whether evil is not legalized in
many of our laws, stabilized in many of our institutions, and glorified in some of our boasted economic mores.
The Devil will be stripped of his disguise only as the Church
brings into the world a sense of sin adequate to the social
realities of modern life.

D. In any effective analysis, the attitude of the person or
the institution toward his function in a given situation is an
important factor. If a person feels within himself that he
is a responsible agent for the growth of scientific knowledge,
he will exert himself accordingly. If, on the other hand, he
feels no pressure to put himself into this field, his personal
contribution to scientific advance will be accordingly limited.
Correspondingly, the attitude of the Church toward its own
rôle in social change will determine the extent to which it
exerts itself as a responsible agent for such change.

There have been periods when the Church has won its
claim to be supreme in society; in Rome and Geneva it has
sat in the seats of ultimate political power. There are sufficient grounds, however, both in principle and in practice, to
indicate that the Church should never assume temporal control of society.

The other attitude has been to work out a modus vivendi
between the Church, as the representative of Christ, and the
State, as the representative of Cæsar. Generally speaking, the
Church has insisted upon autonomy within its own sphere,
the spiritual, and has not sought to impose its authority in

the affairs of the State. This attitude accounts for the lack of ethical earnestness on social questions.

The reason for this attitude toward its own function lies partly in the way the Church has conceived its relationship to culture. Certain characteristics of American church life are peculiarly illustrative of this.

When America was settled, the Church was the center of culture in a peculiar way. Thrust into a barren wilderness, with the struggle for survival so pressing, the settlers looked to their religious institutions to maintain the ties which bound them to their spiritual heritage.

This rôle of the Church, as the preserver of culture, continued as the march westward was undertaken. Every time a new frontier was settled a struggling community faced the problem of preserving its essential culture. The Church on our movable western frontier symbolized the cultural roots of the people.

From the beginning, too, Americans were faced with a people whom they thought barbaric in their culture, savage in their ways, and heathen in their religion. The cleavage which these settlers felt between their own cultural attainments and the cultural debasement of the Indians gave the Church a mission to impart the spiritual heritage of the white man. For converting the Indian also meant taming his spirit to the ways of the "superior" white race.

This same situation was repeated with the negro; once again the Church stood as the custodian of an advanced religion and culture. The two were not, and could not, be separated. If the religion was the white man's, so was his culture; and everything demanded that the negro accept both in accepting one.

And then there came the tide of immigrants to our shores. Not Anglo-Saxon in race, foreign in tradition, the Church confronted these newcomers as an institution whose own roots were deep within the native culture. The chapels and centers established among these many foreign-speaking nationalities were looked upon as strategic centers to assimilate the immigrants into the cultural stream of their newly adopted land. Whatever appraisal one may bestow upon the success of this undertaking, the fact remains that once again the Church dispensed culture.

Largely through the force of circumstance, then, the Church has been cast in the part of the carrier, if not the preserver, of the prevailing culture. And to add that this was also a welcome task, is not necessarily to impute economic security as the dominant motive. For cultural stability is a concern to men, and even more so to a religious institution whose interest is in spiritual values.

For the culture in any Christian community is signally a product of the influence of the Church; the Church has created much of what is accepted as of spiritual value, and stability lies in the maintenance of that cultural pattern. An institution that is fulfilling the rôle of cultural guardian is not going to give itself to criticism of that culture and its roots. Such analysis as is made will be directed toward supplying sanctions for the status quo, rather than toward exposing errors that call for a thorough overhauling. The true task of the Church should be that of Conscience for the prevailing culture, bringing ethical insight that sees beyond the attainments of the present. Not until the Church realizes that the Gospel has more to gain in a culture based upon a more ethical economic order, will it go out as a responsible agent to effect basic and far-reaching social charges.

III

It has been pointed out that analysis is congenial to the religious temper; and analysis of the world of men and affairs is always present when religion is represented by its prophetic spirits. None have with so much daring and precision laid bare the soul of men in respect to their economic and national relationships as have the prophets; and while Jesus Christ is more than a prophet, yet he is one with the prophets in this. The prophetic spirit sees into the heart of society as over the shoulders of a God of consuming righteousness and redemptive love. Social life, in all its ethical ramifications, is the subject of prophetic concern and agony of soul.

For one thing, the prophet takes hold of facts and data as something that almost burns his hands, so aware is he of their import. Where is the injustice that characterizes every society more vividly marked than in the accusing blows that fell from the lips of Amos? Where is the hollow strength of nations more immediately apprehended than by Isaiah and by Jeremiah? With what unmistakeable definiteness does Jesus reveal the false conceits that society takes so seriously, and to its own destruction. With a single parable, such as that of the Good Samaritan, he definitely deals with phenomena of contemporary society, and with conditions that still cry to God for change. Truly the prophets are stoned, and he who is more than a prophet is crucified, because they come down from generalizations to specific moral ills that characterize the everyday life and the accepted practice of the world.

The prophet goes deeper in his analysis than the fact itself; it becomes significant because it is a symptom of an order of reality that is more profound than the fact. Not as a statistician, nor as a student of sociology, but rather as one tremendously on fire on behalf of a righteous God does the prophet approach social analysis. Disparity of wealth is not a mere economic phenomenon, it is a sign of a moral disease. The perversion of justice is not a legal concern so much as it is evidence that the processes of justice are the tools of interests fulfilling their lust for greed. A political alliance between states is more than a diplomatic concern; it is a sign of spiritual poverty on an international scale. For the prophet, everything points to the righteousness of God.

The analysis of the prophet probes still deeper into the ethical structure of life, so that he holds the conviction that the moral law is in the very substance of life itself. The universality and the binding nature of physical law, which is the assumption of modern thought, corresponds to the view of the moral law held by the prophets. Moral obligation does not zig-zag through life, carefully making its way between this that it binds, and that which it leaves unbound. Life in its totality, in respect to all men and to all circumstances, must conform to the will of the Righteous God, which is disobeyed only at a loss too great for life to sustain.

The analysis of the prophet is also concerned with experience; for the prophetic spirit sees the unity of moral experience. Moral personality is one, and to divide it into degrees of moral earnestness is to make it less of a personality. The ethical life is supremely a quality of soul, resulting from an experience of moral reality. It is something which we are, or are not; not something that we have now, and can discard later. To compartmentalize moral experience is to violate its basic unity. This prophetic insight into the unity of such experience is expressed in Jesus' words, "Ye cannot serve God and Mammon."

Dr. John A. Mackay, in his book entitled "The Other Spanish Christ," relates an incident that poses the ethical problem of the Church. He declares that whoever has visited Seville during Holy Week will never forget the scene of woe which the Cathedral presents throughout the midnight hours of Easter Friday, with its High Altar shrouded with a huge dark veil and its immense nave filled with women who groan and lament the night long. But, he continues, as soon as pealing bells announce that Christ is risen, the populace rises from its mourning to attend the first bull fight of the season.

People come within the influence of the Church, molded by the atmosphere and values and practices of the world of bull fights and other social phenomena. And they pass from out the influence of the Church to enter again into the stream of the formative influence of the world. In analyzing this world with prophetic insight and in seeking to transform it with prophetic self-abandon, the Church will create a new individual who will in turn create a world of social relationships that will be an earnest of the coming of the Kingdom of God on earth.

THE CHURCH AND THE MIND OF CHRIST

FREDERICK KUHNS

CHAPTER IV

THE CHURCH AND THE MIND OF CHRIST

HUMANITY is uprooted. So Maurice Hindus informs us. Not alone in Russia have revolutions been fired. The social structure has been shaken. Blessed institutions are crumbling like shell-torn cathedrals. Inherited systems, many of them now unwanted, have had their day. New concepts of goodness, truth and beauty are replacing the traditional philosophy of our fathers. Tomorrow's morals will be different from yesterday's. New occasions are upon us. Will they teach us the inevitable new duties?

The advent of Jesus in the period of the Cæsars shattered social systems more ancient and benevolent than twentieth-century capitalism. Forgotten values were restored to significance. His religion generated new values men held were destructive of commonplace virtues. Christ does not confront a disordered economic process and unsavory politics for the first time in this year of grace 1935 A.D. The religion of Jesus supported all human values seemingly disregarded in our time. His mind introduced a new reagent into the laboratory of human experience. It precipitated new issues for men to face bravely and compounded new principles of living that augured hope.

Paul's injunction, "Have this mind in you, which was also in Christ Jesus," was and is audacious counsel. It is the bench-mark from which the building of the human order must proceed. Social systems being what they are, as followers of Jesus the men and women who make up the Church cannot nor should they ask to escape the practical considerations implied in those tremendous words.

Much doggerel about the Church failing to measure up to the ethical teaching of Jesus leaves me unwarmed and unmoved. After winnowing the wheat of genuine inspiration from the chaff of foggy argument, we are thrown back again and again to the personality of Jesus for a scale of values as a measure of human advance. The research of the scholars on this one point is convincing enough. The personality of Jesus alone is of abiding significance. His teaching is the normal outreach of what he became. In fact, his teaching is hardly different from that of any of the great Hebrew prophets. He did, of course, teach forgiveness with a new vigor. If Jesus may be said to have learned by doing, then it is true to say that his ethical teaching resulted from his fellowship with man through the gamut of human experience. "He was tempted like we are tempted." Still he worked his one talent and developed his latent spiritual capacities in a manner such as only a high calling can bestow. His life is the controlling influence it is in society because of his wise employment of individual energy. Free spiritual initiative is of the essence of his faith and work. When a philosophy of individualism is being read out of court it is important to recall that Jesus stressed individual enterprise. When Paul spoke of growing up into the stature of the fulness of the Christ, he must have had that in mind. A man should seek to train up by calling out at every opportunity what singular capacities he might have. The Beatitudes as set forth in

Matthew's Gospel are nothing if they are not a catalogue of the various spiritual necessities of mankind. Undisciplined and uncontrolled, they lead to frustration of tremendous social possibilities.

Only a community of spirit-filled people will make Christianity a living religion. Only religious faith will amend and dictate moral activities. This is not merely a first-century thought-pattern unless I have mistaken modern psychology, especially the psychology of religion. Human nature being what it is, "the mind of Christ" is the one place we can begin to labor for a better world. Yet I, for one, refuse to compromise this principle by treating Jesus as normative for religious experience. To make of him a spiritual absolute is to side-track individual initiative. To discuss Jesus as the only prism, as it were, through which the vari-colored spiritual rays of the universe have passed or shall be allowed to pass, is to short-circuit the primary spiritual powers latent in man. And these primary powers are urgently needed for inducing a high potential in our moral performance. We cannot afford to deny to the common man that priceless experience that Jesus said is the privilege of the pure in heart. They must be allowed to see whatever spiritual achievement is in store, not suppose that faith has been delivered once for all to the saints of some remote time. In Ralph Waldo Emerson's words, "I have no expectation that any man will read history aright, who thinks that what was done in a remote age, by men whose names have resounded far, has any deeper sense than what he is doing today. The world exists for the education of each man." This is a Christian judgment and a Christian method of procedure. Like the old spectacle-maker, we too must seek to find that which is true whether or not it accords with our presuppositions and prejudices about life. Jesus may have been the religious genius of the first century. Little doubt is left that he was. But as astronomy could have made no headway if Galileo ordered it to stop where he took leave of it, just so would humanity make no gains if we anchored at any given point in time.

None the less, the leadership of Jesus, to which he is justly entitled by reason of his own worth, suffers from contempt and indignity. Christians debate the attributes of the Godhead while humanity remains a crawling mess. A new society awaits the emergence of a new race, as Paul said. In Christ there is no Jew or gentile as such. All are sons of the highest. It brings one up short to think of such a prospect. To possess the mind of Christ is to be fired with a redemptive purpose in living. Paul confessed, not immodestly, "For me to live is Christ." Perhaps we cannot understand that unless we read it in terms of hidden motives and purposes in a man's credo. "Many are called, few chosen," was Jesus' way of stating mankind's chief difficulty. Not all in his day were able to triumph in spiritual affairs. Hindrances of many sorts thwarted man's attempt to be full-statured. And woe unto him who proved a hindrance to his brother. It were better for him never to have been born.

Not the least of these hindrances to pinnacle spiritual performance is man's own wish to dwell in ease and comfort. It is better to be undisturbed, we are apt to say, than to suffer the necessity of change. We let things take their own course. Rather than treat a disease we run the risk of surviving it. In the realm of morals this is only the blindest kind of service to the insights of Jesus. We should beware that we do not let into our minds what he called "dark light." We must be amenable to change, turning, conversion.

A business man of my intimate acquaintance told me only recently that, looking back over a career of forty-odd years in the service of a great corporation, he had about reached the conclusion that business, as we know it in America, is non-moral. The interesting fact about this statement is that it is made by a Christian gentleman, a church member and a heavy supporter of missions. In other words, it is the insight of one who has his money on religion. If he were a poor man and unsympathetic to Christianity, one might be able to deny the truth of his statement.

We do face a basic necessity of our age to Christianize business and all human services. We speak much in these days of re-employment. Let us ask ourselves whether we are re-employing men in occupations that serve the Kingdom of God. Let us also not forget that Paul's preaching in Ephesus threw some men out of work. The high demands of the religion of Jesus do not necessarily guarantee everyone employment on his own terms. Still, many who sit in their Sunday pew care little for preaching upon economic issues. One of my best friends is a man who tells me nearly every Sunday that economics should be kept eternally out of the pulpit. I still love him and I still preach about any issue that I feel called to preach about. We respect each other's claim. Most congregations, be it said, prefer their minister to stand where they stand on such matters. Here we see a definite invitation to forsake the basic thing that religion is. Religion is a judgment. Let the modern rabbi and minister recall that the congregations in Israel expected their prophets, and Jesus, too, to stand where they stood. Amos was chased from the city to the country, Jeremiah was dumped into a cistern and Jesus was crucified. To use a modern phrase that any newsboy might understand, they were "taken for a ride." These things happened because they refused, in the isolation of their own inner integrity of spirit, to live on some one's else level, but chose to dwell apart from man as though to live for God.

To reconcile this conflict of divine service with the parochial interests of men is no small part of the preachers' task in modern times. When the private prejudices are invaded, loyalty often ceases to a man whose qualifications to lead are brilliant. It is fascinating to note, as one reads into the biographies of the spiritual leaders of the race, how their own expectations always exceed those of their immediate adherents or descendants. Is loneliness the price of great leadership?

Christianity is a prophetic movement. Conceived as a continuation of an ancient and unequalled lineage of voices in the wilderness of man's own muddling, it risks the test of "fruits." To affirm that the chief interest of Christianity is worship is to belie its origins. Worship must be surcharged with content that seriously offends the conscience. The peace that passeth all understanding isn't God's unless our souls are troubled and our consciences torn. Can the churches succeed in developing a service of worship along lines that will sear the consciences of the worshippers Sunday after Sunday? It is a foremost duty of the hour. The Church must refuse to be a purveyor of comfort unless it is the comfort of wrestling with an angel. Not that the preacher must make a nuisance of himself that he may prove his allegiance to Jesus. So long as we speak with our understanding we shall be true to a wise instinct. Even so, some of the first Christians were overjoyed to be called "fools." The making of the whole family of God is at stake. We must make humanity Godlike. This the Church conceives its mission to be doing. To emphasize anything less is to be truant to Jesus, lacking in his mind and faithless to ourselves. This is the religious meaning of the teaching concerning God as Father. Any other use of the term is apparent childish sentimentality.

While economic conditions in particular may alter our conduct, they should not be allowed to engulf our spirits and defraud us of character. The supreme fact, startling as will appear, is that Jesus overcame everything that threatened his own peace. Let the sociologist make of it what he can. Indeed, adverse economic, political and social conditions in his time only nerved the man to utilize every human capacity to the utmost to steer away from disaster. Religious faith intensifies our ordinary daily capacities to avoid shipwreck just as it invigorates all intellectual effort. We cannot explain how it happens, but it is a fact of experience. "The fear of the Lord is the beginning of wisdom." Reverence is the prerequisite of learning. The Church can serve the present by focussing attention upon and creating interest in the development, in individuals, of the spirit of fair-play, justice and love; and, among groups, of many shades of opinion, urging co-operation with all men, of whatever race, nationality or religious faith, in establishing any and all agencies necessary to fulfill the basic drives and hungers of mankind. The Church must increasingly find it possible to minister to the growing acquisitiveness, both individual and collective, that threatens the very existence of society.

Criticism of the Church descends by the ton from the hopelessly misinformed. Certainly the Church should heed all honest criticism. The Church should lend every encouragement to all honest efforts to set the problems of economics, politics and sociology in the light of reason, experience and conscience; but, in my judgment, should never undertake to present or promise any one hard-and-fast solution to the many issues that are involved in a steady advance toward the Kingdom of God. We must come to terms with that precious stuff known as human "personality." We find it everywhere we may go. A serious student of human affairs, traveling in Germany, France, England, Italy and Bulgaria one summer, and in China and Japan the next, said that human beings are pretty much alike all over the world. We are only at the threshold of a new era in human understandings. God is with us in our efforts to familiarize ourselves with the new peoples, who happen paradoxically to be very ancient peoples, that our commerce and communications are making neighbors. The world is a small place, after all. Regard for personality wherever we meet it is a test of our allegiance to the mind of Christ. And certainly Paul's idea of our being "temples of the Holy Spirit" approaches the findings of our best psychologists, that is to say, those psychologists who insist, on scientific grounds, that we are more than scampering mice or yelping dogs.

Again, the Church must be reconciled, not only to God, but to men of various temperaments and dispositions and heritages. There are other civilizations than our western Latin culture. We should forget that the Bible contains, as has been alleged, the only inspired words of decision ever uttered by an Almighty God. We would do well to teach the growth of the Spirit in every religious tradition worthy of the name, as a "source of psychological power to ourselves," to use H. A. Overstreet's fine phrase. Books like "Re-Thinking Missions" are the harbingers of the coming day of finer understanding and wider sympathy as they also herald the time of mutual effort for the building of a world community that will be blessed. We must as well "re-think our cities," as Overstreet suggests, in his book, "A Guide to Civilized Loafing." Seen for what it really is, the religious bond makes us kin with the world as it affirms our kinship with the mind of the Eternal God. This undying religious message of the Church we must singly and individually illumine with the incandescence of our own personality. We must bear in our own bodies these "marks" of Christ if our ministry is to be valid in the present hour. Such a message in the last analysis is truer to human experience than the dogma of any political movement. The mind of Christ is the call of God to men to assist wisely in the worthy enterprise of fashioning the whole natural world and the whole organization of human affairs according to specifications wrought out, as it were, in eternity. We are caught up into the holy purposes of God. They transcend the limited impulses of man and partake of something more than transitional technique. We must refuse to be opportunists to the extent that we compromise humanity's fundamental longings. We must evoke the highest possible religious response of which men are capable. This, as the history of Christianity abundantly shows, is never without acknowledging and living for definite ethical obligations. To achieve the courage and the wisdom of Christ's mind is the most alluring adventure that the Church, to the very last man and woman, is privileged to have for its task. It will prove equal to the terrific demands and the great strains made upon it by doing this well and other secondary matters when convenience may permit.

NEW CHURCHES FOR OLD

BEDROS KEVORK APELIAN

CHAPTER V

NEW CHURCHES FOR OLD

"My name is Mr. B——," he said, as we sat down at the annual dinner of the local alumni club of our college. He was much pleased when he discovered that I had graduated from the theological school, and added: "You have the best thing to give to the world." This was an unexpected but appreciated surprise. Gifted with a winsome personality and penetrating mind, he had all the earmarks of a first-class layman. I envied the minister for having such a leader in his church.

"What church are you working in?" I inquired.

"None!" he answered firmly.

I smiled and waited for him to continue.

"I'm looking for a church that will give me a God for today," he added, "and so far I have not found it."

Our chance acquaintance did not end there. We have talked considerably about the deeper needs and issues of life, both personal and social. His father had been a minister on the frontier line in the middle northwest. His brother, until recently, had kept the ancestral torch burning in the southwest. In spite of such a religious background my friend was hungry for the "living God" who alone could satisfy his innermost longings and help him adjust himself to the rapidly changing world of our times. But up to that time he had not found the church where the living God could feed him and use him to accomplish His purpose.

Another instance happened at a suburban country club.

"Tomorrow is Mothers Day," commented one of the "boys."

"It is the twentieth anniversary of my mother's death, too," said another, "and I think the world of her."

"Why not attend church in the morning and meditate upon the memories of your mother?" I suggested. "There will be plenty of time in the afternoon for a round of golf."

"If I were near enough I would perhaps come to your church. I was brought up in the church and know a good deal about religion. My uncle was a minister. But truly, I have no use for the church."

"Why?" I asked.

"The ministers speak in a language which I do not understand."

These are not isolated cases. Daily one meets men and women in all walks of life wistful, sometimes consciously, often unconsciously, but always seeking a God for today expressed in terms which they can understand, and who can give them spiritual health to enable them to stand firm in the shifting sand underneath their feet and against the raging storm overhead.

Recently an honored business man said to me bluntly, "Peter, it is you ministers who brought us into this mess, and it is you ministers who can take us out of it." He has not been inside of a church for decades.

"How can this be?" I inquired.

"By permitting us to follow wrong ethics," came his answer.

No testimony has been introduced from the underprivileged class—the exploited workers and the poor. Would it be considered fantastic to state that they have asked for bread and have received a stone, have demanded justice but have been met with violence? In this class struggle the church as a whole has been on the side of the privileged class. To be sure it has given succor to the wounded even if it has come from the crumbs that have fallen from the rich man's table. Is it a wonder that there is such a growing and aggressive hostility on the part of the exploited class against the church and even against religion?

Our purpose is not to condemn the church or deny the contribution it has made to progress. Like all other institutions or organizations its record is a mixture of virtues and vices, black and white, positive and negative. It has both nursed and stoned the prophets; it has championed liberty and persecuted the non-conformist; has preached love and nursed hatred; has proclaimed peace and engaged in war; has denounced the world but sold its soul and betrayed its Lord to the princes of Mammon. Judged by the standards of the world its record may be creditable. But judged by the purpose and mission it is organized to accomplish, it is found wanting. People are organizing against it or deserting it because it does not grapple with the problems of personal life and with the social issues of the day. What it preaches, teaches and does is so irrelevant and extraneous to those needs and aspirations of life which religion—particularly

Christianity—is expected to meet and realize. The statisticians of the various boards may attempt to acquit the church before its critics by pointing to its proportionate increase in membership, ability to carry on even through the present economic depression and by its holdings and influence. May not such evidences of strength be the weakness of the church? The church is the tree of religion, and must be judged by its fruits, the quality of its membership and ministry, as well as by the success it achieves in accomplishing its purpose. The vineyard of the Lord is not producing sweet grapes to heal and harmonize life both in its personal aspects and social relationships. As long as it fails to accomplish this it will still be found wanting even if it enlists in its membership all the peoples of the world, and commands their wealth.

The chief mistake of the church has been to mistake its purpose for its program, to regard itself as an end and not as the means to an end. What is a church for, to keep on being a church or to be a flexible human organization to do something, with that something determining the character of its organization and program as well as the technique of its ministry? The church as an end in itself has no justification nor any religious value. To claim divine authorship and apostolic sanction for any church is to misunderstand both the mind of Jesus and the experience of the disciples, the original founders of the church. All attempts in the past, and even now, to claim authority for a particular type of church and ask people to accept its doctrines and practices as final on the ground that it was instituted by Jesus and transmitted through the apostles to the present ecclesiastical atuhority—be it a bishop, pope or official board—are futile and injurious.

The church is a human laboratory, a congregation of truth seekers. Therefore the nature of any church should be determined by the truth it seeks to attain. What is this truth for the realization of which the church should be organized? *To seek, interpret and apply the will of God to all human needs and relationships.*

Jesus was reluctant to have his followers wrap themselves around him in adoration, or follow him as a soldier follows mechanically his commanding officers. He would not make himself the ultimate end of life's quest. He would not even encourage a candidate to call him good. He invited the people to join him as he led the procession in a common adventure to seek the will of God and throw their lives unreservedly on the side of God for humanity. So could they become the children of God, grow in His likeness and be the heirs of His love and grace. The seeking and doing of the will of God was so central in the consciousness of Jesus that he denounced as iniquity at least three types of good deeds done in his name, on the ground that his followers might do all these things and still fail to do the will of God. "It is not every one who says to me, 'Lord, Lord,' who will get into the realm of heaven, but he who does the will of my father in heaven. Many will say to me at that day, 'Lord, Lord, did we not prophesy in your name, did we not cast out demons in your name, did we not perform many miracles in your name?' Then I will declare unto them, 'I never knew you; *depart from my presence, you workers of iniquity.*' " [1]

The account of the life and teachings of Jesus in available sources is much limited. There is no complete statement as to what exactly is the contents of the will of God for all people

[1] Mat. 7:21-23. Moffat's translation.

in all times. We have no indication that Jesus even wanted to make such a final and universal statement about the will of God. He simply revealed the way whereby one might find what God's will was for the specific situation. He could depend upon the Spirit to teach, guide and strengthen him.

Still there is enough in the gospel narratives to convince us the central factor of the will of God. Jesus assumed that God and man stood on a common ground, and man, bearing the image of God, was capable and destined to grow fully in those values which make life worth while and of which God is the perfection. God is interested in man, far more than a good father is interested in his children. It is His will that His children should grow in the fullness of life, to rise up in the spirit of love and grace, maintain peace and serenity in the midst of difficulty and frustration, to develop a sympathetic and understanding mind, cherish a courageous heart and magnanimous purpose, and withal to experience a joyous and triumphant life. This is the meaning of Jesus' saying in the gospel of John, "I have come that they may have life, and have it more abundantly."

On the above assumption it would not be difficult to discover the implications and technique of realizing the will of God for humanity.

1. No material object, thought, event or organization that can contribute to the development of human personality can be alien to God, and nothing that hinders the growth of personality can be in harmony with the will of God. Life should not be divided into two compartments, one "sacred" and the other "secular" as the church has arbitrarily done. Whatever is helpful in the making of persons is good and divine, and therefore should be sought and disseminated by the

church, and whatever is injurious or makes it harder to develop persons, no matter how strongly sanctioned by the church, state and the public, should be denounced as wicked and destroyed. How much do our present industrial system, our social and educational relations, the teaching and practices of the church help make better and happier people? This should be the criterion to evaluate the present social order and guide us to establish the new.

2. Available opportunities for the development of personality should not be limited to a group, class, race or country. Human beings are equal in the sight of God and members of His household. Attempts to corner the resources of help for the good of one section of humanity is sin. All resources of help should be thrown wide open before all the members of God's household. If there should be any preference in the order, the weakest and the neediest should come first, both in the case of individuals and groups.

3. The development of personality depends upon two conditions: one is the successful and complete integration of the inner life. This means harmonizing one's impulses, thoughts, purposes and emotions, and experiencing that at-home feeling in the universe through fellowship with God as the loving source of our spirit and the perfection of our aspirations. The other is the re-making of the entire social fabric to nourish, sustain, encourage and preserve human personality.

As to the technique of the fullest realization of personality through inner integration, serene mastery of circumstances and non-manipulable factors of life, and right social adjustment, Jesus gave us what is apparently a simple but is really a very subtle formula. "Whoever wants to save his life will lose it, and whoever loses his life for my sake and the gospel's will save it." The road to the making of character and perfection of personality is devotion, prompted by love, of all that one has, is and can be to the common good, and to the welfare of the divine family, the social order of unified and harmonized humanity. It is the inborn right, therefore, of every individual throughout the world to have all possible opportunities and help thrown before him that he may grow as a son of God in the rich and triumphant life, and toward a completed character and perfect personality. Moreover this is to be carried out here on earth in the flesh, and not in a post-mortem realm.

The present social order is destructive to personality, therefore wicked. It produces, encourages and justifies selfishness both in individuals and groups. Its objective is mainly material gain. Property rights supersede human welfare, thus permitting industrial exploitation even through the enlistment of governmental aid. It widens and intensifies the cleavage between the classes, races and nations. It completely ignores love and its application to human relationships. To realize "a harmonized man and harmonized society," in such a sinful order is impossible. The mission of the church is to help replace the present wicked order with a new righteous order. The church as it is constituted is not even conscious of this task. It has become an integral part and defender of the present vicious socio-economic order, calling Jesus "Lord, Lord," but refusing to inquire what God wishes it to do. The gospel it preaches is not Christian. Its organization is ecclesiastico-centered and divisive; its theology irrational and adulterated with mythology; its worship, unreal; its educational technique, magical rather than psychological; its ethics negative and individualistic; and its objective, otherworldly. The salt has lost its savor. The light has gone out of its altar, and lo, the whole world is in darkness.

To be sure there are individuals in and outside the church who are facing the issue realistically and are endeavoring to bring themselves in harmony with the will of God. Nevertheless what we have said above is true of the church as a whole. Our need is not for a substitute for the gospel but for a new birth for the church that would seek the truth—the will of God in history, in the hearts of its people and in the social turmoil round about—and which would undertake the adventure, experimentally and courageously, to create a new social order in which God and His children could have a favorable chance to work out their common purpose. Such a transformation in the church would necessitate the remaking of its entire structure and program. Starting with the shifting of its aim from saving souls after death to the building of a completely "harmonized man and harmonized society," it should reorganize its machinery, rebuild its edifices, rewrite its theology, reformulate its worship, revise its educational technique, redefine its code of ethics, to fulfill its mission for the realization of God's will on earth as stated above.

The Christian gospel has both a positive and negative side. On the positive side it is the way to the good life. On the negative side it is a campaign against sin, against whatever obstructs the way and hinders the realization of the good life for all. The church has weakened its position in the present crisis and has betrayed its Lord by its silence against or indifference to the sins of our age. Its excuse has been that it stands for positive and not negative values. This is sheer stupidity, cowardice or selfishness. A good deal of the strength of the church should be directed to unearth clearly the viciousness of our civilization, recognize its guilt and remove its sins. Where are the preachers who are sensitive to the sinfulness of our socio-economic system as well as to its fruits, and are condemning it as a thing to be hated and destroyed, as the abolitionists condemned slavery and the prohibitionists the liquor traffic? The number of people on the relief roll of the nation is on the increase. Yet we have enough provisions and material to feed, clothe, shelter and provide comfort and cultural opportunities for every family in the United States. Still we underplow corn, kill pigs, limit the production of farms and factories, and thus increase human suffering instead of applying the injunction, "Bear one another's burdens, and so fulfill the law of Christ." But which church raised its voice condemning this national act as a sin against God and man? Why are there so many in need? Not for lack of goods, but because of our calloused conscience that has allowed the rights of property, controlled by the few, to have preference over the claims of millions of needy human beings, citizens of the same country and children of the same God.

Even the politicians tell us that politics (science of government) is corrupt. But the church goes by and sees nothing, feels nothing and does nothing. Is not the spirit of nationalism and patriotism today almost synonymous with approval of the present state of its unethical and militaristic policies? What church feels the sting of this sin and is waging war against nationalism which supports the militarism of the nations and so hinders international peace? Much is said about good will among the races within the same country. Sometimes it is expedient and sometimes a necessity to endorse such views. But the very spirit of exclusiveness is a sin against God, because God's purpose is that we must work for a social order in which racial or class barriers are eliminated. Where is the preacher who can denounce his parishoners as sinners when they move to a more fashionable avenue or exclusive suburb because they do not want to have as their neighbors, Negroes, Jews or undesirable foreigners? Is such reasoning or emotional adjustment sinful? On the contrary it is generally thought of as a mark of success. Many ministers would rather congratulate their parishoners when they become rich enough to be exclusive with the hope of keeping their membership and of securing their financial support. Of course this too is sin, this time the sin of the minister and the church. But who is conscious of it to the point of saying, "God be merciful unto me a sinner?"

Against the desire of the congregations for a comfortable gospel we need men like John the Baptist, to unearth the sins of our socio-economic debacle and call us to repentance. Then we may be ready to listen to the positive aspect of the gospel and receive the grace of God to follow the new way.

Denunciation of the sins of the present order and attempts to reconstruct the whole structure and program of the church must be followed by active participation in the transformation and rebuilding of the structure of society. The main task in this field is to change the economic order known as the capitalistic system, through the instrumentality of the government. Industry and commerce have been competitive in method, profit-seeking in motive and self-centered in objective. These practices have led to the centralization of the country's wealth in the hands of the few, subjecting the many to destitution and despair. Under this system it is not possible for an individual to rise to his full development, nor to harmonize his inner life and maintain a normal relationship to society.

To give the right opportunities of self-realization for all is possible in this age only in a communal social order, in which all resources of the community are shared by all members of the community according to the needs of each. To assist in the creation of a government that will make this revolutionary transformation of our economic order should be the main task of the church today. Due to the emergency of the present crisis, as well as to the physical, moral and spiritual loss suffered by all, tomorrow may be too late.

True, man does not live by bread alone but neither can he live without bread. It is useless to offer God to the people when they need and want bread. The question is not God *or* bread but God *and* bread. If the body is the temple of God, how can God dwell in it or work through it when it is dilapidated and ready to fall to pieces? Charity has been a cardinal virtue in the church. To provide for the needy is to serve Christ, it has said. If it is ardent to build hospitals for the sick and soup kitchens for the hungry, should not the church be more concerned for an order in which human needs could be eliminated? Isn't it better to prevent unemployment than nurse the unemployed? How can it dare call radicals enemies of the country when they are attempting to find a preventive to human needs? Would not such a venture, experimental as it may be, be a better way of serving Christ and discovering God? How can the church preach brotherhood and send missionaries to Africa while it permits the innocent boys of the shameful "Scottsboro Case" to rot in jail? We cannot square our conscience by simply visiting the prisoners. We must prevent their getting to the prison. The church regards it a virtue to support the Red Cross which ministers to the victims of war. Should not the church be more concerned to prevent wars and thus save youth and the country from its diabolical consequences? Why be afraid of a change of systems and governmental policies when it is the only method to discover the way to life. Only he who tries and follows the lead to the end will reach the goal even though the trail be winding through thick woods. It is the way that the scientists, prophets and the heroes of the faith have followed. It is also the way of the Cross. Why not have the church follow it in the huge task of social reconstruction?

Kindness, expressed in benevolent acts when the need arises, should be perfected by creating an order in which charity will be displaced by justice and acts of benevolences by a coöperative order in which the wants of all shall be the concern of each. It might be more Christian for the church in the present crisis to cease its acts of charity and direct its energy to eliminating the present unjust and destructive economic order and to replacing it by a coöperative order. Such a daring venture might possibly entail less suffering than we are already experiencing. But suffering or no suffering the permanent solution of the present tragedy can be accomplished only through such drastic change. The present situation is becoming intolerable. To continue to waver means to postpone the day of judgment.

We need a new system, a new set of rules, a new order more than a "new deal." Even with better cards in hand the game is hopeless. Religious tradition, the constitution, the government, and other established institutions are all means to serve the welfare of the people. They should be revised and even abolished if this is necessary to start the new coöperative society. This is the will of God for this generation. Will the church dare to do the will of God?

The church should not ostracise radical movements in America as expressed by the Socialist and Communist groups, nor should it limit its mission to the accomplishment of their objectives only. It should lead, transform and supplement their claims and "beat them to it." To them it should say, "Come, let us reason and work together that we may find the way of life, the full life for all." Economic justice and security must be established and guaranteed for all. While that is the main goal of the Socialists and Communists it should be the starting point for the church. The final aim of the church is to transform humanity into a divine family, a communism in which the members, in addition to sharing material things, will share also their spirits, a growing mutuality of love and fellowship both among men everywhere, and between man and God. For only then can we have "a harmonized man and harmonized humanity," and grow toward a realization of the highest values for which all aspire.

It is the genius of the prophets of the Bible to be dissatisfied with the present, dream of a better future, and to inspire the people to live and labor sacrificially for the realization of the better day. Beginning with Abraham who was discontented with the status quo, and Moses who conducted a revolution for liberty and self-determination, to the seer of Patmos who sustained the loyalty of his readers by the picture of a new heaven and a new earth, religion is an adventure in search for the new, the higher and better. In a rapidly and perilously changing world the church must either lead the procession to the new day or suffer the consequences of a lost opportunity and gross neglect of its mission.

To change our mind from making life an enterprise in the seeking of our own personal safety, security, satisfaction and salvation, to an adventure in the creation of a new world in which love and coöperation would encircle the globe and control all the institutions and organizations of society is the meaning of repentance and the first step in Christian discipleship. He who makes this crucial decision and takes the step is born anew. Recognizing the spiritual kinship of humanity he gives himself to the task of making the family spirit rule all the children of God. He has become a new creature in Christ, a citizen of God's kingdom.

"Who are my mother and my brothers?" Jesus replied, when he was informed that his mother and brothers had come to take him, because they thought he was out of his mind. "And glancing round him in a circle he added, 'There are my mother and my brothers! Whosoever does the will of God, that is my brother and sister and mother.'" To have faith in the gospel means primarily to believe that all people everywhere will some day do the will of God and thus live as a new family, the family of God, devoting all that they have and are to the realization of God's will on earth. This is the new evangelism the church is called upon to undertake.

RELIGION AND THE GOD-STATE

EDMUND B. CHAFFEE

CHAPTER VI

RELIGION AND THE GOD-STATE

And I saw a woman sit upon a scarlet colored beast, full of names of blasphemy, having seven heads and ten horns . . . and upon her forehead was a name written "Mystery, Babylon, the Great, the mother of Harlots and abominations of the earth." And I saw the woman drunken with the blood of the saints, and with the blood of the martyrs of Jesus. . . . Rev. 17:4-6.

In these stinging words the writer of the last book in the Christian Bible lashes out against the Roman empire. That under the symbol of Babylon he means that mighty empire, practically all scholars now agree. Nor need one be a scholar to know that fact, for the writer John does not leave the reader in any doubt about it. As he develops his burning philippic against the Roman system, calling it a harlot, a beast, a dragon, he takes pains to give such open hints as these:

And the woman which thou sawest is that great city which reigneth over the kings of the earth. . . . The seven heads are seven mountains on which the woman sitteth.

"See," he says, "I mean Rome which sits on her seven hills."

And in these words he describes the emperor:

Here is wisdom. Let him that hath understanding count the number of the beast for it is the number of a man; and his number is six hundred three score and six.

And this, as we now know, was an open invitation to the reader to write the Hebrew letter equivalents to these numbers. When this is done we read plainly Cæsar Nero. There can be no doubt about it. The Roman empire hated the early Christians and the early Christians hated Rome. In persecution after persecution the Roman authorities and the people tried to stamp out these dissenters. They threw them to the lions; they soaked them in oil and burned them as torches; they tried every way that a people skilled in cruelty and refined in torture could devise to exterminate the disciples of the Jewish carpenter.

And why did they do this? All the religions of the earth had flowed into Rome and she was tolerant of them. The gods and goddesses of Greece, the mysteries of Egypt, the dualistic faith of Persia, they were all there and the Roman authorities looked on with kindly eye. But with the Christians it was different. Even such a good emperor as Marcus Aurelius persecuted them. Why was this? It was not because of any rites or ceremonies which the Christians practiced although scandalous stories were circulated about these. Nor was it because of anything the Christians believed about the Godhead or a future life—all this could be matched in other faiths. Nor was it because of their manner of life, for even their bitterest foes admitted that the Christians were kind and generous even to their enemies. It was none of these things. Rome turned with an insane fury upon the Christians for one thing. The disciples of Christos would not bow down to the emperor or his image. They would not take part in the universal emperor worship. The Christians had to flee to the catacombs because they would not admit that Rome was above all and beyond all. The Christians were driven from the haunts of men and called the enemies of all mankind because they would not give complete supremacy to the state. In the faith of the Christian, Christ was above Rome and this Rome would not tolerate. The Christian believed that his first allegiance must be to Christ. Rome said it must be to Rome. On this issue the Christians and the Roman empire drew the line of battle. Resistance to the claim of the empire that the Christians should worship the state was the first great conflict in which the blood of the Christian martyrs was shed. It was on this issue that the Christian community fought Rome and it was on this issue that the Christians perished by the thousands and tens of thousands. The Christians were true to their Jewish tradition and the first commandment of that tradition, "Thou shalt have no other Gods before me." Nor did it alter the case that this God was not one of wood or stone but an imperial government which could clothe itself with divinity.

All know the story. The Christians defied the might of Rome, its laws, its armies, its courts, its public opinion. Every weapon was used to break these humble followers of a Galilean peasant. But eventually the Christians won, for in 325 A.D. the Emperor Constantine gave full and complete recognition to the Christian faith and made it that of the empire itself. Many of us are now convinced that this political victory was of no real value to the spirit of true religion but it is not this which is our concern now. I would only point out that this conflict with the state and the deification of it was the first great battle waged by the Christian faith.

Today, by a curious turn of the wheel of time this old conflict is again arising. Once more the idea of the God-State is emerging and men are again being asked to yield not only their property and their lives but their very sense of justice and right to the nation. Once more the state is endeavoring to stamp out any loyalty which looks beyond itself. We see this phenomenon in Germany where the Hitler government would make the Church a servile handmaiden of the Nazi state. We see it too in the Soviet government of Russia which would outlaw religion altogether. We see it in Italy where Mussolini, although an atheist at heart, would use the Catholic Church as a national unifying force and stamp out all religious dissent from it. We see it in Japan where like ancient Rome, the emperor becomes a symbol of the state and one hundred per cent loyalty to him is demanded. We see it very definitely in our own United States where the doctrine is arising that no one can be a citizen unless he is willing to fight in any war which congress may declare, no matter what private religious scruples he may have against it.

Just how far we have already gone along the path of deifying the state is shown by the religious ritual which all countries are building up about it. There is a national anthem, a hymn of praise, which must be sung with the greatest respect and fervor. And we must rise when it is sung or played. Then there is the flag which must be displayed in a prescribed way and no other. Rules and regulations are laid down as to how it is to be washed and how destroyed when it has become worn and threadbare. Moreover the salute to it is definitely prescribed and made a part of the curriculum of our schools. There can be no disputing the fact that public opinion is to a large extent backing up all this. Nationalism is becoming in very truth "Man's Other Religion." And, we may add, that other religion is to millions more real and potent than any of the historic faiths.

Perhaps I can bring this home to you by asking you to think for a moment of what would happen if one were to take a Bible or a cross and tear or break it in pieces or trample upon it before an audience of average Americans. The audience would not like it but no one would be in bodily danger if he were guilty of such an act. But think for a moment of what would happen if one were to take the American flag and deliberately trample on it or rend it in twain. A man would be lucky if he escaped without being maimed and certainly he would be hauled into the courts and sent to prison. Some may recall how Bouck White burned the flags of all the nations back in 1916 or thereabouts in token of international unity and the six months sentence he drew for it. Now I am not for one moment advocating that either the Bible, the cross, the flag or any other religious or national symbol should be treated with anything but respect, but I am pointing out that the whole drift in our world today is toward the deification of the state much in the same way as the Roman empire deified it. This re-emergence of the God-State is creating a tension in the religious life of man whether he be Christian or Jew, Moslem or Buddhist.

Now the first question which naturally arises is why this increased reverence for the state? Why should we in this third and fourth decade of the twentieth century behold a rebirth of the cult of the mystical absolute state? To this question several answers are possible. There is the answer of Spengler, the German philosopher, who years before the rise of any of the European dictatorships was predicting with assurance the coming of the Cæsars. A few brief quotations will make his meaning clear.

This is the end of democracy. . . . As the English kingship became in the nineteenth century, so parliaments will become in the twentieth, a solemn and empty pageantry. . . . Men are tired to disgust of money economy. They hope for salvation from somewhere or other, for some real thing of honor and chivalry, of inward nobility, of unselfishness and duty. And now dawns the time when the form filled powers of the blood . . . awaken in the depths. . . . Cæsarism grows on the soil of democracy, but its roots thread deeply into the underground of blood tradition.

There now sets in the final battle between democracy and Cæsarism, between the leading forces of dictatorial money economics and the purely political will-to-order of the Cæsars.

Indeed the final words of Spengler's epoch-making "Decline of the West" deal with this very theme. For us, he says:

whom a destiny has placed in this culture and at this moment of its development—the moment when money is celebrating its last victories, and the Cæsarism that is to succeed approaches with quiet, firm step—our direction, willed and obligatory at once, is set for us within narrow limits, and on any other terms life is not worth living. We have not the freedom to reach to this or to that, but the freedom to do the necessary or to do nothing. And a task that historic necessity has set will be accomplished with the individual or against him.

Now when we recall that Spengler had conceived his philosophy before the war and had it fully worked out before the war closed, we cannot but be impressed with the uncanny accuracy of his prediction. Dictatorships have appeared; more may be on the way. And these dictatorships are taking the natural and inevitable course of mobilizing everything that will add to this centralization of autocratic power. It is for this purpose that Mussolini and Hitler would strive to make the state the supreme object of loyalty and devotion. In so far as Spengler is right and there is a drift to Cæsarism we must expect that the state will be clothed with the attributes of deity.

There is a second answer which may be made to our query as to why there has come this increased reverence for the state. That answer is found in the colossal failure of the world war to achieve a peaceful world. All over the world, and notably in our own land, men fought to be done with war. It was a war to end war. The world looked forward to a day when the nations should not arm against each other but rather should coöperate for a better and happier humanity. But that vision was not realized and instead of more internationalism there came a fiercer nationalism. If there was to be no effective league of nations to look after the interests of all, then each nation felt it must look after itself. Thus the race in armaments was renewed and the armies and navies became greater than before the war. Moreover the battle was transferred to the economic front and every possible obstacle was put in the way of trade. Tariff walls were built higher and higher and England, which never had believed in the protective policy, embraced it. The obvious result of all this has been to make the French more conscious of France, the Italians of Italy, the Japanese of Japan and Americans of America. Nationalism was accentuated. The state loomed ever larger in the thought of men and reverence for it increased.

Also a third answer may be made to our question. A third force is making the state assume more importance in men's thought. That force is found in the hearts of youth. Young men and women have become impatient and disgusted with the attitude of their elders toward the great social evils. Moreover they are "fed up" (to use an expressive term of the war) with the humdrum of a scientific culture and all the standardization which has grown out of it. They are in rebellion against it. In most of the churches too they have found little that really touched life. They have longed for something to which they could give themselves with all the abandon which is the right and the joy of youth. The social class conflicts to which economic radicals invited them somehow did not strike fire; they did not seem idealistic enough or big enough. But the fascist program of a unified state above the class battle made an appeal hard to resist. The youth in many lands came to feel that here was a great truth for which they could crusade. So all over the world they gave and are giving their uttermost loyalty to the state. With complete devotion they have lost themselves in it. All this has helped to give the state the place of God in their lives and in the lives of those who are about them.

The rise of Cæsarism, the failure of the world war to achieve a more neighborly and unified world, the appeal of extreme nationalism to youth—all these help to explain the growing reverence for the state of these last two decades. This development has made nationalism, to millions, a more potent religion than the historic faiths. But there is still another force working in the same direction. That force is found in the decline which has taken place in religious certainty. As the state has grown stronger the faith of the people has grown weaker. The development of the historical method and the critical appraisal of religious documents have made it difficult to appeal to religious authority with the confidence of the men of the past. The writers of the sacred writings we now know to have been men of life passions with ourselves. Moreover the whole scientific approach, of which this historical method is a part, has made it anything but easy to believe we are in a friendly or a caring universe. When our astronomers can tell us that on a map of the known universe made the size of a city block, a period would be 50,000 times too large to represent even the outermost limits of our whole solar system—to say nothing of our puny little earth—it is hard to believe that the power in and through this universe cares for us who are but little specks on this earth. And if to this damaging testimony of the astronomers we add that of the biologists who so stress our biological oneness with all life, new meaning and poignancy is given to the cry, "What is man that thou art mindful of him or the son of man that thou visitest him?"

The simple fact is that religious faith has been eaten away by what some one has well called the "acids of modernity." Yet it still remains the fact that man wants something outside of himself to which he may give himself without reserve and he still wants something outside of himself upon which he can rely, from which he can derive help and strength in his hour of need. While they never analyze it, there are multitudes who for this reason are drawn to the worship and the deification of the state. They find in it an emotional substitute for Christianity or whatever their old faith may have been.

Moreover, as we examine this phase of our subject, we must note another fact. Just as the inner religious life of man has been confused and weakened by scientific development, so the outer religious forms have been weakened by the growth of the secular state. Since the French Revolution this development has been marked. Increasingly the Church has been disestablished. Other countries followed the action of France, and today the same thing has happened in Mexico, in Spain, in Chile and in various other parts of the world. Nor is this trend confined to the so-called Christian countries. Mohammedan countries have shown the same tendency. In Turkey we no longer have the close tie-up between the mosque and the government which formerly was a matter of course. Perhaps we can sum up these trends in the statement that in the inner religious life the citadel is being attacked by mechanistic science and in the outer it is being assailed by the withdrawal of official support formerly given as a matter of course to organized religion by the secular government. It is quite possible that other causes besides those just sketched are at work, but of this fact there can be no doubt: the historic faiths are declining in their power over the minds and hearts of men, while the secular governments are clothing themselves with the attributes of deity and are demanding of their citizens a loyalty which formerly was given to God alone.

And why can't religion resign itself to this development? Why can't it accept the state as its god and fall down and worship it? Why can't it be content to play a subordinate rôle? The answer lies in the very nature of religion, whether that religion be Christianity or Judaism or any other faith. Religion is the consciousness of having direct and personal relations with the universal power which controls the course of nature and of human life. True religion always implies a cosmic reference. It is the assertion that there are absolute and eternal values, values which demand the utter devotion of man. Historically it has never tolerated—and as long as it remains itself can never tolerate—any usurpation of this supreme place in the heart of man. True religion demands always that man's first loyalty be to God and the eternal and absolute values which that term implies. The basic attitude of religion was well expressed by the apostle Peter when he and others were hauled before the council. The account found in the Book of Acts is most expressive:

> Then Peter and the other apostles answered and said, "We ought to obey God rather than men."

Religion must oppose the deification of the state because this God-State, mighty and powerful and worthy as it may be considered, itself is after all but a part, a very little part of the whole reality for which man always longs. Allegiance to a geographical locality is a poor substitute for allegiance to the Almighty God of beauty, truth and justice.

Moreover it must never be forgotten that Judaism and Christianity and other ethical religions have continuously insisted upon reverence for personality. But the God-State does not hesitate to sacrifice human personality in the interest of itself. It assumes to tell its citizens what they must do and what they must think. For the individual it cares little or next to nothing. If it needs his life in war it takes it ruthlessly and with no compunction. How different all this from true religion which makes personality and reverence for it its basic principle. Moreover the very genius of true religion is its universality. It looks upon all men as the children of one Father. It opposes the narrow nationalistic view of the state. It teaches that men are equal in the sight of God and it looks forward to the realization of a world, mark you a whole world, not just one land, based on brotherhood.

It is then because religion implies a cosmic reference and asserts absolute values that it cannot permit itself to be subordinated to the God-State which even at its best is but sectional and partial. And it must refuse to bow down to the Cæsars of today as it refused in the days of the Roman empire. It is considerations such as these which were in the hearts of the early Christians as they refused to worship the emperor or his image, and it is considerations such as these that are in the minds of the German Christians today as they battle to prevent their churches from becoming merely adjuncts of the Nazi state.

If what we have been saying thus far be true, if we are witnessing the rebirth of the old idea of the God-State and the worship of it, if true ethical religion in contrast to this nationalistic faith can never bow down and worship a God which in many respects is a modern Moloch, then it would seem as if a conflict lies ahead. This is indeed the case. On every hand there are signs of it. Just as before the Civil War the Dred-Scott decision so aroused religious folk that they said boldly that they recognized no obligation on their part to help slave owners extend their slaveholdings, so in these days there are religious men and women who are saying that there are limits beyond which they do not recognize the right of the government to command them. There is the issue of education and the effort now being made to make compulsory military training a part of it no matter what religious scruples there may be against it. Other issues will occur to you.

But the line of battle in the years ahead will be found in two fields, the economic and the international. On the economic side there is a strong and rapidly growing body of religious opinion which says that the present economic system is ethically wrong, that it is unjust and ought not to continue. Now it is easy to envision an attempt on the part of the great money kings of this land and other lands to maintain the status quo with all the legal machinery of the God-State of which we have been speaking. Just as the super-patriots have attempted to intimidate the ministers of Evanston, Illinois, so have the Patriotic Order of Sons of America attacked well-known clergy of Philadelphia because they have shown interest in the Sacco-Vanzetti case, in civil liberties, disarmament, increased navy building, and various other economic and political matters. To oppose the present industrial set-up tends to become treasonable and laws are passed and will be passed which aim to solidify and fortify the interests of the possessing classes. Not a few religious folk will oppose such legislation as unjust, and in order to be true to their conscience, which is the voice of that religion of which we have been speaking, they may refuse to obey it. Thus a conflict of the first magnitude will develop between ethical religion and the religion of the God-State. Particularly may we look for such a development in the field of free speech and press and in the field of education.

However, the most imminent line of battle is on the question of participation in war. It is now generally known that there is an ever-growing body of opinion among the leaders and the rank and file in our churches and synagogues which definitely repudiates war as such, no matter for what alleged purpose it may be waged. A questionnaire prepared by the magazine, *The World Tomorrow,* revealed a tremendous drift toward the position that all war is contrary to true religion and that a follower of Jesus and the Hebrew prophets could not consistently take part in it. It has become evident that departments within our government already feel the force of this opinion and fear it. This is evidenced by the fact that more and more willingness to take part in war without any questioning of its justice or injustice is being made the test of citizenship. Madame Rosika Schwimmer was refused citizenship and this refusal was upheld by the supreme court because she would not promise to bear arms for this country although the question in her case was purely academic. Professor Douglas C. MacIntosh of Yale was also refused citizenship even though he was not an absolute pacifist and expressed himself as being quite willing to fight in any just war. The mere fact that he reserved the right which any religious man must reserve to decide in his own heart and conscience as to the justice of the particular war was held by the court to disqualify him for the sacred duties of American citizenship. And this in contrast to the fact that the man who killed Mayor Cermak of Chicago and nearly assassinated our President was admitted to citizenship at about the same time that Professor MacIntosh, professor of ethics, was denied it. And in St. Paul, Minnesota, the Rev. T. F. Rutledge Beale, minister of the People's Church, was denied citizenship although he was willing to support and defend the Constitution. Mr. Beale maintained that the Kellogg Pact, solemnly signed by this government and now a part of the law of the land, outlawed war, thus making it eminently right and proper for its citizens to do the same. Mr. Beale contended that it was the duty of the individual to repudiate war even as the nation had repudiated it. But his petition was denied.

There can be little doubt that there is increasing tension here between the religious man, who feels that the most sacred obligation laid upon him is that of being true to his conscience, and the God-State, which tends increasingly to admit no such thing as the right of private conscience.

To show that struggle and tension in all its stark reality let me describe a scene which took place in the Military Tribunal of Paris. I quote from the *War Register,* the international magazine of the War Resisters movement.

Standing before the colonel and other military authorities in charge of the proceedings is a young Protestant theological student. His name is Jacques Martin and he has carefully considered the stand he has adopted against all war.

"Well," said the judge, "you have refused to submit to the law of our country?"

"Yes, that is right," said the young man. "I obey a higher law. I cannot disobey what I conceive to be the will of God."

"A very beautiful theory," said the Judge, "but a Utopian ideal, incompatible with moral and civil law."

"But," continued Jacques, "I can make no other choice." In persuasive tones the question is put:

"But what about the right to defend one's self?"

"I would only defend myself in so far as it does not mean taking the lives of others."

"Unfortunately everyone does not think as you do," admitted the Colonel. "Why," he further asked, "did you not leave France, since you despise her laws?"

"If I despised the laws of France, I should certainly have left the country. But I respect them and that is why I have come to place myself at your disposal. I know the consequences but I would testify in my own country to the better, higher way."

Then one of those defending the prisoner spoke up. "There

are two religions, Colonel, your own which is barbarous, and which, alas, is still that of the state. And there is the religion of the prisoner, which is that of the gospel. You will only succeed in making martyrs and your struggle will be in vain. Remember that Rome tried to do the same thing and was defeated."

Then a witness spoke up, "I have the impression of being in the midst of just men—but of those present, I feel that the one who is most just is the accused."

This did not win much approval from the court and Jacques Martin was sentenced to one year's imprisonment.

And it must not be forgotten that after that year has expired he may be called up again and resentenced on and on until he is broken in health or until he is above the military age of fifty-four. Such are the head-on collisions which are taking place as the God-State seeks to compel the worshippers of the God of all mankind to fall before it.

In thus calling attention to the cleavage which is growing in our modern world between the worship of the universal God and the worship of the God-State I am not oblivious of the fact that some will say that no civil state can exist unless it is to have full and complete authority. Thus these folk would say to me: "Mr. Preacher, what you are preaching is nothing but anarchy." I want to deny that charge most emphatically. The really religious man will obey the state except in the most extreme cases. He will not frivolously or merely to satisfy his own desires or appetites defy its laws or decrees. He will not lightly stand out against it. He will so stand out only when it is a matter of fundamental conscience when he knows that he must obey God rather than man. Moreover it is to be noted as a matter of historical record that the Quakers and the Mennonites and other sects opposed to certain phases of the claim of the state have coöperated with it in all but the more exceptional cases. They have followed the rule of Christ to render unto Cæsar the things that are Cæsar's and unto God the things that are God's. But in that realm of conscience they have believed God to be supreme rather than Cæsar. Moreover I would point out that such outstanding churchmen as Dr. Fosdick, Bishop McConnell and dozens of others who would stand out resolutely against any war they thought unjust cannot be considered anarchistic in any rational use of that word. Indeed these men believe that in being true to their God they are in the highest sense being true to their country. Only this they will not do—they will not give to their country the worship that belongs only to God. In the words of the Westminster Confession of Faith:

God alone is Lord of the conscience and has left it free from the doctrines and commandments of men.

By a strange turn of the historical process, the mood and manner of ancient Rome is again upon us. Once more men seek to attain a full and complete national unity. Once more they are learning to hate the suggestion that there can be anything greater than the state. Once more we have a nationalism which would deny justice and the essential oneness of mankind. Once more we have a spirit which would compel the individual to do what he believes to be wrong. Once more the devil is saying to the worshippers of the cosmic God, "All this will I give thee if thou wilt fall down and worship me." But the religious man can never cease to seek for justice and brotherhood and peace no matter how much a God-State would strive to compel him otherwise. God grant that we religious folk may not have to make the choice, but if we do, may we have the courage and the stamina to speak as did those youth described in the Book of Daniel when they were asked to violate their religion and their conscience by worshipping the image of gold set up by the king as a test of loyalty. Listen again to their reply:

"O Nebuchadnezzar, we are not careful to answer thee in this matter. If it be so our God whom we serve is able to deliver us from the burning fiery furnace and he will deliver us out of thine hand, O king. But if not, be it known unto thee, O king, that we will not serve thy God nor worship the golden image which thou hast set up."

There speaks the voice of true religion, a voice that Rome could not still and a voice which will be heard when our modern Cæsars are laid in the dust and even the God-State is but a memory. The Church must heed that voice!

CAN THE CHURCHES ACHIEVE UNION?

H. LINCOLN MACKENZIE

CHAPTER VII

CAN THE CHURCHES ACHIEVE UNION?

ARDENT advocates of Church union describe with enthusiasm the recent achievements in the movement towards Christian unity. They point with pride to the United Church of Canada, to the union of the Established Church and the United Free Church in Scotland, to significant unions in India and in China, to the Cogregational-Christian combination, and to adopted resolutions of conferences and assemblies of the Methodist and Presbyterian churches. All of which is not to be decried, but none of which touches the essential problems that confront churches which seem to be hopelessly separated by great chasms of Faith and Order. A study of the chief mergers reveals that success has attended earnest efforts only where there existed a common faith and practice, and only where religious idiosyncrasies originated and perpetuated schisms. Unfortunately for Protestantism, little or no progress has been made affecting real differences, since Calvin's attempts to reconcile Luther and Zwingli ended in failure. Even tentative approaches to Rome by English high churchmen have been met by flat refusals to negotiate on any terms save those laid down by the Pontiff. Indeed it is a notorious fact that the Roman Catholic hierarchy cherishes as the only outlook for reunion the penitent return of the Protestant secessionists. The Protestant Episcopal Church maintains a similar attitude towards all other denominations. It is to be expected that a coalition of forces will continue among the unorthodox evangelical sects as they face the moral demands of the age and the more potent factor of economics. But in the meantime, a graver menace confronts the Church in the growing disposition to relegate the religious instinct to the limbo of the infantile period of the race. Not however, through a frontal attack, but by quietly ignoring and practically discarding all so-called supernatural influence, while in its place are being substituted the handmaid of Psychiatry and the more utilitarian ægis of Science. A great host today seeks and receives the aid and benefits of science in many instances where formerly they would have turned to the higher and less misleading ministries of the Church.

Thus the dissenter and the protagonist of Church union stand upon common ground, in that both must ultimately face an ever-increasing foe—the unbeliever in any and all religions. And when the final issue is joined it will not be in the arena where diversified sects contend, but in a universal anti-religious cohesion of forces that will utterly ignore the reality of the Supernatural. Therefore the Church of the living God must be prepared and should now gird itself with greater armor for the coming trial. It is this foreseen contest of forces that more than anything else prompts the writer to affirm what seems to him to be the only thorough-going platform upon which all believers in the Divine may unite. Other reasons, of course, suggest themselves such as (1) the ineffectiveness of the Christian ideal in influencing a complex world to accept standards of living exemplified in the first century of the Christian era; (2) inadequate conceptions of religion arising from partial and self-willed views of the

Divine, resulting in petty jealousies, ill-will, and dangerous prejudices; (3) lack of power and real convictions on the part of the church-going population, so that the neutral and the religious antagonist is unimpressed; (4) the ridiculous spectacle of churchmen advocating coöperation, harmony and human brotherhood when they themselves do not make practical demonstrations in the household of faith; (5) inconsequential matters on the periphery of Christianity which myopically are magnified, through unfamiliarity with basic and central principles of the good religious life. The last, and not by any means the least, consideration that I wish to present is the schismatic missionary effort of churches that has become the subject of sardonic laughter by the unprejudiced observer.

Other, and perhaps more potent reasons for a union of Christian forces might be enumerated, but the oncoming Armageddon for the contention of a world in which it shall be determined whether God or Mammon shall hold sway over the conscious will of man, looms as the primary desideratum in any presentation.

Ecclesiastical historians have recorded that Protestantism arose as a protest against too much authority in religion and in an untoward expression of what the New Testament revealed as Christian virtues. Now a declaration of religion based upon individual judgments is bound to be divisive. The children of Protestant churches that from the beginning formulated creeds and organizations that expressed individual preferences may become impatient over consequential weaknesses, but they must of necessity study the causes of disunion before a rapprochement can be made.

Before the sixteenth century divergence, there were others

of probably greater significance, having their origin in the first and second centuries. The New Testament records the early struggles between Jewish Christians, led by James, the brother of our Lord, and the ardent defenders of the liberties of Gentile converts, championed by St. Paul. In the second century the Christian faith was nearly wrecked by internal dissensions whose party leaders could not agree. Indeed as early as 96 A.D., Clement, a leader in the Church at Rome, writes to the Church in Corinth that "We should be obedient unto God rather than follow those who in arrogance set themselves up as leaders through abominable jealousy." And the Master Himself had to meet the early opposition of His own followers to one who was not a member of the group but who, nevertheless, performed good works in the name of Christ, with the great pronunciamento, "He that is not against us is for us."

Again the history of Christianity during the first five centuries is one of controversies and dissensions that finally resulted in Rome and Constantinople dominating other Churches independent of each other—perpetuating the Roman Catholic and Greek Catholic schism. Earlier, about A.D. 195, the Roman Church excommunicated the Asian churches because they could not agree on the day on which Easter should be observed.

It is not remarkable, therefore, that divergences of Faith and Order traceable to the inception of Christianity should characterize religion today. It would be strange, religion being what it is, if the contrary were true. Uniqueness is an essential characteristic of a vital religious faith. Any approach to church union must take this into consideration. If today the trend is in the direction of unification, even if imposed from without through economic necessities, slow progress will be made until the débris due to individualistic expressions of religion, sentiment, prejudices, and illusions is cleared away. For in the Church Universal there can only be maintained as a common basis of support one essential article of faith: belief in God. But within there must be latitude for individual convictions and beliefs which groups may discover to be helpful, and forms of worship, rites and practices, that strengthen and inspire, will need to be tolerated. Perhaps in its initial stages a supreme head or an episcopal hierarchy will be necessary, but ultimately this concession will be regarded as a matter of economy in administration, since the Protestant affirmation of the soul's unhindered access to God will be accepted by enlightened minds everywhere as the heart and genius of religious faith.

Nevertheless, greater progress than ecclesiastical overheads suspect is being made in this direction among the lay members in many communities. Many members of the evangelical churches base their preference on convenience and "good preaching" regardless of the denomination. Children are sent to the nearest Sunday school which largely determines the support and adherence of their parents. Others attend their own denominational church for sentimental reasons. When I was a student-pastor in a small community where seven churches existed each church was maintained largely because of the associations and sentiments connected with them by the inhabitants. The clergy alone were guilty of seeking to emphasize doctrinal differences as a basis of support.

There exists, however, a generation—my own—that disavowed the old orthodoxies, and many left the Church altogether. These, and their children, now constitute the hope of the Church. They are without labels and are ready for cultivation in a Church that seeks to interpret the mystery of life, and that will give them new meanings and values for aimless living. The present perfunctory service of worship can never do it! It belongs to yesterday. And the old order fadeth. Sectarianism will not win them. It offers a stone, while they cry for bread.

Among certain ecclesiastics one of the chief barriers to the unification of all Christian Churches is the ancient conception of Apostolic Succession. According to the earliest available data as recorded in the Acts of the Apostles, the gift of the Holy Spirit was received through the laying on of hands, first by the Apostles, and later by their successors. This act of consecration bestowed on the candidate the grace and power which enabled him to teach and to proclaim the Gospel. Thus his ministry was authenticated, and what is considered of even greater importance, he was properly commissioned to administer the sacraments.

The Roman Catholic and Protestant Episcopal Churches arrogate to themselves the sole right to this ancient prerogative, inasmuch as each claims to be the direct heir of the apostolic Churches. So far, however, as it is at all possible to trace in a historic manner the successors of these ancient sees, no one would care to deny the Roman Catholic Church's right to make the first claim. But if it be admitted that such a privilege is the only guarantee of a true Church, then this Rock on which Christ's Church was built has already been split beyond restoration. For Rome cannot erase the schism of Avignon, when the succession met with its fatal blow in a dual papacy. In a world, where, as history records, strife and disaster disrupted empires, there can be no arrogation of spiritual rights on the theory of *direct* succession.

The real intention of the apostolic act was not to insure the perpetuation of a dominant Church, but to transmit the divine power of fulfilling the mission of the Master, Jesus Christ. Wherever His Word is obeyed, and His work carried on, there is the only Apostolic Church, and the final court of appeal is the written record of His teaching contained in the New Testament. Whosoever will take up His Cross and follow after Him is a disciple and a successor in the ministry of the Great Cause.

To talk then of "Apostolic Succession" and the "true Church" is to speak in conundrums, so far as the generation we have in mind is concerned. The faith of their fathers is lost and can never be re-won. It is doubtful that it would serve them if it could be re-captured.

Let it not be thought that it is our intention to disparage in any degree the great work which the servants of Christ in every age have accomplished. Nor do we mean to imply that the Churches which they founded are altogether lacking in the things of the Spirit. We salute them, their work, and the memorials they raised in ancient and beloved institutions. But it is with the same emotions and feelings that one regards the splendor of ancient Athens, or the glory of an old cathedral. They are to be venerated and cherished as highwater marks which it is incumbent upon our generation to surpass if we can.

The call today is to face our age with the same heroic spirit and daring by which they conquered. To them God was a pillar of cloud by day and a fire by night, as they travelled the wilderness, blazing trails for those who would come after them. Their work and their ideals are for us to build upon. Our mistake is one of standing still, and not venturing forth to apply with equal zeal and valor the spiritual forces at our command. We have been content to rest upon the laurels won. The world suffers because the fires of faith have been allowed to die down. We must kindle them anew, and striking again our tents, march on. Hunger and cold and the harder experience of misunderstanding and animosity may be encountered, but we shall seek the hill-top where the everlasting glory dawns.

Frankly, I am skeptical about the possibility of uniting the old-line denominational Churches: Evangelicals, Episcopalians, and Roman Catholics. Sentiment and emotions are too dominant; and dogmas, creeds, peculiar practices and petty jealousies cannot be reconciled. The way must come through a new conception of the function of the Church. As Lincoln said of a country, so we may say a Church should be: "By the people, for the people, and of the people." But for this, adequate leadership is essential— leaders who emphasize above everything else the spirit of Christ, and who will exemplify in their lives the type of service which He and His disciples rendered to their age. A Church that functions solely in the interest of people, and not to maintain itself as an institution will rapidly cease to think of itself in terms of a denominational tag. Its primary concern will be to direct baffled souls, and to bring peace and healing to a wounded world. In this noble work its ministers and priests must exemplify as never before a way of life that will impress the world as being Divinely directed. When this occurs the adherence of this new way of life will need to face some of the old problems relative to Faith and Order.

But as in the beginning days of Christianity the peculiar purpose of the movement will determine its moulds. I wish to outline what seems to me will be determining factors in such an attempt to restore the House of God.

A primary consideration will be the theistic conception. God is not worshipped today in any real sense, because He is inadequately conceived. The old glamour that surrounded the Deity of sectarianism is gone. Modern minds do not sing the old hymns because their theology is out-moded. The songs of Zion no longer express the new embryonic thoughts of God. One cannot sing about what one does not feel. Isaac Watts, William Cowper, Ray Palmer, Robert Robinson, Phoebe Cary, Charles and John Wesley and F. W. Faber wrote hymns expressing the faith and theology of their day, and they were sung by people with that faith. But for a modern congregation to sing some of these hymns is nothing short of blasphemy. To sing words which do not coincide with one's experience is to be profane and sacrilegious. And to inflict such hymns on youth as we do in our Sunday schools and young peoples' societies is pitiful. Consequently it is doubtful that the new Church will be a singing Church. That will have to come later. Will it be a praying Church? Can one really pray unless there is something greatly felt that makes prayer essential? The new leaders will need to commune with God. The evidence of their power from such communion will in due time inspire the desire for real prayer among their followers, even as Christ's disciples were led to seek from Him the true way of prayer.

Let no one suppose that such a movement, within the Church, which is now due, will be in any sense the true and only way. It is an anachronism to think in such terms of anything relating to earthly experience. And like all other expressions of the human soul there will follow later organizations and the sure doom of stratification, but its mission will then be accomplished. Unification will have been established. The pathetic aspect of present-day auditorium religion practiced by all churches is that it does not recognize itself as a thing of the past. It does not know it is through. It persists all unaware that the world that matters has passed by.

The primary concern of the new Church will be social and not theological. Its roots will be embedded not in time-worn creeds but in living issues. The world will be regarded as a vast laboratory in which experimentation ought to be the chief concern. One of the encumbrances of our present society is its underlying philosophy that there are institutions and orders that willy-nilly must be perpetuated. The new order will advance on the assumption that only the useful has value: a bridge that is no longer capable of carrying the traffic that must cross is torn down. But we do not apply the same wisdom to our social or religious institutions.

One of the great things about Jesus was the uncompromising manner in which He dealt with the ecclesiastical hierarchy of His day. It was quite obvious to Him that God was God, and Mammon was Mammon. Therefore new wineskins for the new truth. Calvary was inevitable. He would have wasted His time had He endeavored to unite the old sects. He knew that time, as time has, would take care of Pharisee, Sadducee and Herodian alike.

Any new alliance of religious forces must deal in a like manner with old-time institutions of religion. Even our theological seminaries will have to undergo the same renewal. They now exist as recruiting stations of sectarianism.

They were founded by ecclesiastical groups that still have to be mollified if their students are to be accepted as ministers. Furthermore, the financial sources from which support is solicited and from which foundations have been secured, cannot be ignored. Moral, if not economic obligations commit their leaders to points of view which are wholly inconsistent with the demands of a brave new world.

It is becoming a commonplace to say that the sectarian Church of today is helpless, if not inconsistent, in the face of the topsy-turvy world in which we live. But it needs to be pointed out that the Federal Council of Churches, the offspring of sectarianism, is likewise impotent. It is too dependent upon the whims of its denominational sponsors to be of any real consequence. Its status is pretty much that of the Y. M. C. A., in comparison with the churches. It may only do the things that common consent allows, whereas what is important and crucial is to do things that will never receive the vote of old-time groups.

Churches that preach platitudinously about peace, the evils of a competitive and acquisitive society, that inveigh against concentrated wealth, political chicanery, and racial discriminations, while they themselves partake of and practice all the evils and sins they denounce, are in great need of rehabilitation. Can the blind lead the blind? Can a corrupt tree bring forth good fruit?

Church officials in every communion are apparently much more anxious about financial deprivations than they are concerned about what is happening to people's souls. And plenty is happening! Concern for investments and the maintenance of positions are in themselves so exhaustive and depleting that unbiased thought and clear vision become impossible. So priests who become bishops, pastors who become superintendents or secretaries are as good as lost to churches that require of their shepherds and saviours the disinterestedness of the Son of Man who had not where to lay His head. Indeed the greatest hindrance to church union today is not altogether ecclesiastical differences so much as vested interests. A man is elevated to a place of eminence and at once he regards himself as a guardian of the status quo. He becomes skeptical of new ideas, afraid of changes, and a coward in deciding issues. So, as in the days of the Master, the hosts of Satan wear fine raiment and live in great houses, while in the highways and hedges, the lame, the halt and the blind are betrayed by those whom they trust and are uncared for by those whom they support.

Jesus was concerned with the Kingdom of God. If the conception means anything today it is to be discovered in the realm of spiritual values. Consequently a society organized primarily to exploit raw materials, and specifically engaged in the amassing of wealth, operates without regard to spiritual values. And the Church has been satisfied to traffic on the left-over time of the bedeviled masses, while it continually countenances by its silence the prostitution of those whom it seeks to spiritually fortify. It consents to be a hospital for those whom an inimical social order wounds. It is an ambulance at the foot of the cliff to succor the belated traveller who falls because no one builds a fence strong enough to avoid the disasters.

The rejuvenated Church will not be a hospital with an ambulance, but a socio-religious order with a program. Its creed will read something like this: God is a spirit of personal goodness permeating the universe. He may never be seen but always experienced. Jesus was supremely, but nevertheless a limited, incarnation of that Spirit. Everything is sacred. Selfishness is the greatest sin. Coöperation is the greatest virtue. Service that enables individuals to rise to higher levels of appreciation and spiritual enjoyment is the greatest good. Life is continuous beyond death. The world is a kindergarten in which the Divine may become known. Noble character is its greatest fruit. Conformity of beliefs is unnatural. The bond of unity is belief in God and the desire to further common interests. He only has the right to rule and govern who exemplifies the highest virtues in coöperative effort and altruistic service. The strongest and perhaps wisest credo of such a new Christian alliance will not be in any formulation of platforms or doctrines, as such, but in the new social structures that it will engineer. Such a Church will enlist the trained intellect, the skilled technician, the pure scientist, the professionally trained, and each one, according to his talents and abilities, will be encouraged to find his place of service dedicated to the common good.

The mistake of the passing ecclesiastical order has been in its exclusion of areas of life that are the chief concerns of men. The assumption has been that the ethical and spiritual teachings of the Church would be carried over into the affairs of the everyday world. To realize that this does not occur, it is only necessary to observe the unchristian ethic that obtains in nearly every concern in which man is occupied. Men do not labor as under the eye of God, *sub specie aeternitatis*. Neither do religious considerations enter into the purposes and plans of multitudes. The Oxford Group's principle of "daily guidance" is nearer to what ought to be. If the Group renders no other service than calling the attention of its followers to this specially neglected privilege, its contribution to religion will be inestimable. For surely God's kingdom is established where the Divine will is in all things manifested. To seek Divine direction in one's life at all times is to have an insight and a power commensurate with one's tasks.

It appears then that much of the final purposes and good intentions of Christians who seek to practice their religion are nullified by the indifferent who are dominated by selfish and ulterior motives. Consequently we live in a semi-pagan world. Perhaps this is being too generous. If so, and I am inclined to think it is, it follows that the ethical standards of the followers of Christ are not high enough, and their influence is not great enough, to offset the deeds actuated by irreligious motives, schemes, and ambitions. This, in itself, should bring one to a full realization that there is something radically wrong. The weakness is to be discovered in the manner and method in which religion is dispensed from week to week in all Churches. Either the dynamic of faith that should actuate its membership is too weak, or it is not functioning properly.

In this connection it may be of interest to note that the average church attendant does not indicate any serious misgivings with the established religious routine, or if it is at all questioned there is no indication of responsibility for something better. If, therefore, a new order is to arise, it will be necessary to re-educate Church people so that they may not impede progress through misunderstanding. Men and women with inspired vision will need to function as prophets and teachers of the new order in expounding through pen and voice its basic principles, and probably what is of more immediate importance, to point out the inadequacy of the old régime. This is of especial importance where solutions to intolerable conditions are wanting in areas of life where despair grows with age, as men and women face maturity and old age with a feeling of not having lived well, and without making any worthwhile contributions to the common welfare. It is of paramount importance that in any approach to this task of re-educating the adherents of churches, it be pointed out that a political order which has dismally failed in its many attempts to establish peace and prosperity for all, permeated by the good life, is no longer worthy of the confidence and trust ordinarily imposed in it. Hence only a new order with its leadership consecrated to the interests of all must be indicated as the primary essential in the rehabilitation not only of the Church but of the world.

If one asks for a life-giving program capable of bearing this load, the answer is that some such technological structure as has been announced by the Committee on Technocracy is nearer to meeting the requisites of a complex world than the old two-horse combination of political parties and laissez-faire industrial monopolies. This, of course, will sound the death knell of unrestricted individualism, and the rights of private ownership which is now maintained wholly in the interests of the wealthy few. Subtract the evils occasioned by unregenerate nature, and all of the great deleterious forces that prey upon the rights and privileges of men and women, can be traced to the uncontrolled rights of private monopolies, and the desire for profit and power occasioned by the present competitive system.

The new Church will need to be as emphatic in zealously pointing out the sin of a society that has to provide pittances for old age and insurance against unemployment as it is in proclaiming against the sins of murder, theft, adultery, and other forms of corrupting influences. In a just order of society, there will be no more need for old age pensions and unemployment insurance than there is now a necessity for such safeguards in behalf of multi-millionaires. These provisions are again the old ambulances in the valleys of necessity, established to carry off the victims who fall over our inadequate walls built to fence the dangerous cliffs of an unjust and unnecessary profit system. A statesmanship that combines the collectivism of the Soviets with the technical ability of American industrial engineers, based on the ethics of the Sermon on the Mount, is capable of converting materials and energy into a subsistence level that will tower above the peaks of capitalistic prosperity as Mount Everest towers above the Himalayas.

In the new dispensation which is opening before the world, nationalism, one of the chief causes of friction, must be relegated to the out-grown and more primitive socio-political organizations of tribalism and feudalism. There is no reason or justice in any group of people maintaining suzerainty over vast tracts of land, when other groups are herded in areas which do not afford adequate subsistence. To be afraid that such races as the Orientals and Latins will dominate is to cry "wolf." Such fears are alone justified in a nationalistic régime that can only be permanently maintained by military force. Large military expenditures are part and parcel of this primitive arrangement of which war is an inevitable concomitant. In other words any new church alliance that seeks to initiate international accord, must work towards the removal of all national boundaries, so that eventually the peoples of the earth will know but one vast domain as their Fatherland in which all races shall have equal rights and privileges. Only then will it be possible for the peoples of the earth to bow down and worship one God—the Father Almighty, supremely revealed in His Son, our Lord and Saviour, Jesus Christ. The Ten Commandments and the ethic of the Sermon on the Mount may be taken as the basic law by which man shall govern and be led. This is one way in which the Church Universal can be established, and the Kingdom of God made a reality.

The complete separation of the Church from the State, although it may be justified from a purely historical stand-point, can never be ethically justified. The practical outcome has been that the State ends by being wholly dominated by secular interests; a gargantuan monster without a religious spirit, whose creed is solely one of national expediency. Such a political anomaly could never have happened had there been a United Church. But to please all, the State had to remain neutral. Now the union of the State and Church can-not be achieved, if it proves at all desirable, so long as the prejudices of men are rooted and embedded in ecclesiastical pastures, from which will require an international moral earthquake to shake them loose. At present group ethics and group loyalties are morally incapable of such a righteous achievement. It has been tried ever since Nicæa with advo-cates whose names are venerated by every Church historian, but without any notable consequence save the "justification" of the status quo. Believers in divisive arrangements will go on fighting each other over the spoils of their own systems, but those whose power is Light, Truth, Justice, Equality and Fraternity, will march on to possess the earth.

The opportunities that would be created by a new international alignment for the neglected development of man's latent talents and abilities are beyond any adequate portrayal. Suffice to say that it would be a renaissance such as the world has never known. The spectre of fear and want would not hang over mankind to cloud the imagination and to condition all work. The type of education which is now administered would give place to new schools that would operate as essential units of the larger world order. Each school would be a model unit of the actual world wherein the problems, interests, and desires of the race would be studied and experimented upon so that the student would naturally step from the place of concentration to the field of operation.

A radical change such as is herein implied can only be brought about by a complete change in an educational system that has been derived from a social order built upon a competitive-profit foundation. Unless radical changes occur in the minds of school boards who largely govern what is taught, one may not look for leadership in this direction. There are, however, many dissatisfied superintendents of schools, principals, and teachers who would be willing to follow wise direction. Even so, many of them are hamstrung by economic necessities, and these with other unenlightened pedagogues may constitute a formidable barrier against any contemplated changes. They too will fear the socialization of private property and the regimentation of the nations of the world, a fear engendered by a politico-social arrangement that has provided jobs and bread for those who are reasonably prepared to become parasites at the capitalistic feasts that rugged individuals provide for their own pleasure. Most of these pedagogues have unwittingly contributed to the kind of training which hapless youths receive to fit them for the docile rôle of unquestioning obedience to things as they are. A wisely directed propaganda prepared for their consumption may save them but this is extremely doubtful. Nevertheless the Church must capture the schools as one of its first citadels, for a new educational system that will gear in with a reconstructed order must be marked by the religious spirit. This, of course, will be in direct contrast to what now obtains, inasmuch as our present educational system has relegated religious instruction to the Churches, none of which have been at all able to cope with the task. Nor does a sectarian set-up permit it, owing to the great lack of time and funds. Indeed the pathetic state of denominational Sunday schools is in itself a severe indictment of schismatic religion.

Contrary to the opinions of those who are afraid of a world where there is room and plenty for all, the leisure problem will disappear. First, because leisure is a mold that grows only in an unorganized state and is the result of a lack of proper training and enlightenment. And secondly, a world organized to develop spiritual values, that sees all things from the spiritual viewpoint will promote those desires and capacities that through expression receive the greatest satisfaction. To properly understand this possibility one needs to distinguish between "rest" and "leisure." "Leisure" is the time spent without the thrill of having something to do that challenges innate capacities, while "rest" is the time required to restore depleted energy.

Living and working in a world in which the need for basic necessities of life is no longer a nightmare, there will be ample opportunities for rest, inasmuch as the absence of hurry and rush so characteristic of present-day activities will characterize all occupations. Indeed the only problem will be the lack of time in which to see and to do all that a new age of interests will provide. The freedom to study, travel, work, and play, that now belongs to the few, will be enjoyed by the many.

While some may prate of the liberty which now obtains under the present capitalistic system, an increasing number grow skeptical concerning its actuality. An economic system that fails to provide ample subsistence for multitudes of deserving people and that requires those who are gainfully employed to goose-step in its line of march, is more and more creating conditions of enslavement. In such a world only those who have abundant means of support are at liberty. Even so, it must never be forgotten that ultimately there is only one kind of liberty that must be obtained at all cost, the liberty that a person enjoys who is freed from the tyranny of sin. An order such as we may now visualize is designed to insure against the temptations to evil that arise in a highly competitive system which breeds avarice, engenders lust, encourages dissipation and intemperance, thus making the good life impossible for any one. In it unsatisfied needs clamor for satisfaction while the disappointing quest for things with which to satisfy them leads multitudes into all sorts and conditions of sin that accumulate with the rapidity of national and private debts. Souls are always for sale in a market where material, mental, and spiritual values are maintained at a high premium. Once these values are made available to all "without money and without price," the old temptations will disappear. To be sure the New Order will bring others in its wake, but they will have the redeeming virtue of being of a higher type. The fact that mankind continues to battle against ancient sins that enslave is in itself a sufficient indictment against an unregenerate organized order of society that ever produces unregenerate souls. A higher plane of living must be realized in the world of secular forces before these old evils can be conquered. Mending old dykes is a futile task when less effort and cost will build new ones.

To argue, therefore, that liberty will not be enjoyed under a religious system of collectivism is to overlook the debilitating effects upon human lives everywhere as a result of the more drastic form of regimentation which a capitalistic order has imposed upon the world. In it only a comparative few are free—the 1 per cent who own—in America—59 per cent of the wealth. C. Lester Smith, who "makes" or inherits a fortune can go to Florida or Europe when he so desires, and indulge his atavistic and predatory instincts in collecting antiques, but such privileges can never be enjoyed by Tom Jones, born in poverty and lacking in the type of character, talents and abilities that would make him become a member of the "rugged individualistic party," a party that alone insures the wealth, position, and authority peculiar to this group. Where the competitive-profit system permits one C. Lester Smith to rise to the top, millions of Tom Joneses must remain at the bottom. Such is the tragedy of the old order. It can only make a like provision for humanity the world over. Better to experiment a thousand years than to remain indifferent to such a world.

The praiseworthy efforts of the wealthy who build hospitals and endow institutions, are being seriously questioned, inasmuch as provision is only made for those who are mutilated by the process in which wealth is secured. What is of still greater condemnation, charity and philanthropy are made necessary by the unfair practices of those who deprive workers and their children of the rewards of industry. Owing to this type of vicious practice the latter become the objects of benevolences, and to a large extent, the patients of hospitals and asylums. They likewise must patronize or attend, upon the donors' terms, the libraries, museums, and colleges, which they were deprived of planning and building in the interests of themselves and their children. The new world may be so ordered that hospitals, asylums, and all charitable provisions will be gradually eliminated. (Today these are all steadily increasing.) The casualties of our present order will be cared for in such a way that they will not wish to transmit their maladies and weaknesses to oncoming generations. Thus the unfit will be eliminated. Man will be encouraged to use the same wisdom and intelligence in breeding a superior race that has been successful in producing superior breeds of cattle and varieties of improved agricultural products. The experience gained in these fields of experimentation is waiting to be applied in the production of a superior race.

This sketchy outline of a program for the Church's regeneration may constitute a challenge to those who are ready and willing to follow the gleam and to buckle on the armor of faith.

A brief summary of the position taken may not be amiss: My contention is that church union as it is now proceeding will inevitably hit the snag of hopelessly entrenched doctrinal and age-old encrusted beliefs that will make further progress impossible. Therefore, instead of spending futile efforts in this direction, the better way is to re-think the raison d'être for a Church at all. I have indicated that this is supremely the mission of seeking to fulfil the work begun by Christ and His Apostles, which was to obtain abundant life for all. Consequently, a Church that envisions such a program must concern itself with all that directly affects the welfare of mankind. Its main emphasis will therefore be social and not theological. An adequate program of action will include the building of a new social structure that will make adequate spiritual and material provision for all men everywhere. To accomplish this, all social institutions, whether religious, political, or educational, will have to undergo drastic changes. Rights and privileges, now enjoyed only by a comparative few, will be extended by the new methods of social engineering to all. Such an actional program will necessarily cut across all boundaries and barriers in its initiation of a lasting unity based upon a totalitarian view of life.

A RADICAL CHURCH AND ITS YOUTH

STANLEY U. NORTH

CHAPTER VIII

A RADICAL CHURCH AND ITS YOUTH

ALL things are relative. That is why I find myself among the Younger Churchmen. Not that I am young any more, but that I am younger. So too, does it happen that I am writing a chapter on "A Radical Church and Its Youth" in this present symposium, for I would certainly be classed as a rank conservative by the Left Wingers, whereas my capitalistic friends look upon me as a trifle half-baked. Probably they are both right. For whether one is a radical or a conservative depends upon the company he keeps.

I suspect the editor of this volume asked me to contribute, not because I rate as a radical, but because in working among young people I have insisted upon a realistic note being struck. And that is radicalism with a vengeance to a large section of the Christian Church. So far, however, I have not lost my job. And that, I take it, is an inescapable problem of a prophetic ministry, to lead as fast as one can without destroying one's leadership.

The topic assigned to me was phrased differently from the title I have used. It was "Youth—A Radical Church as it Ought to Be." That is a large order. And I simply do not qualify; but what I shall write will be interpreted, I hope, as an honest attempt, however inadequate, to arrive at a solution of a very real problem.

A church, as I see it, can be radical in two senses. It can

be radical as the Community Church, made famous by John Haynes Holmes, is radical. There is a place for such a church in the religious life of the nation. Its rôle will necessarily be prophetic and its greatest influence needs must be of the future rather than immediate. The fact is that the prophet today is no more popular than he has ever been. Tomorrow, however, he will be acclaimed, and the loudest voices, ironically enough, will be those of the conservatives. In the meantime the prophet will gather about himself a comparatively small group of disciples, while the big body of people, who are traditionalists, will seek pews that are more conducive to their peace of mind.

It is not about a radical church in this sense with which I am at present concerned. I personally have profound respect for John Haynes Holmes, yet the fact is that Mr. Holmes would not last beyond the first sermon in a vast majority of Christian churches. What then shall we of the Christian ministry who have come to sense the revolutionary character of the gospel of Jesus do about it? My answer to that question is that a church can be radical in a second sense, which I have chosen to call realistically radical. It will be replied that such is exactly what the Community Church is, realistically radical. It looks upon a world that is filled with deceit, bigotry, injustice and intolerance and it calls things by their right names. That's realism! Granted. But that is only half of the picture. Realism must recognize not only its problem but also the materials available for its solution. The extremists will object that that is pussy-footing, not radicalism. Which suggests the question: When is a radical? Was Jesus a radical when he proclaimed the seven woes but not when he told the story of the Good Samaritan? Was Jesus a radical when he cleansed the temple but not when he reasoned with the Scribes and the Pharisees? Was Jesus a radical when he went to the cross but not when he prayed in the garden of Gethsemane?

We usually use the term "radical" to imply divergence from the traditional in marked degree. The conservatives use the term loosely to serve their particular purposes. The New Deal to old-line Republicans is radical. Let there be a strike and immediately the Chamber of Commerce attempts to attribute its inception to radicals. While the vigilantes, as happened recently in the San Francisco episode, organize and make the inevitable violence of a strike look like child's play. My point is that radicalism is not just a matter of action; it is first of all a matter and a manner of thought. Action will vary according to experience. Violence is not its characteristic, or else Jesus was no radical. Violence on the part of radicals is all too often a matter of desperation. It is an answer to violence by police and militia and company-paid deputies and those self-constituted authorities, the vigilantes. The real menace to our institutions is not the radical but the reactionary who uses the state to defeat the ends of social justice. Massachusetts by its judicial murder of Sacco and Vanzetti, and California with its crime against Mooney and Billings, have not only intensified radicalism, they have spread it. As a symptom violence is an evidence of loss of faith by the people in the justice of their courts and in the integrity of *their* political officials. It is reactionaries, not radicals, who breed disillusionment.

It may be that realistic radicalism, as I use the term, will end in violence, but it never begins there. It recognizes the plain fact that the big body of people are conservatives. And the further fact that without conservatism, no reform, however valuable, could be made permanent. Radicals are not made of prosperity but of adversity. The nation has suffered since 1929 but it still has its memories, and so it wishfully hopes for a return of "good times." The losses inflicted by the depression have been tremendous, but they have, in general, been widely distributed and philosophically accepted. The millions of unemployed with their dependents have known distress to a degree that back in the twenties would have been unbelievable but that would have been vastly worse had not the system administered relief.

As is the average father and mother, so is the average young person conservative. Youth has been inconvenienced by the depression, but its life (I mean, of course, the youth of our churches) has gone on fairly much the same. For the high school student the question of college may have been in doubt; for the college student tuition may have come hard and jobs may have been lacking upon graduation. Still, football continues to attract its multitudes, and social life, in general, moves on, if at reduced costs, not at reduced rates.

Such is the situation that the usual minister faces. Let us suppose that he is a recent seminary graduate. The probabilities are that the New Minister Committee picked him because his voice was pleasant and his personality attractive, while his wife had looks and charm. The church wanted a young man who would "pep" things up and put punch into the various organizations. Beyond that Dr. Coffin or some other seminary president had strongly recommended him. But of just what was in the mind of that young man the chances are good that neither the committee, nor the church that extended its unanimous call, was aware. This young man has been exposed, let us say, to Harry Ward and to Reinhold Neibuhr. He might have recovered from the one but hardly from both. His has been no entering upon his task in blind and blissful ignorance. He knows his world, or, at least, he knows enough about it to know that injustice and cruelty and greed and exploitation of the weak and graft and rackets tramp through it, sometimes frankly and at other times, sadly enough, in the garb of respectability. And worse, he knows that all too often Christianity is more of a label than a reality. Shall he, therefore, begin his ministry with an indictment of the social order and re-echo it until his people are moved to action? Certainly not, unless he was as courageously outspoken in his trial sermon. The first thing he will do is to win the confidence and respect of his people. They have personal needs to be met. He will meet them. They are caught in the system, and more, they are parts of it. There inevitably comes a time for bold denunciations, and a self-respecting man needs must speak, but that time is not every Sunday at eleven o'clock. That is no radical church, it will be said. And if the sermon topics are concerned with religion rather than with revolution that will prove it. And yet, just as the safety of a ship involves the man on the bridge as well as the crew, so too the radicalism of a church is to be measured by the man in the pulpit not less than by the cutaways in the pews. And if that man be radical as Jesus was radical, he will be saddened by calloused sin and yet gladdened by the capacity for kindness, to both of which he is a daily witness. And he will proclaim the love of God not less than the death of sin.

I am saying, you see, that a church which is realistically radical takes its complexion from its minister and teacher.

As pastor he must minister unto his people's individual needs. As teacher he must lead his people into ways of truth and into a sense of unrealized needs. The people of the church are conservative because their backgrounds and experiences make them so. They will become liberal or radical only as their experiences change. Therefore, the realistically radical church will be a church of new experiences; while the pulpit will be an interpreter of life as it is and as, under God, it might be. There will be a minimum of denunciation and a maximum of life revealed in its true colors, some very beautiful, some very ugly. The ugly will be impressive and challenging because the man who speaks is sure of his facts and, what is fully as important, is sure of his religion. This is no radical church in the sense of being—as the Community Church is—radical; but it is radical in the sense of becoming. Life is its laboratory and its field of activity. It will act where it knows; it will seek to know where it is ignorant.

Fundamental in this realistically radical church will be the principle of tolerance. It goes without saying that there should be intolerance of wrong. The difficulty is that wrong and right not infrequently get their clothes mixed. You will recall that the deacon in *David Harum* would not transact business on Sunday but had no scruples over cheating a widow out of her home. The church that I am attempting to describe will seek to transcend its moral and spiritual blindness. It will turn the light on its prejudices and bring out into the open its conditioning. There will be committees that will be engaged in exploring for truth and right in areas of controversy and conflict. There will be serious attempts to clear away class, racial, and national suspicions and misunderstandings. And along with its passion for social justice will go a missionary-mindedness, for the abundant life is not something one possesses by getting, but by sharing. The individual does not live who knows it all or whose life cannot be enriched by insights received from those toward whom, all too often, the attitude of Christianity has been patronizing.

The realistically radical church, then, will provide as many enriching experiences as is humanly possible. There will be a minimum of indoctrination, a maximum of illumination through projects centering in problems of race, industry, slums, unemployment, rackets on the one hand and in recreation, art, beauty, the theater, music, worship on the other. The young people of the church will share in these experiences. In many cases they will be the pioneering group. A common criticism (and significant) is this, "All the good times are planned for the young people." And yet those very good times, over the lack of which the complaint is made, have been in many cases ventures in understanding (such as a Harlem Reconciliation Trip) which adults could organize and participate in as easily as does youth. This sort of technique is being extensively followed among our churches in contrast to the old prayer meeting Christian Endeavor. I do not mean to deprecate worship as an influence and a force in the lives of young people. We have too little significant worship. God is a name, not an experience. I do mean to say that worship to be vital must arise out of a sense of need. That need may be to express gratitude, or to exult over beauty, or to build a more just world. Youth is receptive and pliable. What may not be done for the future in terms of life-experiences provided for youth? After all, diet is just as important in terms of mind and spirit as it is in terms of the physical body.

A few illustrations of what has actually been done follow. In a recent summer conference a Jewish rabbi was invited to be a member of the faculty. The experience was mutually revealing to both the young people and their guest. The rabbi will hereafter think more kindly of Christians, while the young people gained an insight that no amount of preaching could ever have produced.

Another conference was exposed to Tucker Smith with his revolutionary Marxism and listened, incidentally, to the most exalted appeal for the foreign missionary enterprise that it has been my privilege to hear. At this conference, too, there happened to be a young Communist from the mountains of the South. Having come expecting to shock the Northern bourgeoisie he was somewhat shocked, himself, as he witnessed three hundred young people listening with keen interest to a scathing indictment of the capitalistic system by the President of Brookwood college. I am not suggesting Communists be added to the faculties of our summer conferences, and yet this experience proved that the Christian church needs to know the forces which make for Communism. Our young people had no knowledge of the sort of suffering experienced by this young man. Life to them had been easy and sweet; to him it had been cruel and bitter. And it was altogether wholesome for these two extremes to meet. George Coe pointed out long ago that we learn primarily not by precept but by practice. Only as experience is added to experience is youth to be initiated into the ways of vital religion. Youth is not going to be Christian through mere exposure to the Bible; it must be exposed, as well, to life.

Along this same line a valuable series of projects has been carried out in the New York City area with week-end conferences. An entire week-end was given to the discussion of a single social problem. On one occasion colored young people and leaders were brought in, to be entertained in fine homes of white people and to think through with white people their inter-racial problems. The fact of their presence was valuable, but the conviction and ability with which they spoke was invaluable. What strange ideas we get about people concerning whom we know little or nothing. How illuminating is acquaintanceship.

This has proven true to those groups who have gone on "Reconciliation Trips" to one or another of the pulse centers of New York City. "I never knew before—" "I never suspected—" are some of the frequent remarks. There are aspects about such trips that are undoubtedly superficial, yet to the young person who has all of the ways of civilization to learn and (sad but true) no few of its biases to unlearn, if life is not to be warped, a trip to Chinatown, or to Harlem, or to the German section and the like, if properly directed, means seeing how other people live and feel and what they do and think.

A different method but a similar type of project was carried out recently by a Presbyterian group who invited a German student to America to be a guest in their homes for a period of weeks. It gave an opportunity for a German young man to see American home life and to catch something of the spirit of our people, and an opportunity for American young people to talk with a native youth fresh from turbulent Germany. Those concerned will always feel differently toward each other because of this experience.

Illustration can be added to illustration of how young people can and are being given pictures of true life that challenge interest and loyalties. And certainly a church that seriously functions along these lines is a radical church, for it will ever be looking for new truth and ever striving to create a revolution against limitations. And this church will be realistically radical because it will frankly recognize the nature of the materials with which it is dealing and will strive to transform those materials into the Kingdom of God as effectively and as quickly as human influence can operate in a human world.

THE CHURCH AND PROLETARIAN MOVEMENTS

DAVID MUNROE CORY

CHAPTER IX

THE CHURCH AND PROLETARIAN MOVEMENTS

THE most casual student of economic and religious thought and movements in the last hundred years cannot fail to be impressed by the similarity between the Christian ethic and the working-class idealism as proclaimed in Socialism and other proletarian systems. This relation has not always been a conscious one, and we note here a decided difference, generally speaking, between German (or Scientific Marxian) Socialism, and the movement in Great Britain. Whereas the "Scientific" Socialism of Germany has rather consistently exercised religion and religious ethics as "an opiate of the people," "a tool of the propertied classes," etc., the Socialism of Great Britain, France and the United States, if not avowedly religious in character, has no quarrel with the church and has drawn much of its best leadership from Christian sources.

I. GREAT BRITAIN

There can be no question that the presence of religious-ethical elements in the program of Socialism has increased its popularity and practice in Great Britain. Edward Bernstein in relating his experiences in England during the early days of Socialist propaganda in that country declares: "It repeatedly happened to me, and no doubt to others also, that laborers or artisans, who had heard a socialist speech for the first time, came to me at the close of a meeting, and explained to me that everything I had said was in the Bible, and that they could show me the passages, text by text."

A prime reason for this close rapport between the Socialist movement and Christianity in Britain has been the essentially democratic and popular character of Scottish Presbyterianism and English non-conformity. Keir Hardie grew up in the heart of Scottish piety; like Amos of old, he was neither a prophet nor a prophet's son, but a working miner, the first Labor M.P. and the guiding genius in the founding of the I. L. P. Hardie had no use for the cant and cowardice that were apparent in much of the church life, but he loved the Gospel. "The world to-day is sick and weary at heart," he wrote. "Even our clergy are, for the most part, dumb dogs who dare not bark. So it was in the days of Christ. They who proclaimed a God-given gospel to the world were the poor and the comparatively unlettered. We need to-day a return to the principles of the Gospel which, by proclaiming all men sons of God and brethren one with another, makes it impossible for one, Shylock-like, to insist on his rights at the expense of another."

Hardie's earnest Christian spirit and his high moral idealism helped to keep British Socialism from ever being tainted with the sour anti-religious bias so common in the movement in Germany and Italy. "Socialism is a great moral movement," he declared. "I am a Socialist because Socialism means Fraternity founded on Justice, and the fact that, in order to secure this, certain economic changes are necessary is a mere incident in our great human crusade. My protest is against economics being considered the whole of Socialism, or even the vital part of it."

J. Ramsay MacDonald, Hardie's younger compatriot, was always a loyal member of the Kirk and had equally strong convictions on the basic relation of Socialism to Christianity. In striking contrast to some German radicals who envisaged the ultimate "Klassenkampf" as taking place between Christianity and Socialism, in his book, "The Socialist Movement," published shortly before the World War, MacDonald saw the great Armageddon of the future as the conflict between Christianity and capitalism:

> The competitive system cannot be reconciled with Christianity. It is a struggle for the survival of those whose only virtue is that they are the most adaptable; religion can never abandon the desire to supplant such a struggle by a method of selection which will secure the survival of graces and virtues. It must frequently result in glaring instances of the triumph of the unjust and of the otherwise unworthy; religion must always regard such results as indications that the conditions which produce them are alien to it. . . . Above all, religion must resent the attempts made by commercialism to measure virtues by their economic advantages and to appreciate—or depreciate—saints in accordance with whether they are or are not useful in counting houses. . . . As early Christianity had to challenge and change the life of Rome, so later Christianity must one day challenge and change the life of modern capitalist society.

In England the Christian character of political Socialism has been as strongly marked as in Scotland. Whether coming from the ranks of the Labor movement, or from the clergy, including that of the supposedly aristocratic Church of England, Christian Socialists have maintained the identification of the Gospel with the movement to free the toiling masses from the bonds of economic slavery. Labor has produced such Christian leaders as Arthur Henderson, a Methodist lay-preacher, Fenner Brockway, a Christian pacifist, and George Lansbury, prominent in the Christian Socialist movement. The Anglican Church has produced a long succession of Socialist leadership. To simply list the names of some of these is a revelation of the social conscience in this "free" state-church: F. D. Maurice, Charles Kingsley, John Malcolm Ludlow, Henry Scott Holland, Bishops Westcott, Gore, and Barnes, and Archbishop Temple.

Maurice's two-fold program, the Christianising of Socialism and the socialising of Christianity, bids fair to achieve a greater success in Great Britain than in any other country. While the churches are by no means wholly converted to the coöperative commonwealth, and Labor is certainly not animated by religious idealism alone, the real leaders in both camps stand upon a common ground, and as every present indication would show, the trend is once more slowly but surely leftward.

II. FRANCE

In France the relation between the Catholic Church and the proletarian movements, both economic and political, is an excellent illustration of the old adage: "Necessity makes strange bed-fellows." The Third Republic has always been notoriously bourgeois and anti-clerical. From the very beginning of the proletarian agitation there has been a close rapport between clerical and working-class groups. Even in the violent '48 in the last century, the social-political movements were headed, for the most part, by loyal Catholics; litterateurs like Lamartine and Lamennais, politicians like Buchez, and even practical saints like Ozanam, united in denouncing the bourgeois character of kingdom, empire, and republic in the outwardly changing but essentially identical state.

The Paris Commune of 1871 proved a severe jolt to Catholic Socialism which had made considerable headway in the Second Empire under the leadership of Le Play, and the result was a somewhat more opportunist policy which issued in the foundation of the Action Liberale by the Comte de Mun. While the criticism of the movement that it inculcated a voluntary and benevolent program rather than a self-conscious working-class movement was widely made, it cannot be denied that the pressure of the Catholic trade unions and the support of the Action's deputies in the Chamber often resulted in the passing of Socialist legislation which the radical blocs could not have achieved without his assistance.

During and since the War period the Church appears to have regained some of its lost popularity with the working-class, and such preachers as Père Sanson sound an authentic note of Christian social action before vast audiences.

French Protestantism has always been preponderantly bourgeois in the composition of its membership, but recent years have witnessed a growing interest and activity along social lines. Edouard Herriot, the perennial mayor of Lyons and the holder of many a cabinet post, is an elder in the Église Reformée and one of the most prominent of the moderate Socialists. An excellent monthly, *Le Christian-isme Sociale* is published at St. Etienne and members of its editorial staff count such names as the Monods and the Gounelles. A typical article is one appearing in the issue of February, 1931, entitled "L'Action Sociale de l'Église," from the pen of Theodore H. Gounelle. I quote some of its ringing paragraphs:

The limits of the Kingdom of God do not stop before the Empire of the Cæsars and the leaven must make the whole dough rise.

The Church, indeed, must not only protest against the actual social régime, she must proclaim and prepare a better Society.

If the Church is to be disinterested in social problems, the world will be disinterested in the Church.

The Socialist daily, L'Œuvre, has also a strong Protestant following, and there is at least one *pasteur* who has been an active member of the Chamber of Deputies.

In short we may say that while there has been a marked defection of the population from the church, this is neither a new nor a working-class phenomenon, it is as old as the French Revolution, and is more marked among the middle-classes than the proletariat. Working-class movements with the usual exception of the Communists have not been anti-religious. The republican bloc has shown the strongest anti-clerical tendencies, and even proletarian groups outside the church such as the guild or work-shop movement of the last century, headed by Louis Blanc, have been permeated with a spirit reminiscent of primitive or medieval Christianity.

III. GERMANY

If the identification of the Christian ethic and proletarian idealism by the plain man has contributed to the strength of the socialistic movements in Britain and France, the same may be said of Germany. In central and eastern Europe, however, the alliance of the church with the official bureaucracy rendered the church as an *institution* and religion as a *dogma,* odious to the laboring classes that espoused Socialism or other forms of proletarian revolt as a protest against the existing order of which the church was part and parcel. The lip-service paid to religion by the leaders of the Nazi revolution has not provided the basis for a return to the church on the part of the estranged German worker, and the extreme Nazis with their German Christian program, or their sentimental return to the old German mythology, have alienated the bourgeois church people, Protestant and Catholic alike. But for those who have waxed enthusiastic over the active resistance of the Evangelical Church, and such groups as the Pastors' Emergency League, it should be recalled that this was simply a defense of the church against the encroachment of the state upon its own private domain and was in no sense a protest against the political or economic fascism of Hitler and his cohorts. In fact, the point is made by one of the latest writers on Nazi Germany—"Ernst Henri" in "Hitler over Europe"—that the resistance of the clerical forces was in effect the protest of the disillusioned lower middle classes who had not experienced the relief expected from the Nazi program.

Dr. Paul Piechowski and Fraülein Gertrud Hermes, in their careful case studies of scores of German workingmen, have made an excellent case to prove that while the average German proletarian has repudiated the church he has incorporated much of her ethic and even of her eschatology in his new philosophy.

Piechowski, in his "Proletärische Glaube," speaking out of his long experience with working-class groups, and his own tireless efforts on behalf of social amelioration, points out the significant fact that for many workers, Socialism (or

Communism) has the value of a religion. I select several answers to a questionnaire widely circulated by him among Berlin workingmen. The following opinions are taken from the replies of a typical Socialist workingman, unionized, married, and forty-two years of age:

> Socialism is a Religion.
> Jesus was a proletarian teacher, but later generations have made a god out of him.
> Catholic piety is humbug and Protestantism is not much better.
> The "Jugendweine" [taking place on Palm Sunday] is a substitute of real value for the old, meaningless confirmation.
> Prayer is a form of self-deception.
> The Old Testament has portions of real value, but the Bible is no better than other books, etc., etc.

Piechowski's conclusion is that a great conflict is impending not merely between the two forces of Christianity and Socialism, but within each group, in the first between the Christian Socialists and the conservatives, and in the second, between the religious Socialists and the materialists. The only salvation for society will be a *"Gemeinschaft"* between all men of social vision and goodwill for their common ideals.

That Socialism has actually become the religion of large numbers of the German proletariat is the claim of Piechowski and in this contention he is supported by that acute observer, Professor Tillich, in his book, "Religiöse Verwirklichung." After surveying the religious-ethical character of the movement, he declares: "Thus Socialism may be considered as a religious phenomenon: it may be looked upon as the manifestation of the human situation in our own time."

Gertrud Hermes in her acute analysis of popular Marxist ideology, makes the interesting observation that quite unconsciously the irreligious proletariat has reproduced many of the phases through which traditional Christian thought has passed. Beginning with a buoyant optimism in the ability of man to realize his ideals, and with a kind of "animal faith" in the essential order and harmony of all life, provided only certain conditions are met, the thinking proletarian often arrives at an impasse producing disillusion akin to that experienced by religionists who seek a release in a powerful eschatology, and so the irreligious Marxist also embraces a *"Katastrophen-theorie,"* which envisages an economic Armageddon as the inevitable outcome of the present irremediable conditions. Only from the ashes of the past and present can a new civilization arise. This final dénouement is usually depicted as a great "Klassenkampf," which again, as Tillich has pointed out, borrows its imagery and even its idealism from the Christian view of the final victory of the Kingdom of God.

The relations between the churches and non-religious political and labor groups in Germany have been far from cordial. Protestant "Socialism" has left an ugly bequest in an inflated nationalism and a sinister anti-Semitism, which in part was a reflection of popular feeling and partially due to the early influence of its leader, Pastor A. Stöcker. There is no doubt that there is a very real relation existing between the old "Christian Social Party" of 1895, and the Nazi program. The Catholic Church in Germany found in Bishop von Ketteler a sincere and able protagonist of the religious guild socialism so popular in the social program of that church, but von Kettler's emphasis on industrial reconstruction was soon swallowed up in the political Catholicism of the Centrist Party. It cannot be denied, however, that church leaders and the Centrist Party often collaborated with leftist groups in order to enact socially useful legislation.

The Third Reich received the support of many patriotic and socially minded churchmen, Protestant and Catholic, who felt that the widely publicized Nazi program with its safeguards for the German home and the German church against the threat of Communism, together with its controlled economy in the interest of *"Das Deutsches Volk,"* would bring new life to the church. The extravagances of the Nazis, however, have alienated the support originally gained in this quarter, and at present writing (July, 1934), it would appear that the Church, Catholic and Protestant, was one of the leading centers of opposition to the totalitarian program of the Nazis.

What the lasting effect of the Nazi régime, which is certainly riding for a fall, will have upon the social program of the German Church is hard to say. The official liquidation of the radical parties has only intensified the opposition of a large section of the German proletariat to the church. The radicals, as in Austria, have their own martyrs, and may well develop an ideology out of their struggles having many of the characteristics of a religious faith. Socialist ideology, as Heinz Marr has so ably indicated, is in a period of transition between an older materialism and an as yet unrealized idealism, a period that "knows no longer a materialistic one, and has not yet a faith." In Socialism, rather than in the church, the Social Gospel may be rediscovered. All great German religious movements have been the joint product of a *"Zeitgeist"* and the natural piety of the German masses. One need not be a Hegelian to hope that out of the thesis of individual liberty, the corner-stone of the German Protestant tradition, and its antithesis in the social control of the Marxist ideology, may arise a new synthesis that will do justice to both great heritages.

IV. RUSSIA

In Russia, popular religion (cf. the writings of Tolstoi, Dostoievsky, etc.) has always contained many social virtues that were deeply rooted in the village life, and when later radical movements and eventually Sovietism disabused the minds of the *moujiks* of the gross superstition and earlier servility that had characterised popular religion, they all unconsciously retained the social ideal of mutual aid that had been preached by many a humble parish priest. Some of these clergymen played a prominent part in the Dumas at the beginning of the present century. In the First Duma (April, 1906) three priests were active members. In the more conservative Constitutional-Democratic Party, Father N. Ogniev proved to be one of the most forceful speakers. S. N. Tseretelli who quitted the priesthood for a political career in the Socialist group, was several times arrested for his political activities. In the Second Duma, there were also several active clerical delegates, notably Father G. Petrov, a prominent publicist who was forced to quit the church because of his radical views, and the courageous Father K. A. Kolokolnikov, a member of the radical Social Revolutionist Party who suffered persecution for his bold stand.

If no other name were mentioned from the ranks of the clergy, that of Father G. Gapon, should be sufficient to dismiss the charge that all the clergy were to be found on the side of the oppressive bureaucracy. It was Father Gapon who as head of the Union of Russian Workingmen led a peaceful demonstration before the palace of the Czar which turned into the unjustifiable slaughter of these unarmed citizens— the massacre of "Bloody Sunday" (1905). Gapon who had not flinched under the fire of the soldiers, but had sought to give aid to his stricken followers, publically condemned the Czar in language reminiscent of Hebrew prophecy:

With naïve belief in thee as father of thy people, I was going peacefully to thee with the children of these very people. Thou must have known, thou didst know this. The innocent blood of workers, their wives and children, has forever between thee, O soul-destroyer, and the Russian people. Moral connection between thee and them may never be any more. The mighty river during its overflowing, thou art already unable to stem by any half measures, even by a Popular Assembly. Bombs and dynamite, the terror by individuals and by masses, against thy breed and against the robbers of a rightless people—all this must be and shall be. A sea of blood—unexampled—will shed. Because of thee, because of thy whole family, Russia may perish. Once for all, understand this and remember, better soon with all thy family abdicate the throne of Russia and give thyself up to the Russian people for trial. Pity thy children and the Russian lands, O thou offerer of peace for other countries and blood drunkard for thine own!

Otherwise let all blood which has to be shed fall upon thee, Hangman, and thy kindred!

GEORGE GAPON.

Postscriptum—Know that this letter is the justifying document of the coming revolutionary terroristic occurrences in Russia.

G. G.

Gapon escaped to England where he wrote "The Story of My Life"; returning to Russia, he disappeared under the most mysterious circumstances. On April 11, 1905, a body was found and identified as that of Gapon by his lawyer. It was later reported that Gapon had entered into secret negotiations with government officials and had been murdered by his former associates, but this statement has been regarded by many as "inspired" by his opponents.

The "First Revolution" of 1905-06 was followed by a period of reaction. The Church, completely dominated by the reactionary Holy Synod, forced most of its radical clergy to doff the cloth, and proved a willing ally of the state. The result was that when the radical forces again asserted themselves they found much less support in church circles than twenty years before. The new tide of unrest which found its peak in the great Leningrad strike of 1914 was only checked by the World War, and most of the Socialist leaders, including the venerable Plekhanov, united behind the government in what they considered a righteous war, only the exiled Lenin, Trotzky, and a few others called upon the masses to obstruct the prosecution of the war in an effort to cause the collapse of the state.

The Revolution of 1917 was headed, at first, by the moderate radical groups: the first cabinet in which Kerensky was the dominant figure, included a portfolio for the Procurator of the Holy Synod—a post held in this and the succeded cabinet by V. N. Lvov, a Constitutional-Democrat.

The coup of October, which placed the Bolshevik (majority group of the Social-Democrats) in power, initiated a definite anti-religious policy on the part of the government. At first definite gestures of friendship were made toward various Protestant groups, especially the Baptists, in an effort to weaken the Orthodox Church, but soon all religious movements came under the restrictive measures and the force of the atheist propaganda of the increasingly powerful Soviet government. The present outlook for the churches in Russia is certainly far from encouraging. With a rising generation consistently and constantly indoctrinated in Atheism and the program of the churches rigorously restricted to worship and other spiritual functions, it is doubtful if organized religion will be able to play an important part in the state. It is possible, however, that Communism will develop an ideology that is actually religious. Such an acute observer as Harold Laski has recently written "Communism is as genuine a religion as any in the experience of man," to which Professor Reinhold Niebuhr rejoins that in so far as Communism is religion, it is "a bad religion." Certainly it is difficult to conceive of any system as religious that repudiates the existence of Deity, however altruistic and enthusiastic it may be. The future of religion in the Soviet Union is an enigma.

V. THE UNITED STATES

The prolonged continuance of a "laissez-faire" economy in the United States was rendered possible by the prevalence of free land and fluid capital in a nation that was underdeveloped and not even populated in many desirable areas. The nineteenth century for the United States, despite varying shifts in politics and industry, was characterized by one great constant factor, the Western expansion. This era was marked in the preaching and work of the churches by a corresponding emphasis on the individual. The "revival" was a characteristic phenomenon, and whether conducted by a Finney who thundered the wrath of a righteous Jehovah, or by a Moody who proclaimed the redeeming love of the Christlike

God, its great purpose was the salvation of individual souls. Only in the battle against the liquor traffic did the Protestant churches show anything like a united front on a social issue, and here the Catholics did not join them. Slavery, war, economic pressure which was on the increase with the growing industrialization of the East and Middle West, found prophetic voices in the churches raised in protest, but denominations, preachers, and people showed, on the whole, much greater interest and activity in personal religion than in the social ethics of the gospel.

At the turn of the century, owing largely to the efforts of men like Josiah Strong, Washington Gladden, Francis Greenwood Peabody and Walter Rauschenbusch, the church took a new interest in social work. Settlements, neighborhood centers, institutional churches, all in the name of "applied Christianity" sprang up in our larger cities. There was some preaching upon the "social question," but *the main emphasis was upon social work rather than upon social change.*

Despite considerable support from the churches in the pre-war period, the organized peace movement collapsed completely under the war propaganda attendant upon America's entrance into the great conflict. A recent book by Dr. Ray Abrams is a candid, factual indictment of the utter failure of churchmen to oppose a war that was essentially capitalistic.

The period of artificial prosperity following the post-war adjustment (1922-1929) lulled the church at large into an amiable acceptance of the economic status quo. Several of the seminaries, however, such as Boston, Auburn, Yale, Pacific, Chicago, McCormack, Rochester, and notably, Union (New York), maintained a critical attitude toward the social order, realising the basic weaknesses, moral and economic, that underlay the outwardly imposing structure.

The Wall Street crash of November, 1929, and the continually increasing unemployment and suffering throughout the country, greatly increased the rising tide of criticism of the whole economic fabric. In fact it might well be said that large sections of the church apparently realised and attacked the evils of modern capitalistic society with greater zeal and acumen than did the organized labor movement. The grim realism of a writer like Reinhold Niebuhr, the perspicuity and activity of a lecturer like Harry Ward, the influence of such authorities as Bishop McConnell, Sherwood Eddy and Kirby Page, have inspired hundreds of ministers to join in the struggle for economic justice with those engaged on both the economic and political fields. The very strength of this significant trend is, however, its main weakness. It is basically a movement for and not of the working-class, and of the ministry rather than of the laity. This is all the more regrettable as the American churches, Protestant and Catholic, can claim a much stronger following from the working-class than their sister churches on the European continent. The fact remains that it is the colleges and not the mills, mines and farms that have supplied the active leadership and even most of the following for Christian social action in the United States. The widespread dissatisfaction among the working-class and "white-collar" church members in this country needs both intelligent direction and an emotional orientation in a great popular crusade. If such leadership is not forthcoming, a type of fascism reminiscent of the "Know Nothing" and Ku Klux Klan movements may capture the rank and file of American Christians (especially

Protestants), with a specious bally-hoo playing up prejudice and patriotism.

Those actively engaged in the creation of an intelligent, ethically conditioned social conscience and a militant working-class program in the church have been carrying on their work along various lines.

There are now in all the larger denominations, commissions on social welfare which are served by socially awakened churchmen, and through these groups an increasingly informed social consciousness seeps down into the more or less inert masses of the denominations. The Methodists have been particularly active in this field, and issue a most informing little semi-monthly publication, "The Social Service Bulletin." The Congregationalist-Christians in their last General Council (Oberlin, June, 1934), adopted a carefully worded resolution pledging the denomination to work for the abolition of the profit system. The Episcopalians have produced many active leaders in this field and are represented by the Church League for Industrial Democracy. We have not space to describe further denominational activity, official and unofficial in the field of social welfare.

There are also the freer and more radical non-denominational organizations and publications. The Fellowship of Socialist Christians is a well-disciplined group of Christian radicals, the well-known Fellowship of Reconciliation is active now upon the field of economic as well as of international strife. The Ministers Union, modelled along the lines of trade union organization, is committed not merely to the security of its own profession, but to the welfare of the whole working-class. There are many other local groups too numerous to mention. As regards publications, *The World*

Tomorrow, edited by a corps of Christian socialists, was one of the most influential radical journals in the country. The most informative little bulletin, "Economic Justice," published by the National Religion and Labor Foundation, gives timely reports and comment on the economic struggle.

On the Interdenominational front, invaluable service has been rendered through the activity of the Federal Council of Churches. The Department of Research has issued an illuminating Information Service, and most reliable studies, and the annual Labor Sunday Message of the Department of the Church and Social Service has received wide publicity.

Here and there, churchmen, especially the ministers, have taken an active part in the economic struggle, but many of these radicals, like Norman Thomas, A. J. Muste, and Devere Allen, have found it expedient or necessary to quit the ranks of the organized church in order to enjoy freedom of action. Some like the Rev. Herman Hahn of Buffalo (Evangelical), Dr. Frank Kingdon of New Jersey (Methodist) and the Rev. L. Bradford Young of Brooklyn (Episcopalian), have maintained a regular church connection and have, at the same time taken an active part in the economic struggle on the political and industrial fronts.

Symposia, conferences and questionnaires have revealed a remarkable growth in interest on the part of the Protestant clergy in social and economic reconstruction. The poll taken by Kirby Page with the collaboration of *The World Tomorrow,* the results of which were published in May, 1934, showed a remarkable leftward trend of thought.

The Roman Catholic Church has been loath to enter general movements for social action, but in its own conferences have shown a keen insight into these problems. Discounting the spectacular utterances and activity of popular figures like Fathers Cox and Coughlin, great credit is due to the research and keen criticism made by such real students of economics and sociology as Fathers Ryan, Ross, Haas and Gillies. The Catholic Church has, however, been hampered in presenting its social program, by its traditional distrust of socialism, whereas the Protestant bodies have, in the main, adopted socialist or neo-socialist positions.

The basic weakness of the whole American church approach has been its failure to enlist the consecrated and intelligent support of the laity in a great crusade for social reconstruction. In marked contrast to other lands, the informed clergy are, as a whole, far ahead of the laity in their appraisal of and program for the new society. Unless this gulf is bridged, socially minded ministers are going to find themselves serving unresponsive congregations, and on the side of the laity the old story of European radicalism will be repeated—the socially minded members forsaking the church for radical movements where they may find scope for the furtherance of ideals that were originally discovered in their religious study and experience.

The church, her leaders and her people, are facing a tremendous challenge here in America, she can no longer "go halting between two opinions," but must choose to serve the Baal of the money-bags and eventually be repudiated by a growingly self-conscious working-class, or else choose the stony way to a new Calvary of self-identification with the struggles of the exploited, and so laying down her life for the brethren, rise again to lead a new and classless society with her eternal moral and spiritual resources.

IS THE CHURCH PACIFIST?

FRANK OLMSTEAD

CHAPTER X

IS THE CHURCH PACIFIST?

FOR many long centuries war has been an accepted part of civilization, but never has war been so much of a threat to so many people as it is today. On the one hand we are still suffering from the World War. The suffering of its thirty millions of victims still stirs us, grief for their loss is not yet erased by time, and the economic consequences of its waste and destruction of material resources are even now filling the world with want. On the other hand we see the nations frantically arming for a new conflict. Europe is a powder box, filled with the flint and steel of fear and hate. England recognizes the significance of the new air weapons by declaring that the Rhine has become her frontier. Japan nourishes the inseparable triplets of increased armament, increased debts, and increased necessity for international rape and robbery. China is not only threatened from without but is torn by internal warring factions of divers sorts. And the United States, which might arouse the people of the world to demand from their government a new sanity, shows no sign of possessing, in this field, leadership with vision above the crowd.

In the background lurks the ever threatening war between classes, although strangely enough the Communist threat is today one of the major factors working for the prevention of premeditated war in Europe and Japan. Capitalist leaders are well aware that another major conflict will weaken their hold on the reins of power—an opportunity which will not be lost by the disciples of the Soviet, who are alert though driven under cover. The warfare which the Communists could bring, even though it were another war to end war, would be far more deadly in its consequences of destruction and hatred and bitter desire for retaliation than the older type of conflict between nations. Even for those Christians who see the present economic system as contrary to the principles of Jesus, the possibility of a class war constitutes a threat to Christian idealism which cannot be viewed with even a mild degree of approval.

In the consideration of possible class war it is well to recall that the Bolshevik revolution in 1917 offers no legitimate basis for comparison. That quick and effective upheaval was almost wholly without violence. It was the product of a speeded-up process of education which involved four years of war, nearly two million dead, streets and hospitals filled with torn and broken bodies, and the twelve or fourteen million men in uniform repeatedly betrayed at the rear by their German-sympathizing officers. Both German and Bolshevik propaganda had been showered upon the Russian front, which under these circumstances was peculiarly receptive. True, the methods of class war persisted for ten years thereafter—have not wholly ceased—but there was nothing comparable to the conflict situation which would develop in America were New York to be seized by the Communists and Chicago by the Fascists, with deadly strife for power, not only between the two sections, but dividing every block in both cities. Our Civil War and its aftermath of bitter resentment and hatred would be mild in comparison.

No man can accept class war and call himself a pacifist, nor can he support defensive war and lay claim to that name. The churchman who says that he can imagine a war which he would have to support is usually thinking of defensive war fought against invaders on our own soil. Such a man is almost certain to end up by supporting any major conflict, for every war in history has been for both sides a defensive war, appearances notwithstanding, for always the best and safest defense is an offense. This country is still filled with people who believe that the Germans were prevented only by our entry into the war from seizing our entire country and making this a subject people. When the war propaganda machine gets going with its censorship of truth and its host of falsehoods, our qualified pacifist is bound to feel that this again is a war that must merit his coöperation and blessing. The fact is that we must think much more deeply than we have into the Christian basis for pacifism.

There are two approaches to pacifism. The mind may reject war as futile, or the emotions may lead us to an intuition which prohibits us as individuals from killing. In the early days of the church, the latter basis seems, up to the time of Constantine, to have made the Christian Church unqualifiedly pacifist. Today the intellectual approach is far more common and promises to be more important, unless there is an extensive revival of an emotional, religious nature which will strike through to the type of experience engendered by Jesus. Probably much of the anti-war progress since the World War has been of the intellectual variety. True, this rational indictment of war has been accompanied by some fine spiritual appreciations. But it has in the main been a movement of leaders, of twentieth-century church leaders, who are guided by their heads rather than by their hearts. This interpretation is borne out by the fact that few Southern Methodists and Baptists responded to the *World Tomorrow* poll, while a much larger percentage of those addressed in the more liberal and less emotional Northeast not only responded, but voted pacifist.

It is probable that the leaders are well to the left of the average church congregation in their stand on war. Judge Ulman of the Baltimore Superior Court ruled that twenty-six denominations have by their rational action put themselves on a par with the Quakers in their attitude toward war. National assemblies, general conferences and synods draw together the leaders of their respective denominations and pass resolutions or even enact legislation which make war a matter for the personal conscience. They even list it as a sin. This has made twenty million church members theoretically pacifist. At the same time, with tens of thousands of boys from those denominations compelled to take R. O. T. C., the group who refuse to train to kill their fellow men is numbered in the dozens. The bulk of the twenty million do not yet know that they are against war.

This analytical leadership against war has led to a strange contradiction noted by Kirby Page. State or national gatherings of churchmen solemnly pronounce war a sin, often the greatest sin of our age, and then proceed to absolve the individual, if he feels that his conscience leads him to help his country commit that sin. That which is a sin emotionally is not thus lightly left to the individual. This sin is mindmade and is flexible. It does not hit deep into the spirit, even of those who have promoted the action against war.

The line of reasoning which leads to the repudiation of

war is easily obvious to the informed and thoughtful churchman. The World War gained no end for which it was
fought—did not save democracy or protect helpless women
and children, nor end the crime of war. It did not even
collect the moneys due our bankers, whose adroit pressure
had much to do with our joining the Allies. Moreover there
was no victor. The tragic loss of life and property left all
grappling with gigantic problems, calling desperately and in
vain for those best brains now turned into Flanders dust.
Death for a great cause is not unreasonable in the Christian
tradition, but thirty million deaths all for naught are bound
to call to mind the sacredness of human life. The church
cannot lend itself again to such tragedy.

Reason can also discover the conflict of war with religion through the breakdown of morals occasioned by the conflict. When murder is legalized, hatred must replace love,
and brutality must be cultivated as a virtue. Cases may be
cited of men who rose above such levels, but those who
know war know that if all had done so, fighting would have
soon automatically stopped. The higher values of life simply
had to be shed like civilian clothes, and the result left little
room for the Christian virtues of love and mercy, of honesty
and chastity. The impartial intellect has no difficulty in seeing that such reversion to barbarism destroys in a day that
which may have taken the church years to build.

The intellectual Christian also attacks war for its damage
to the goodwill and spiritual understanding built up by years
of ardent missionary work. True, the missionaries had
sometimes been over-zealous in presenting not only Jesus as
the Prince of Peace but the Christian Church and Western
civilization as his peace-promoting agents. The tragedy of

disillusionment was none the less real. Much true spiritual value had been engendered, however, for the missionary work of religion strikes a pure note. The gasp of astonishment, if not horror, which went up from so-called heathen lands aided a similar reaction at home. This horror certainly marks some gain from the days of the crusades. It also was partly due to missions that the excuse had to be offered by Christian apologists that Christianity had not failed—it had never been tried. The World War was a terrible blow, nevertheless, to the spread of an understanding of the significance of Jesus. The un-Christlike action of supposedly Christian countries set back immeasurably the process of sharing with other lands that message of Jesus to which we had been exposed, but which we had not taken. It is now obvious that the spread of the gospel demands the effort to prevent the identification of the church with another such prostitution of humanity.

When it comes to the emotional rejection of war through spiritual development, the number which is involved is much smaller, but not less significant. In this there is bound to be a much higher percentage who will see it through to the end than in any other group. In fact, the definition of true spiritual development might well involve the attainment of an inner norm, by which conduct is evaluated, instead of by the pressure of public opinion.

Why did so many men in the ministry who seemed to see spiritual truth give themselves so wholly to the last war? The question cannot be answered without a digression to analyze the real nature of spiritual life. This point is of great importance, for whether Christianity will be pacifist against

the rising tide of Communism and its emphasis on the class
war depends largely upon the content which life has at a
spiritual level. Does the spiritual life contain a means to
an end as well as an end? Many a Christian is in revolt only
against imperialistic war until he knows the answer. His
mind alone will not make him a pacifist when class war is
concerned unless his mind can see more power in spiritual
religion than it has seen up to date. As a matter of fact, that
power is there, and there is good reason for thinking that
it may soon be more generally discovered. And it will be
seen that a Communist with all his zeal and devotion to a
class is not religious at all in the full sense of that word. In
fact he may be less religious than is a trained seal, or a dog
in the movies.

Life is truly religious when it begins to use all of its
latent possibilities. Today man is able at his best to feel both
a sense of solidarity with the human race, and a sense of conscious relationship to that which is greater than himself and
outside of himself—to the creator spirit, to God. To claim
that a Communist is religious when he identifies himself
with his class but senses no unity with the great unseen, is
like calling Dillinger religious for his loyalty to his immediate group of fellow murderers. It is true that that impulse
extended becomes religious, but so does the digestive process
—that is, we could not be religious without it.

Some will say that this definition of religion excludes such
bodies as the Buddhists. So it does, and a great majority of
Christians as well. We have not recognized the true nature
of religion, and the result is that few have claimed the high
privilege which awaits them. Truly a trained seal is more

religious than most church members. The seal is extracting from his equipment the very maximum of achievement. Al Capone or Lenin or we ourselves have not done that unless we have learned, possibly through a course of training as arduous as that of the seal, to actually communicate with the mind and heart that is back of the universe.

Is it such a wild idea to talk thus of man enlarging his powers so that he can hear as well as talk with God? A brief review of the development of life on earth ought to convince us that it is not unreasonable to expect such a thing. Life at every step of its ascent from its beginning has become possessed of larger powers. The amoeba is versatile compared with the one-celled vegetation of the seas. The newt in its life cycle has a freedom in water and on land that makes the amoeba seem helpless. We get a similar feeling when we contrast the newt with the dog, the latter has a universe so much larger. The four-year-old boy gives us the same feeling in regard to the dog. The boy's father contrasts vividly in powers compared with the boy, and Einstein might again dwarf the father.

As life has become more complex in its forms through a series of great growth mutations, it has progressively become able to use more of the universe around it. The mathematical figure may help us to get the picture. Any vegetation, as a weed or a tree, uses a point in space. The simpler animal life, as an earthworm, uses two dimensions of space, the boy three, the man dimly senses a fourth, which has become fairly real to Einstein.

The striking thing in this survey of life is that always new powers are released at each new level of life. A worm has motion and sensation by which to interpret the world around him more fully than can the weed. The dog feels and moves still more freely, having a far larger degree of consciousness, and can perform feats impossible for the earthworm. And man with his self-consciousness, longer memory and enlarged power to relate concepts and develop ideas, becomes a veritable god to the dog. If our imaginations can then grasp the possibility of another step up to a level above man, may we not reasonably expect that we will gain fuller powers that will let us occupy that larger universe glimpsed by an Einstein and explored in part by Moses and Isaiah and Jesus, by Joan of Arc and Fox and Wesley?

In short, it becomes predictable in a world where like begets like, that eventually the likeness of the great Creator Spirit should emerge in the product of the life stream. Like forms of consciousness at the higher levels can communicate. Today such a likeness has come to pass and now at least a degree of conscious, two-way communication has become possible for all who will meet the laws of the growth of the spirit. Although only a few have demonstrated it, this ability is as real—and as indescribable—as is the power of vision.

People who have thought that far, and have begun to explore the nature of those higher laws of growth, find that war kills that divine awareness of God's presence. It kills this ability to feel as he feels and the consequent identity of purpose with his will. It kills too the sense of oneness with all higher life with our fellow men. For such people war becomes impossible. No man in his senses will cut off his own hand, and no man whose senses have become aware of the oneness of life at its highest levels will destroy the most vital part of himself by sticking a bayonet into the body of a fellow man, or by blowing him to bits with shells.

Those who know anything about life on these higher levels know that such life is at once the most valuable product of the ages, and the most desperate need of modern society. The social system must be changed, indeed, but as the Soviet itself is beginning to realize, that does not end the social problem. Progress is impossible without that social cement which is to individuals as mortar is to bricks, and which for the great bulk of mankind comes through real religion and is a self-revealing experience of the accessibility of God. It is not to be wondered at that the high authorities of the Soviet have begun to talk about a "spiritual incentive."

Out of the higher experiences of life comes the privilege of living at a new tempo with a resulting enlargement of power, so that it becomes possible to reach out into the lives of others and to aid in drawing the higher type of life out of them as the sun pulls the color and fragrance out of a rosebush. This is significant creative power. This is sharing in the creative process at its peak, becoming the parent of spiritual children. It is life's highest function and the hope of the human race.

Here is where the spiritually motivated pacifist comes in. He knows that to pump lead into his fellow men will destroy not only other lives of countless worth, but will as well ruin within himself the dearly bought power to be still and receive the impact of God's spirit upon his own. Then and then only does he become able to truly love his fellow men. Dimly he senses that there is creative power in this new relationship that can do more than all the Communist armies that united labor could produce. Here is the window through which he sees the faith that could move mountains—or create new capacity for selfless vision and wise action among the leaders of the world.

This is true Christian pacifism. Some glimpse of these higher privileges of life is what made the early church so solidly against war. Today there is many a saintly mother who is such a war resister and who would give all she is and has to let her children share her knowledge. But the present generation of church members is handicapped by much newly gained physical privilege, and finds too difficult the task of making room for a more subtle and hard-to-gain power. Our imaginations, instead of being released by science, have been made too dull to recognize the possibility of such an enlargement of life. The human race stands at the threshold of a new inheritance and does not claim it.

Out of the disillusionment of the present economic break-down, however, has come a new sensitiveness to the intangible values of life. The swing of young people to pacifism is of course partly that they have thought through the World War and its failures; it is also due to the intuitive sense of high possibilities within themselves which they feel the war method will destroy. They are ripe for true spiritual development, and if a movement were to be started which would be truly religious and not in conflict with their minds, it would sweep the youth of the country into an anti-war mood that would make a resort to arms a practical impossibility.

Some will say that the youth of the church are already

pacifist. Certainly all over the country youth groups are recording majority votes that they would under no circumstances respond to their government's call to another conflict like the World War. Those who know human nature are not taking these results too seriously. If the hysteria of another '98 or '17 should come, the number of youth pacifists who would survive the social presure to war would be small. This is no reflection on the sincerity of their present attitude. It simply means that the price is greater than they know, and they are not generally equipped to pay the cost.

It is in preventing the deliberate manipulation of our press, radio and pulpits toward the development of such an hysteria that the pacifist sentiment of the church may be most useful. In this connection, one of the most promising possibilities lies in a movement which was initiated last winter. A group of twenty ministers assembled on Armistice Eve to discuss the single question, "What would I do if war were declared tomorrow?" Two hours of discussion brought out the fact that all felt that they would have to oppose the war. All, with one or two possible exceptions, were resolved to oppose it even if faced with the certainty of arrest as the result of their stand.

Need was felt for some kind of movement to link likeminded ministers throughout the country. Sentiment was strong against another costly organizational project, so that it seemed like an inspiration when one of the group suggested the group-chain idea. Each member was to contact six or eight other individuals in the larger centers who in turn would each reach a like number of friends in their vicinity. These in turn would reach out, and so on. In this way it was felt that many of the progressive leaders of the congregations of the country could in a crisis be reached by letter or wire without overhead expense, each carrying the cost of contacting his own group. Two chief purposes exist for the emergency; one to counteract propaganda leading toward a declaration of war, and the other to offer, throughout the country, centers where pacifists may gather for mutual support and council upon the declaration of war.

Even this movement, sound as is its educational and psychological basis, will at the crisis depend for its real power upon the number it enrolls who are having a continuing experience of God rather than ideas about God. In the fatal year of 1917 some powerful preachers of peace were swept into support of the war to end wars. They believed heartily in what they preached about peace and good will and God, yet they swung to an enthusiastic support of war. We must conclude that they had failed to capture in life that which would have made it impossible for them to so act. Otherwise they could not have so grossly violated the spirit of love—love for all humanity—which would have become a part of their natures. If another conflict cannot be prevented, we must look for very similar results from our present pacifist leaders. A few will, like a few Socialists, see it through on an intellectual plane. The majority will sink or swim in terms of the depth of their own spiritual experience.

The Church of today is far more pacifist-minded than it was ten years ago. But the Church as it stands today is able only to delay a declaration of war. It is not able in itself to prevent another war. It lacks the spiritual depth. Only another great spiritual revival can release force adequate to stay war. The potential to end war is, however, latent among the great masses of church members. They have a theoretical belief in the peace ideal of Isaiah and Jesus, the latent faith that God is real and that the still small voice can be heard. So much does the world need and want it that another great prophet may arise from our Church filled with the larger life of God and a boundless love for humanity. If he comes, it may be hoped that he will break off the nationalistic shackles from statesmen and citizens alike, and lead us into a warless world.

THE CHURCHES AND WORLD PEACE

JOHN ELLIOTT

CHAPTER XI

THE CHURCHES AND WORLD PEACE

1. THE CHURCH RENOUNCES WAR

THERE is no question that the churches are up in arms about peace. They are awake as never before to the absolute impossibility of harmonizing the way of Mars with the way of Christ. During the past ten years they have grown increasingly bold and vocal in their denunciations of war preparations and in support of agencies and legislation that would seem to tend toward peace. Conferences, general assemblies, councils of the different denominations vie with one another in drawing up resounding resolutions expressing their contempt for warfare and urging their members and the government to abstain from the tragic road of international conflict. If one were to judge solely by the exalted resolutions that have been passed, almost the entire twenty million members of Protestant churches in this country would seem to be lined up as fighters for peace. War is called, in no equivocal terms, a sacrilege to God and man.

Although resolutions are easily passed, and all who have attended ecclesiastical gatherings know how often the resolutions express the views of a bare majority after hasty debate, still the avalanche of condemnation that the war system has received at the hands of church people in recent years, points the direction in which hundreds of thousands, perhaps millions of Christians have been moving. For a resolution expresses an ideal toward which we are striving, the embodiment of our finest Christian feeling. Not all who vote for the resolutions will defend by their personal work and reputation the convictions they expressed so easily at the time. But the church and its many agencies have now gone on record before the world as believing that Christ and war are mutually exclusive, and that loyalty to one means antagonism to the other.

This at first may not seem such a forward step as it truly is, for no one who can read the gospels of the Bible could have any doubt but that Christ would have his followers divorce themselves entirely from the force, bloodshed and hatred that all men know war to be. Yet in past centuries the churches, while holding as their master the Prince of Peace, never stressed the peace program of Christ; indeed minimized his teachings when it came to applying love in the sphere of international relations. The Church of Christ has sold its influence and its power in every war to the forces of brutality and inhumanity, and has committed the further sacrilege of invoking God's blessing upon the evil work of human slaughter. The Church has always found ways of explaining or defending its action, cloaking with high words and noble sentiments the bloody business of warfare. It sought to emphasize the spiritual side of each conflict, and thereby minimize its guilt in sanctioning the anti-spiritual, the evil side. Thus the devil and Christ have been made by the Church to walk arm in arm down the trenches, the devil's work somehow blessed by the presence of possible moral values. Of course the attempt has been made to find moral values in every conflict in which our country has engaged, the

Mexican War, the Spanish-American or the World War. But the Christian Church has been sidetracked from the main line of devotion to Christ's teaching of love, and has spent itself in sideline activities while the peoples of the earth were dying in the head-on collision of evil.

If the Church has awakened, then, to the nature of war and is determined never again to be caught red-handed in evil or used by the forces of brute power, as it has so often in the past, there is cause for great rejoicing. For no modern war can successfully be waged without moral support. Withdraw the moral glory and reason for the war, and few citizens will be rash enough to venture on simply an armed manhunt. If the issue is defense of women and children and the fatherland from a fiendish enemy, instead of defense of trade routes and raw materials from a sharp competitor, then the masses of people will rush to stop the fiend by fair means or foul. But if the Churches of Christ condemn all recourse to war, show all war as immoral, brand it a sin, and excommunicate from membership all persons engaging in war, then the main support will be taken from those who maneuver a nation into conflict. No nation could go against the aroused moral sense of its people.

The General Conference Commission on World Peace of the Methodist Episcopal Church has recently taken almost that bold a stand. Representing not the four million members, of course, of this forward-looking denomination, but speaking as an authorized voice of Methodism, the Commission states: "We believe that war is sin because it involves (a) the slaughter of human beings; (b) violation of personality; (c) vast destruction of property; . . . (f) it puts in place of moral law the doctrine of military necessity;

(g) it distorts the religion of Jesus into the religion of a war god." And then it draws the consequence of this indictment of war. "It follows that no Christian should engage in any war for any purpose or give to it his sanction or approval." The Commission goes on to point out the causes of war and the way to peace as it conceives it.

The Presbyterian Church in its 1934 General Assembly, the highest judicial and legislative body of that denomination of two million members, went on record in equally drastic form. Although not calling war a sin, the Assembly "in the name of Christ and country declares anew its break with the entire war system." It proclaimed its belief that "Christians owe an allegiance to the Kingdom of God that is superior to loyalty to their country, and that in any matter in which the laws of their country conflict with the commands of God, they must assert their duty and right to obey God rather than men." "Christians cannot give their support to war as a method of carrying on international conflict." The Board of Education was directed to make available blank pledges with the following statement, "I will not cross the borders of any nation except in friendship, nor will I support my country in such action." These signed pledges are to be sent to the President and the Congress. Thus one denomination that has never been too radical in its social interpretation of the gospel is placed in the front ranks of the churches attacking war.

The attitude of thousands of religious leaders can nowhere be more clearly seen than in a questionnaire made public in 1934 by Mr. Kirby Page. Of 20,000 ministers answering questions on war and the economic order, 14,000, or 67 per cent of those answering, believed that the churches of America should now go on record as refusing to sanction or support any future war. Thirteen thousand of these ministers declared themselves personally ready to declare their purpose not to sanction any future war or participate as an armed combatant. Now, thirteen thousand pacifist ministers, deadly in earnest about war as an unchristian institution, constitute a tremendous moral power. They are willing for their names to be published and are prepared to take the results that are bound to come. All denominations are represented, and although only a minority of the ministers of the nation, certainly must be counted on in the future to wield a mighty influence for peace. Sentiment is exceedingly strong in the seminaries of the country, and each succeeding year should see a larger percentage of ministers taking this uncompromising position.

One of the most hopeful signs on the peace horizon is the attitude of the churches toward conscientious objectors. The issue has been joined in more than one college or university where compulsory military training was objected to on grounds of conscience. This struggle has been going on ever since the World War, but recently many denominations have come out with sweeping statements backing the rights of their students to refuse military drill. The Northern Baptist Convention, 1934, called on "pastors and people to defend in the pulpit, before school authorities and before the courts, when necessary, all Baptist students who for conscience's sake refuse to submit to military training in high schools, colleges and universities." The Congregational and Christian Churches in the same year affirmed their conviction in the right of conscience in such circumstances and pledged their young people support "in their endeavor to live by the dictates of the religious and ethical conscience." The New England Congregationalists are being challenged to make good their pledge of support in the case of a student of Massachusetts Institute of Technology, and other denominations will watch with a good deal of interest their procedure. Likewise the Methodists have repeatedly declared their opposition to compulsory military training and are backing the court action of two California students dismissed for their refusal on conscientious grounds. The Presbyterians in more vigorous language "announce our support of all conscientious objectors to war, and we hereby demand in their behalf from all educational institutions requiring military training that each objector be excused from classes in military instruction without loss in academic standing or official censure of any kind." They have yet to back their sentiments by court action.

2. THE PROBLEM OF CHURCH AND STATE

There is room then for cheer when we see how awakened many of our churches are to the evil of war. Not all the denominations nor all the pastors have renounced it. Indeed the majority of ministers can safely be said to be opposed to taking a stand against war much stronger than that of decrying it as an evil that all Christians should seek to avert. The discouraging element, however, is not in the attitude one may profess toward peace but the inadequate and almost total absence of a planned program of peace education in the churches. They leave it alone except in very general and platitudinous terms. "Love your enemies" and "The Brotherhood of Man" are the phrases which we too often hope will bring children and adults into attitudes of mind opposed to war. And of course no such result has been produced; men extol Jesus but arm to the teeth, and assume there is no other way out of the situation when so many bad nations are still at large.

The reason for the difficulties which Christians have with the question of war and peace is due to the conflicting theories one may hold as to the relation between the state and the church. Obviously two loyalties are involved, loyalty to the land, people and possessions among which one has lived, and loyalty to the ideals of one's religion that come to claim more as the attempt is made to lead a spiritually motivated life. Now, no man will deny the strong claims of patriotism to one's country, and no one normally would deny that all men should seek the highest good of the whole race. The betterment of mankind is an ideal all men strive for, but the selfishness we all possess is increased when the smaller good conflicts with the larger. No pastor who struggles over the narrow attitudes people take toward foreign missions is unaware of the difficulties involved when the good of the unknown foreigner impinges on the good of those in America. Dr. Albert Beaven has well pointed out that the conflict between state, or nationalism, and religion is the conflict of a lesser or parochial loyalty with a universal loyalty. Christianity teaches a universal loyalty; nationalism teaches local loyalty. To the Christian all men are the same in the sight of God; to the nationalist his countrymen, their life, trade, culture is the paramount good. The rise of nationalism not only in Europe but in our own country is the demand that the rights of a small group take precedence over the welfare of the larger. Loyalty to one's nation, to which one is bound by so many ties, is a more apparent and compelling duty to most men than obligation to guard the rights of men whose land we have never seen and whose language we cannot speak.

Just what is the state, that its demands are held higher than the call of religion? Does a man owe to a political entity, set up for mutual protection of life, property and culture, more than he owes to his conscience, which speaks to him of God? Most men will say, as the Supreme Court of our land has said, that a man must surrender the right of private judgment, even on moral issues, when the state needs defense, though that defense may involve slaying his fellowman.

On the other hand the universal call of religion makes one an internationalist, not watering down one's love to country, but strengthening one's respect for the human race. All men are brothers in Christ, and it is a sin to kill any brother in hatred. The moral sense says that to kill is wrong; the state says killing is right. That is the tension the Christian faces. "Shall I stifle my conscience and obey the commands of men, or is there not something inherently inviolable in the moral obligation I feel to love all men?" War breaks down the solidarity and unity of the human race, which to the Christian is the highest good.

The vital question at issue is whether the state is above morality. The government in itself has no authority except that which its citizens give it, no virtue or fountain head of power other than that freely granted by its people. Every man as a moral being has not only a right but a duty to judge the actions of the nation on ethical grounds. The growth of any civilization depends upon respect for the inner integrity of a man's soul, the conscience he develops and the freedom he has to progress as a spiritual entity. The state has the right to demand his services and his goods, but it has not the right to force the sacrifice of his conscience. Luther and Calvin, both strong advocates of loyalty to the temporal authorities, nevertheless left the clear provision that rights of the individual conscience were inviolable. "God alone is Lord of the conscience" is the Westminster Confession's brave cry, and no prince or president has the right to usurp the freedom of the soul to follow the guidance of God. In any land where the state is glorified as the possessor of all power and the judge of its own morality, the rights of conscience are denied. But that only challenges the Christian further to assert the claims of a higher loyalty than patriotism, a higher duty than obedience to the political state, a duty to humanity itself. The Church finds much solace in the words of Chief Justice Hughes, "When one's belief collides with the power of the State, the latter is supreme within its sphere and submission or punishment follows. But, in the forum of conscience, duty to a moral power higher than the State has always been maintained."

In time of war, however, there never is presented to Christians a clear-cut choice between loyalty to God and loyalty to state. For the many events leading up to the declaration of war are so colored with propaganda, and so much falsehood is given out, that the moral sense is apt to be convinced that the claims of one's country are the claims of God. Every nation places itself in as favorable a moral light as possible, publishes "White Books" of selected diplomatic notes showing how virtuous it has been and how vicious is the enemy, and finally in a blaze of moral indignation war is declared as a religious duty. It was so in the World War and in every war of the past century.

3. Churches Ineffective in Peace Education

Now, if the Christian is to remain loyal to the universal ideal rather than the particular, he must decide long before war looms on the horizon that as a method of settling disputes it is the antithesis of all that he holds highest. He must see that war destroys both the products and the soul of civilization, that it blots out not only life but morality. He may agree to this, yet not be able to say that he will never use evil to accomplish the ends of his nation. Most of us still confuse national defense with personal defense, picturing the enemy nation as a mad dog running loose on the street, or as a burglar breaking into a home at night. But the case of two nations fighting over boundaries or trade routes is not the case of personal defense. One can repulse the attack of the burglar or the dog and still maintain good-will, still refrain from hatred, but one cannot torpedo, poison, bomb and bayonet one's fellowman in anything other than ill-will or hate. War is organized murder, premeditated, annihilating every sense of sacredness for personality that society and religion try to inculcate. Not only that, but there are many other channels for settling international disputes, and war is the failure through selfishness to arrive at a sane, judicial solution.

Building up an attitude of complete resistance to the morality of war is a long and slow process. Only through educating the public conscience to brand war as a personal and social sin will the Church ever develop enough moral strength to stop wars. It is not an impossible task. A good many churches are grasping the Paris Peace Pact as a safe beginning along the lines of peace education. But what a commentary it is upon the Church that it must wait until practically every political state in the civilized world has signed a pact renouncing war before it dares press forward the fight for peace in the name of Christ.

For the churches have waited and are still hesitant about making peace a part of the doctrine they teach. They cling to ancient creeds and easier social issues, such as liquor and Sabbath observance, but dare not make peace the subject of nation-wide denominational effort. Below the surface of the resolutions and the pacifism of a good many clergy, is the tragic ignorance and hostility of the members of our Protestant churches to the issues of international good-will. Peace is considered a political subject fraught with danger. Churches are hesitant to deal with a social issue that is certain to be resented by a good share of many congregations. It is a subject upon which people disagree, and rather than have any argument or dissension in the house of God, they let Satan in the form of war remain. There have been all too many disputes within the churches, but there are some issues which no church, following the Prince of Peace, can afford to sidestep, and peace is one of them.

The effort of the local churches and the national boards of the denominations has centered almost wholly on missions. Study, money, talent and energy have been thrown into the evangelizing effort. Home and foreign missions, with their educational programs, have been the main channels through which the church has expressed its humanitarian interest. Speakers, dinners, motion pictures and a thousand other activities have been used to keep us mission-conscious. And the tremendous outpouring of devotion and money has shown that the church is tremendously interested in spreading the Word.

But it has occurred to few churches or church members in the past that it was incongruous to exert every effort to save the soul and the body of a man through missions, and then murder his brothers by the thousands. We have pleaded that every human personality was worth saving, that there was no cost of life or money too dear to bring a pagan to know Christ. Medical missionaries have told of the joy of healing hundreds in the name of Jesus, while the churches in war have given their spiritual blessing and material resources to the business of maiming, blinding, and gassing the people of other lands. What cruel blindness has made us so insensitive, so callous to human life in time of war? What hypocrisy is there in the human heart that will send a stocking of toys as a token of friendship, and a battleship of death as an expression of hate?

Some of the denominations have laid increasing emphasis upon peace education through the many channels by which they influence their members. Most in earnest about peace are the Methodists and Congregationalists, and they have been striking many a good blow at Mars. Through their publications and social service departments a constant stream of education for international good will is going forth, and the result, or perhaps the cause, may be seen in the Kirby Page questionnaire already referred to. Seventy-eight per cent of the five thousand five hundred Methodist ministers, and 66 per cent of the seventeen hundred Congregationalist ministers who replied to the question, said the church should now state its refusal to sanction or support war. This was higher than Baptists, Presbyterians, Episcopalians or Lutherans. Only 38 per cent of the latter replied affirmatively. Again, more Methodist and Congregational ministers were willing to pledge themselves personally against any participation in war, 72 per cent of the former and 63 per cent of the latter, than in the other denominations. The Episcopal and Lutheran clergy occupied the bottom positions, less than 33 per cent of the sixteen hundred Lutherans being ready to personally renounce war.

A study of the denominational literature and peace efforts shows the Methodist church to be especially alive to the opportunity of educating their members along the lines of international understanding. One of their church school publications that is circulated among 370,000 high school age pupils every week, during the last three years has annually averaged from fourteen to twenty-five articles, poems, lesson materials and the like on world friendship, peace and race relations. The cumulative effect of such peace efforts, over a period of years and augmented by the class room, Epworth League and pulpit, is truly enormous. Would that all churches were as far along the road of banning war from their Christian discipleship as are the Methodists! Yet such work must be carried on year after year, and by all the churches, in order to turn the nation's conscience toward peace.

On the other hand, the Episcopal and Lutheran churches have done very little serious work to place peace among the ideals of the Church. Many ministers of these two denominations are chaplains, which possibly has some effect upon their attitude. The Lutheran Church in 1933 published a pamphlet "Facts and Forces in the Social Order," which is being extensively used by their young people as the basis of their study on how "to live the Christian religion in all relationships." Room is found to discuss gambling, racketeering, profanity and suicide, but not one page or one word is given to a discussion of peace! Nothing is said about world friendship or international relations, an oversight that can only be considered the intention of the Lutherans to stay away from a possibly controversial subject.

The Episcopal Church has a Department of Christian Social Service, but aside from distributing reprints of addresses made at its triennial General Conventions, it apparently does little for peace. The Lambeth Conference in 1930, however, placed on record its conviction "That the Christian Church in every nation should refuse to countenance any war in regard to which the government of its own country has not declared its willingness to submit the matter to arbitration or conciliation." This leaves an opening for the church to support wars that result from broken arbitration conferences, or wars which may result after one's own country has agreed to arbitrate only along certain prescribed lines. It is not a pledge that the churches withdraw support from the war system as such.

The Northern Baptists publish no study material on peace themselves, but are distributing much good material put out by the National Council for the Prevention of War. This is a lame effort for peace, however, for many groups will look with suspicion on materials not bearing the stamp of one's own denomination. Here is a great church practically helpless before the gigantic problem of educating its members for peace. Missionary and world friendship courses of course are good, but they are too indirect to adequately prepare the conscience for the Christian stand against war. Multitudes of missionary-minded folks have little or no sympathy for peace efforts.

4. WHAT CAN THE CHURCHES DO?

What can the Church of Christ do about war? First of all it can bring up the body of its membership to an understanding of the fine resolutions which most national conventions have passed. They have blazed the trail. This means education through every channel at our disposal. Church schools, young people's societies, pulpits, summer conferences, retreats, publications and lesson material, all must be used to overcome the age-old fears and thoughts that make for conceited nationalism, racial superiority, and reliance upon might. There can be no enduring peace without justice, and the churches can point out in manifold ways such as in adult education classes and forums, injustices in the economic and political order which must be adjusted if strife is to be avoided.

Second, the Church can withdraw its moral support from war, making known its present determination that all its material and spiritual resources will be opposed to the settlement of any international dispute by force of arms. It must brand war a sin. Take away the moral reason for the call to arms and few wars can be waged. Some will join any call to battle, but a modern conflict demands the wholesale drafting of manpower, and this will be hard indeed for a government to carry through if the stigma of moral evil is attached to its acts.

Third, the Church should educate its youth to see that the

way of war is utterly opposed to Christ, and that for them to follow Him must mean their sole reliance upon His weapons. His arms were love and good will, His method forgiveness, His power, sacrifice. The appeal of Christ to youth is exceedingly strong, and the Church can do nothing more fruitful for the coming of His Kingdom in the hearts of men, than to say to youth, "If you would follow Jesus you must take the hard, unpopular, and crucifying road of love for all men. The Church hasn't been able to follow Him yet, it has betrayed Him in every war, but it insists that a true Christian will never hate or kill his fellow man." The Friends have been the truest Christians in this regard. They have held inflexibly to the following statement, which the rest of the Church might well take as the ideal: "In all the essential relations of men we believe that moral and spiritual as well as physical disarmament is the way to the more abundant life, whether between the soul and God, or in the home, the school, the factory, the prison. It is equally true as between nations. Only when they are prepared to come together for the solution of their common problems in a spirit of love and mutual helpfulness can they hope for success, and win that peace which is now withheld because they are armed."

THE SPIRITUAL IMPETUS TOWARD SOCIAL PROGRESS

RUSSELL J. CLINCHY

CHAPTER XII

THE SPIRITUAL IMPETUS TOWARD SOCIAL PROGRESS

A SHORT while ago we were all startled to read that 1,200 miners in Hungary had entombed themselves in the coal mine in which they worked. They refused to come up unless their demands for higher wages, and better conditions of living for their families, were granted. These men would not listen to the entreaties of employers or police, declaring that mass suicide was the only alternative to their demands. This is how an aged miner, a man who had been digging coal for fifty-eight years, described the experience:

The pangs of hunger maddened us to such an extent that we ate leather belts, and gnawed at shoes. We couldn't even have the mercy of sleep because the corridors of the pits were so narrow we were forced to stand up. There was nothing but damp blackness for five days.

There are many circumstances which have to be taken into account and explained in this episode, but after we have given full significance to the horrors of the working conditions and the underground days, we are confronted by a remarkable venture of the spirit of man in his relation to the environment of his daily life. We have known of times when the desperation caused by economic or social ills has led men to fight, to tear down and, sometimes, to run amuck and pull down the pillars of life over their own heads and of many innocent people as well. But here was the first great attempt of any considerable number of people in the Western world to lift the conditions of life for others by a sacrifice of themselves.

Now no matter what may be our judgment of such action, this remains true, that the willingness to use a method like that involves the use of spiritual conceptions of life. That does not mean that the idea was conceived in a church, or that prayer meetings were held during those five days they were entombed. It does mean that such a plan could not have been conceived, and carried out, unless the attention of those men had been lifted from themselves and placed upon others; unless they had been thinking of a more ideal time when, through their loss, others might have a more satisfying and hopeful future. No matter what may be the auspices under which such an attitude takes place, its source is a spiritual conception of human life. Has any human attempt been any more thrilling, or stirring than this one in Hungary? Twelve hundred men left their homes one morning, and the light of day, and walked into a mine, vowing to remain there forever if need be. Foolish desperation in the face of economic facts, say some. But the result does not seem to be that, for at the end of five days the company did find it possible to raise the wages of these men from $2.50 to $3.50 a week, and promised a bonus at Christmas. Perhaps spiritual power can even open our eyes to deeper insights into what we call economic facts.

The great light which an episode like this sheds upon our present problem is not just that of technique, though that is most suggestive, but is of even more importance. It is the portrayal of the belief that it is spiritual perception and spiritual power which is both the source of social progress and the meaning of such progress. This is where religion enters into the problem of our disordered social life. It is not a competitor of the social sciences, and should not attempt, by itself, to construct social and economic blueprints. But we are discovering anew today that, though religion is not prepared to sit down at a drafting board and draw the specifications of a new economic order, it does, and must, function in an even more fundamental manner. New specifications of economic planning were made at the close of that entombment. Operators who said that wages could not be raised, suddenly discovered reserves by which a new wage scale could be made. But that was accomplished through the power of a spiritual impetus which was given a chance at reality in life. Such spiritual consciousness not only produces the imperative for social adjustment, it also interprets the use of social advance.

That is just the point at which most emphasis needs to be laid today. The air is full of demands for higher wages, better working conditions, and more security. But there are two questions which have a very great deal to do with these demands to which very little attention is being given. One is how shall we find the power which will persuade us toward social progress, and the other is by what scale shall we measure and interpret social progress when we achieve it. The social scientists do not attempt to touch upon these questions. It has been left to religion to answer them, and so, surely, there can be no criticism if religious people do that which no one else cares to do.

It is well now for us to listen to what one student of

religion has said. "You may," he writes, "give every man a comfortable living; assurance against unemployment, sickness and old age; three acres and a cottage; you may have a warless world; you may have free intercourse among the nations; the Russians may realize all their five-year plans— yet the Kingdom of God may not be upon earth; the world may be better off, but not better. It may still be sensual, greedy, self-indulgent, proud. Into such a world Jesus would still have to come to preach the Gospel of God. He would again preach repentance, a change of mind, and faith as the conditions of entering into the Kingdom of God." When Dr. Richards has told us this he has touched the heart of the problem concerning social progress, that its basic interpretation, both of securing and of using it, is essentially religious. Many of us remember how Alexander Irvine, the eccentric Irish preacher, answered a man who interrupted him at a street meeting by asking, "Why doesn't your Jesus give us bread?" Turning to him, Irvine said, "If the one glimpse of Jesus that you could have was of him coming down the street with a loaf of bread on his arm, or of him upon a cross, which would you take?" That does not mean that religion has no concern as to whether man has bread or not. It does mean that it is concerned with the perpetual source of a spiritual energy which will keep on creating ways of life which will feed more of us, and then of teaching us how to make use of the security of that bread. These concerns are essentially spiritual; nothing else can tell us how to achieve this power, and then how to interpret its use.

If we are going to do this we shall have to begin to love God in a different way than most people are in the habit of doing. Most of us now love God for our sakes, that is, to secure something from Him for ourselves. Now that may be a result of our love of God, but it can never be the beginning. Instead, we must act toward God as Jesus did, that is, to love Him for His sake no matter what may come to us because of it. What does that mean in real life? It means to want to see happen what God wants done. That is loving God for His sake, rather than for ours. There lies the secret of the spiritual impotence of so much religious living. On all sides we hear the criticism that religion never makes its ideals real, never supplies the power to bring its plans to pass. Of course it doesn't, because it is seeking to have God do for us what we want done for ourselves, rather than having us want to do what God wants done in the world.

There was a fascinating story told us recently when the death of the head of the United States Army Medical service in Puerto Rico was announced. Twenty-five years ago he went to the island as a young lieutenant in the medical corps. When he reached his station there were two attitudes he could have taken toward his work. One was that he would try to get from this very secure position everything he could. He would love the army medical service for what it could do for him. The other was that he would love the service for what he could help it do what it wanted to do in that area. He chose the latter. He found that the average life span in Puerto Rico among the natives was very low, and that many died at an early age because life vitality seemed to be drained from them. He began to devote his leisure time to a study of this. Many of his colleagues tried to dissuade him, saying it wasn't necessary in his job. But he doggedly kept on, and bit by bit, he traced the cause to the intestines, and then discovered the hook-worm which was ravaging the people,

He loved his task so well that he loved it for what that task was meant to do in the world. That is the difference between loving something for what it can do for us, and loving it for how we can help it do what it wants done.

Now right there is where we must come to a realization of the difference between what we may call the spiritual and the religious attitudes toward life. It is true, as many are now saying, that religion instead of being an impetus toward social progress, has more often been a hindrance and a bar. There are others, also, who will claim that it has in many cases set the cause of social progress back. That is just why we need to make this difference between the spiritual conception and the general religious one. There are such differences. In the Middle Ages, a few fanatical religious leaders, who were really demagogues, set the simple-minded Christians of Europe aflame with a wild zeal to recover the alleged tomb of Christ from the infidels and the pagans in Jerusalem. With wild frenzy the mob, which increased in numbers as they journeyed, swept out of Europe into Asia, burning, pillaging, and destroying everything, and everybody, they called heathen. There has been no greater expression of inhuman hate, murder, and lust than was evinced by these maddened, religious people who were out to find the tomb of the meek and lowly Jesus.

A few centuries later there began to develop in England a group of people who sensed what they termed "the inner light." They said that if a man would open his life unselfishly to the spirit of God, he would come into the possession of a warm reality of the presence of God, and would possess a new light of understanding and awareness. These people were laughed at, mocked, scourged, and derisively called Quakers. They moved over to Penn's Woods, in America, where they found Indians living. When they bought land from the Indians they did not cheat them, they paid all they could for it. They shared their food with poor and hungry Indians. They tried to teach them some of the stories and ways of life which seemed so good. The final story is that in a period in which Colonial history in America is filled with Indian massacres there is not one recorded story of an Indian massacre in the Pennsylvania colony.

Both of these group experiences could be classed technically under the name of Christianity, but what constitutes the vast difference between them? One was merely a religious or formal expression of what passed for the externals of Christianity, while the other was a deeply spiritual adventure into the inner conceptions of Christianity. The religious expression did not create social progress; it retarded it for centuries. The spiritual expression brought forth social progress simply as a normal expression of itself. That there is such a distinction, and what it is, must now be taught by the Christian church to its people. Jesus recognized them. He had discovered the religious expression which was impotent, and very distinctly he said, "Not everyone that says 'Lord, Lord'." That is, not everyone who goes around with a religious label contains the possibility of creating social advance. Instead, Jesus found that he could discover a very great deal of a willingness to do God's will outside of those channels which were definitely marked religious. He constantly searched for the spiritual attitude, even in Samaritans, that group of people to whom the Jews could not give diplomatic recognition. Jesus was after one thing, the possession of a spiritual power which created social betterment.

The religious attitude is not found in one religion or one sect, while the spiritual is found in another. That is what makes our present religious divisions so ludicrous. It was at the time when the Popes of the Roman church were very religious and very degenerate, that Francis of Assisi developed his spiritual power and brought forth a new creative power for social advance. It was when the Protestant church of England was most observant of religious formality, and was lifeless of any power, that the Quakers, and the Puritans, and then the Methodists, caught a spiritual sense, and a new social imperative developed. The same power resides in those who spiritually interpret non-Christian religions. Every one of us understands how this was true of the Jews, when there were many who were religious and who blocked the roads of progress. But the spiritual conceptions of the prophets literally charged the life of their times with a dynamic power of social advance.

Now we have come once more to a place in history when a social advance must be made. Wars may have once helped some nations for a while, while they destroyed others. But now, one more war like the last one and the game is over for the West. The power will go to the East. It was once possible to carry on a social life in the whimsical, naïve way which is described in the book of Ruth. You remember that Boaz owned the field, and he very benevolently allowed poor people like Ruth to come in and pick up the gleanings of the wheat which he allowed to be left on the ground after he had gotten what he wanted. Humanity rode into the twentieth century in what was practically the social system of Boaz. The best we can now say is that the old vehicle of the Boaz system is like the wonderful one-hoss shay; it lasted a hundred years and a day, and then just fell apart. No one has destroyed this ancient system of the right of the strong to take what they will, if only they leave something for the gleaners. It had to carry the weight of a modern industrialized life in which all of us in the world have a common stake, and it just collapsed.

The question, then, is not whether we shall have social progress, it is when we shall find the creative power to produce such progress. Then, here is the message of Jesus, that we shall not find it in just political and scientific programs, for they are merely the machinery which our power uses. We shall not find it in just religious systems which are mainly interested in correct forms and the maintenance of prestige. We can, and shall, find them, as Jesus told us, and life is continually telling us, in those lives in which spiritual conceptions of living have taken root and have developed power, no matter what their name or place.

This is why those who believe in the efficacy of spiritual power cannot surrender to the pleas of those who suggest that coercion and compulsion, by physical force if necessary, must be used to bring about social advance. It is not because this is a different method that it is opposed, but simply because physical coercion has never been able to create motivations of social progress, and it is those motivations that we seek. Two illustrations of attempted social change may be used to describe the futility of coercion. In the decade before 1860 there was a universal desire in the Northern States of our country that the Negro slaves should be given freedom and the rights guaranteed by the Constitution. Religion and education began to focus their powers upon the problem. But there were some to whom such progress was too slow.

They wanted to break the power of the slave-owners at once and to free the slaves immediately. They were able to instigate a war, and they forced the South to free the slaves. Did they change the mind or attitude of a single white Southerner then? And did the Civil War succeed in changing the attitude of the children and grandchildren of those Southerners toward the Negro? The task of changing the mind and attitude is still confronting those small groups of Northerners and Southerners who are depending upon the only power we possess to work such a miracle, the persuasion of the spiritual resources of life.

So it is proving true in Russia. It was probably necessary that the volcanic action of 1917 should have taken place. Thomas Jefferson stated very clearly that there are moments in history which justify such action by people to whom no other course is open. But the same method was then used to create social progress and it is that which has failed to produce motivations for that progress within the Russian people. It has been possible to force the Russian people to live under the Soviet philosophy. The Czars, however, were able to do that. Yet, in spite of their confidence in force, the Communists of Russia have used the motivations of the spirit in making that which is their greatest accomplishment, that of capturing the enthusiasm of the youth. Maurice Hindus describes the fervor of the young men and young women in sacrificing bread and clothing that Russia may buy machinery. But how was that fervor produced? Not by coercion, but by conversion! The simple fact is, as we all know, that the best and most lasting results of the Soviet experiment have been created when the leaders have appealed to the patriotism, the enthusiasm, and the adventure of the youth of Russia, pleading with them for a release of their spiritual energies. The future hope of the Soviet government does not rest upon the farmer kulaks who have been beaten into submission. It rests upon the youth which has been converted to the religion of Communism, and has felt the power of religion motivating it to social action.

That is the message the church must give, concerning Christianity, to those who call for social advance today. It is not that we differ with some of the secular social programs, it is simply that we have discovered that not only does spiritual power inevitably create and lead to social progress, but it is the only foundation upon which social progress will last. In all the history of the world it has been those who have discovered a spiritual interpretation of life who have been the creators of real and lasting social progress.

Who have been the lifters of the world? In his new book, "Erasmus of Rottendam," Arnold Zweig tells us that it was Erasmus, the religious scholar, alone who broke the hold of the Middle Ages upon the mind of Europe and ushered in the Renaissance, single-handed. The people who gave slavery in America its death-blow were not the politicians balancing free-states against slave-states, or even the Union Army. The freedom of the Negro race will occur through those long years in which spiritually minded men and women will continue to struggle for racial understanding and equality of rights, and will give of themselves for its accomplishment, because the spirit of God keeps them everlastingly at it.

Where is the power of social progress? There is a man standing on a hill above Jerusalem, the city of his people, and when you look at him you find his eyes are wet and his body is shaking with a deep emotion. The sight of the need has broken his heart, and he is weeping over Jerusalem. But the wet eyes of Jesus of Nazareth as they looked down upon humanity, have sent men and women out to face the Jerusalems of the centuries with broken hearts, but with power to change the world.

DOES THE CHURCH SAVE THE INDIVIDUAL?

JOHN I. DANIEL

CHAPTER XIII

DOES THE CHURCH SAVE THE INDIVIDUAL?

"RELIGION, even in the narrow sense," says Gilbert Murray, "is always looking for escape, for some salvation from the terror to come, or some deliverance from the body of this death." Professor Ellwood declares, in broadening this thesis: "The end of all religion is in social and personal salvation, in help over the difficulties, and redemption from the evils of life."

"These difficulties and evils, however, are not all external to the self," writes Charles A. Bennett. "We cannot judge the world about us without *feeling* this world to be judging us. What could cause this reflection except an experience which puts us for a moment at a point outside the self, from which we can see the self through the eyes of another? Thus may we not say that the consciousness of sin is the consciousness of another Mind behind the universe, whose approval we somehow have to win?"

Accordingly, "the doubt which religion generates is a doubt about the moral relation of the human soul to God. The alternative with which it torments man is not that of God or no God, but of God remote, or God near at hand. Religious despair is born of a sense of alienation, and what religion announces as salvation, is the restoration of harmony."

As younger churchmen looking at the church, we see at once that as a vehicle of salvation its task is manifold.

Illumined, first of all, by the modern realization that restoration of harmony is not a matter of the individual alone, there must be an emphasis that relates the individual's quest to that of his fellows. Harmony is here achieved through enlistment in a cosmic enterprise. In this sense, every individual becomes partner in the collectivist crusade of establishing the Kingdom of God, so involving himself, to a greater or less degree, in a dimension of timelessness.

Mysticism offers a second aspect of salvation. While for the most part individual in its emphasis, the conviction of personal sin, to which Charles A. Bennett refers, has its social parallel in the words of Isaiah: "Woe is me! For I am undone; because I am a man of unclean lips, *and I dwell in the midst of a people of unclean lips;* for mine eyes have seen the King, the Lord of Hosts."

Thirdly there is salvation in the less super-worldly sense of salvation from self in the work-a-day life. Salvation in this aspect entails rigorous self searching and discipline. Its inexorable prerequisite is the facing of one's specific sins, confession before God, and consequent surrender. The sense of release and of new power which follows this procedure is strongly affirmed by secular psychologists as well as by religionists. A new, and immeasurably superior way of life, here and now, is the principle involved, and through it thousands have charted paths of spiritual harmony in a very practical and satisfying sense.

Finally, there is salvation by faith, or by grace. The orthodoxies, both of Rome and of Fundamentalist Protestantism, profess to be the channels of its attainment. These orthodoxies are similar in that they promise to the faithful ultimate full soul continuance beyond death—presumably in a state of celestial bliss. Romanism accounts the faithful to be those who subscribe to its dogma, attend services, and otherwise submit to its offices. Orthodox Protestantism holds up the less institutional, but equally dogmatic, standard of belief in the verbal infallibility of scripture, with the Substitutional Atonement as the modus operandi.

Doubtless other types could be added to these four, but we are not so interested in *listing* aspects of salvation, as in discussing what, if anything, an awakening Church offers in relation to them.

II

Returning, therefore, to the problem of the Kingdom enterprise, we may view the Church's mission to be that of spiritualizing the conception of social regeneration. Modern theologians must project the secular vision of the Kingdom out into the realm of eternal verities. Utopian dreams must be grafted onto something more transcendent. But we must first of all repudiate individualism.

Although the greater number of social prophets since the industrial revolution have been cradled in the Church, few have found its fellowship satisfying. Despite the Church's constant protestations of social concern, its individual salvation tradition has remained a dominant note. Numbers of those imbued with social passion have been forced out by politico-economic reactionaries, while many more have simply been cold-shouldered until they came to feel a greater warmth of fellowship, as well as to experience greater effectiveness, in working through non-Christian mediums. Norman Thomas, A. J. Muste and Tucker Smith are only a few of the modern prophets who have left the Church not so much in repudiation, as in despair.

Since the spiritualizing of the conception of social regeneration is one of the major problems of an awakening Church, younger churchmen, as evidenced most notably in conference summaries, are proposing solutions along somewhat the following lines:

1. Greater hospitality toward—and consequent warmer fellowship with—all those who are waging a predominantly social emphasis. It must not be supposed that all leakage away from Christian fellowship will thus be restrained, but there will certainly be an appreciable abatement, and our fellowship will be greatly enriched.

2. An incorporation of the religious consequences of collectivism in the Church's general philosophy of salvation.

3. A transcendent attitude upon the part of the Church that will take the establishment of a coöperative commonwealth for granted—*not as an end in itself,* but as one incidental preliminary step toward the establishment of the Kingdom.

However much those proclaiming the social emphasis may concentrate upon social sin, the fact is that the problem is far more complex than is admitted in their analysis. The religionist realizes the limitation of a conception of social salvation which can be realized in Time. Viewed in the light of possibility of attainment, this emphasis becomes materialistically secular.

No moral realist can regard a Utopia as a substitute for the Kingdom. Were our social ethics perfected, were poverty to be entirely abolished, God would not be displaced, any more than He was bowed out of the picture by the advances of nineteenth century science. On the contrary, as we advance, socially, technically and morally, *our realization of His work for us broadens like an inverted pyramid,* bringing with it an increasing sense of need of His assistance in performing new tasks.

This thought has been likened by some to an incident in "Water Babies" by Charles Kingsley. Tom, a chimney sweep, lost in a maze of flues, finally emerges into the fireplace of the first bathroom he has ever seen. Towels, soap, brushes, bath mats in profusion provoke from him the comment: "What a very *dirty* person must live here to need so many tools for keeping clean."—Then, greatly to his surprise, upon peeping into an adjoining bedroom he saw a child, about his own age, sleeping in a snow-white bed!

Unregenerate man, even though he possesses social vision, can scarcely see further than the goal of secular Utopianism. But there are worlds to conquer beyond this goal! There is a moral enterprise of such dimensions that cosmic resources must needs be brought into play to wage it. Man, mortal and sinful, *needs* God—eternal and sinless. We overlap the realm of mysticism.

III

What is mysticism? Charles A. Bennett defines it: "A way of life, in which the conspicuous element is the immediate experience of God." Not that all who seek this experience do so in quest of power for waging the cosmic enterprise. Many are desirous merely of the personal elation that comes from a sense of communion with the Unseen. In this their motive (however moderate the methods used) is not far different from that of the Hindu mystic in search of Nirvana.

At this very point is seen the practical advantage of conceiving of salvation in its several aspects. That person who is keenly alive spiritually—who has sought after and discovered God for his personal delectation—upon being apprised of the collectivist view of the Kingdom, may turn his inner resources to the end of helping to achieve salvation in other than the individual pattern of tradition.

But, unfortunately, all mystics are not alive to the need for social application of the power that comes to them in communion with God. Having once been afflicted with that agony of despair experienced while alienated from God, they have practiced His Presence and restored harmony. Very many, having reached this haven, have no desire to put to sea again.

Obviously, the Church has here a two-fold mission. It must minister to the sense of personal alienation from God—striving through worship and the sacraments to restore harmony—and at the same time point out the bogus sense of security, the fool's paradise, in which those preoccupied with mysticism may bask.

Our Lord seems certainly to have established the most perfect communion with his Father, in the wilderness preparation, yet it was for him but a means to an end. Repeatedly during his ministry he retired to a remote lake shore or to a mountain top for a mystical experience, but always to use the increased power so obtained, for the more vigorous waging of the Kingdom enterprise.

The return to the world is not only a test of the mystic's intention, but of the *quality* of his experience as well. St.

Theresa, more than any other of the classical mystics, insists upon this. She was much concerned about the genuineness of her revelations, always testing them rigorously with the criterion: "Any love of God which does not increase the love for your neighbor is false." Moreover, since the term "neighbor" implies not only "Samaritans" but posterity as well, the experience of God takes the form in us of a holy passion to be used by Him in bringing to pass a more decent world in which His children—present and future—may live.

IV

Having so far discussed these two complementary poles of the conception of salvation, we encounter the need for release from the personal sense of sin which casts its shadow over the mortal lives of us all. The relation of this aspect of salvation to mysticism is that many hold the surrender of certain areas of sin to be an essential prerequisite to any direct experience of God at all. Again, its relation to the social problem is tersely expressed in the words of Rev. S. M. Shoemaker: "Revolution by consent! Changed lives are the raw material of the new world order."

The need for changed lives—salvation from personal sin —while an age-old emphasis, is being most dramatically championed to-day by the Oxford Groups. Under these auspices we have a definite technique, an application of spiritual method, which appears in an imposing proportion of instances, to work.

Conviction of sin is the cornerstone of this salvation. Next comes confession—in the presence of some sympathetic friend, or alone with God—followed by surrender! This surrender of one or a number of specific sins, which heretofore have been blocking the relationship to God, does make new men and women of thousands who formerly were victims of sloth, selfishness, dishonesty, sensuality, and kindred forms of evil. Moreover, the surrender experience is vitalized by a practical sort of mysticism which seeks in God, and frequently finds, revelations of future conduct. Such practical revelations are termed Guidance, and when checked upon by other members of the Group, afford an index of right conduct which presages greater efficiency to the individual as a unit in the Kingdom enterprise.

These Guidance experiences, as well as the instances of surrendered sin which make them possible, are "shared" by those who have experimented with this aspect of salvation. That it is a deeply satisfying experience few can deny, and if the pattern seems to assume a pharisaical aspect, it must be acknowledged that "Oxford Groupers" have reason for preferring their way of doing things to the moral impotency of so many of their critics.

This is not to say that the Oxford Groups have a monopoly upon "life-changing," but simply to suggest their insight as a technique which no church that is genuinely interested in the complexities of the problem of salvation can afford to disregard.

v

Finally there is salvation in its legal aspect. Wherever orthodox Christianity has been able to retain the unqualified loyalty of its adherents in a given locality, this aspect has been dominant.

In Catholicism, mysticism has always been given auxiliary consideration, and "works" have had a place, but so preoccupied has the Church been with piloting souls safely into an otherworldly paradise, that these accompanying aspects have been dissipated. Fundamentalist Protestantism has concentrated with equal diligence upon the legal requirements for attaining celestial beatitude in the unblushingly personal sense.

If there is anything to be said for these orthodoxies, it is the assurance which they offer to a certain dependent psychological type of person. However, were this assurance morally justifiable, is it not, in view of the new cosmic horizons which lie before us, an extremely precarious haven?

Again, the unqualified loyalty of the faithful is required to reach it, and it is extremely doubtful to the realist whether the Church could retain this anywhere for very long, even if it wanted to. Too many feel that they have caught it red-handed, trying to escape reality in a bogus claim of absolute transcendence.

That era in which the Church can offer individual salvation as its only ware has gone, as a familiar chapter of Russian history most eloquently attests. Presented with the alternative of a completely collectivistic salvation, expressed in materialistic terms, nearly two hundred million persons seem to have chosen (or had chosen for them) the latter.

As younger churchmen, vitally concerned with the problem of salvation, we cannot, however, feel that these are the only alternatives. We feel that before the issue has become too closely drawn in America, there is hope that large numbers of church people will have repudiated their individual salvation pattern, strictly legal or otherwise, for a spiritualized collectivist one; not fly-by-night in character, but in which the treasure depths of mysticism and of ethics will be explored for their contributions.

Among America's greatest secular leaders was one who said, "If I rise, it will be with the ranks, not from them." Our Lord, himself, first voiced the spiritualized counterpart, "And I, if I be lifted up from the earth, will draw all men unto me."

Is there not here revealed a synthesis of collectivism, mysticism and practical ethics which has not been given adequate consideration in theologies of the past? There is even included a note of Hebrew orthodoxy, to which the Nazarene always seems to pay a certain devoir.

To the problems of to-day the first-hand insights of mysticism, with our consequent perception of human sin, are profoundly applicable. The conscious surrender of definite areas of sin is also of tremendous value in training soldiers for more effective use in the Kingdom enterprise.

But the Kingdom itself, by its very cosmic and eternal nature, completely engulfs the individual. The Church cannot save that which in an eternal sense cannot exist. We exist eternally only as we are part of God's Family.

If the whole can be no stronger than its weakest part, that weakest part this moment is our least fortunate brother. Whether our brothers be less privileged in possessions, in talents or in character, we can achieve no Ultimate Salvation without them.

Would we seek restoration of harmony through the Christian Church? Then, true to the Vision of its founder, the Church must offer us a more complete synthesis of the new horizons of collectivism, with the spiritual resources of the past.

WHAT IS THE MATTER WITH OUR PREACHING?

HERMAN F. REISSIG

CHAPTER XIV

WHAT IS THE MATTER WITH OUR PREACHING?

THERE has always been something the matter with preaching. It has never been good enough. The goal of preaching is the emancipation of men and women from ignorance and sin to the glorious liberty of the children of God. To that task preaching has never been adequate. St. Paul failed. Savonarola failed. John Donne failed. Beecher failed. Brooks failed. In this essay I wish only to suggest that contemporary preaching might fail less frequently and abysmally. I will add that if any reader should be so foolish as to make a pilgrimage to the author's church for the purpose of seeing how well the critic follows his own advice, he will wonder as much as I do at the editor's choice. Understanding each other on these two matters, let us proceed with the question.

Much preaching sounds as if the preacher supposed his mission to be the vindication of religion. When I asked a veteran preacher what, in his opinion, is the matter with preaching he replied without hesitation, "We get too much talk about religion and too little religion." I agree. In a time of widespread uncertainty concerning the value of religion, it is probably inevitable that preachers should feel moved to come to its defense. But the value of religion is not demonstrated by talking *about* religion. One sermon on the forgiveness of sins, for example, which sends the people

227

away with a deep sense of release, their spirits ready once more to take up the battle, is worth more than a dozen arguments on "The Place of Religion in Life." One sermon which, beginning with some real human need, helps the people to find in Christ an immediate and potent help is worth more than many eloquent tributes to the greatness of Jesus. Perhaps the best way of stating this criticism is to say that many preachers appear to be more interested in their subject than in their object.

The distinction is important. It is the difference between an essay on friendship and a friend. It is the difference between a treatise on botany and a bouquet of flowers. It is the difference between a lecture on the service of medicine to mankind and the bestowal of health upon the sick. If we who preach will analyse the last fifty sermons we have delivered we will, I suspect, be surprised to discover how many of them have been descriptions and defenses of religion, and how few the actual impartation of life. They are like the advertising profession—much eloquent describing and recommending but no goods. And the result of such preaching, taken at its best, is well described in the words of John Henry Jowett: "Men admire but they do not revere; they appreciate but they do not repent; they are interested but they are not exalted."

An examination of the method and substance of Jesus' teaching sets this matter in high relief. How Jesus found it possible to preach so much and with such effect without even using the word "religion" must be a mystery to many of his modern ambassadors. We are always talking about "religion"—the necessity of it, the character of it, the uses of it. Jesus never mentioned it. His words are God, love, mercy,

sin, covetousness, repentance, sorrow, peace, joy. His preaching is direct, immediate. He is always dealing with the stuff
of life. He does not say, "Religion can help you." No such
meaningless abstraction ever came from his lips. He does
not protest that "what Jerusalem needs is more religion."
He was not interested in religion. He was interested in God
and in men and women. His hearers go away with the life
of God in their souls. They go away, like Zacchaeus, to
restore unlawful gain, or, like Mary Magdalene, to begin a
new life. His teaching is creative, not merely expository;
concrete, not abstract. He addresses himself always to ele-
mental facts and needs.

I should set it down, therefore, as a first requirement of
better preaching that we engage in less exposition of and
argument in behalf of generic terms like religion, Christianity, worship, and that, instead, we deal simply and directly with the original materials of life. For eloquent tributes to the greatness of Christ let us substitute sermons which
channel to specific human needs the insights and the life of
Christ. Let us cross out some of our argumentative paragraphs on the fallacies of the atheist and the communist, sub-
stituting messages so full of light and healing as to be self-
validating. Of books and sermons explaining and defending
religion, arguing *about* religion we have had just about
enough. If we have any affirmative and living message for
this hard-pressed generation let us take it into our pulpits.

Much preaching sounds as if it came from the other side
of a dividing line separating the preacher from the men and
women in the pews. A preacher, as I see him, is a man of
like virtues and infirmities with the rest of men who goes
about among his people with seeing eyes and a thoughtful

mind, takes what he sees to a quiet place of study and prayer, and then, on Sunday, tells his people with humble earnestness what he has found. Be he ever so assured of the importance of his message, he does not forget that he is but a "broken light," that the sins which he exposes are in his own heart, that the spiritual dullness which he condemns lies heavy upon his own soul, that the idealism which he espouses is not the sole possession of preachers. He is a man among men, set somewhat apart, to be sure, but with all his roots in the common life of the people.

But one who listens to many sermons and reads many more —the better to understand the art of preaching—is constantly getting the impression that the man in the pulpit imagines himself somehow outside and above the tragedy and glory of human life. He talks about some bitter human need as if he had never really felt it. He "solves" so casually the "problem" he has chosen for his subject, as if it were all quite simple to *him*. He admonishes us to follow after righteousness as if we were not as eager as he to be righteous. The younger radical preachers of our day, in particular, are not humbly conscious enough of the sources of such insight as they possess. Spiritual aspiration and ethical insight are not hatched exclusively in theological seminaries and ministers' conferences. Nor are they confined to enrolled members of the Socialist party. The world may be in a sorry mess, but we preachers, so glib and self-assured in the pulpit, have got both feet in it. And the reasons for such hope as we can have are as much in the hearts of the common people as in us who think we have a right to admonish them.

This is not to say that the sermon should be spoken with an air of apology, as if the preacher should say, "I know no more about this than you." Pity the preacher who cannot join in the words put into the mouth of Paul by Frederick Meyers:

> *Oh, could I tell, ye surely would believe it!*
> *Oh, could I only say what I have seen!*
> *How could I tell, or how could ye believe it——*
> *How, 'till He bringeth you where I have been!*

Nevertheless, the preacher must remember that, at best, he also is "an infant crying in the night," and that the people in the pews are also the offspring of God. The preacher shares the desperate need of his people: let him talk as if he knew it! The people share the hope for a better world and the desire for a diviner life which animate the preacher: let him speak as if he were aware of it! The simple fact is that the quality which George A. Gordon used so much to stress, "the breath of humanity," is absent from too many sermons.

Much preaching bogs down in innocuous generalities. This is perhaps the preacher's subtlest temptation. His sermon is carefully prepared. He is dead in earnest. But the effect is almost nil because the thought is not barbed with pointed and concrete illustration. Here, for example, is a sermon on "Righteousness Exalteth a Nation." The preacher declares with most solemn emphasis that "our great need is righteous men and women," that "without more righteousness we are lost," that "the real trouble with the world is a lack of honor, unselfishness, truthfulness." Despite his sincerity, however, he reminds us of some lines by Oliver Wendell Holmes:

> *Thou mindest me of gentlefolk,*
> *Old gentlefolk are they;*
> *Thou sayest an undisputed thing*
> *In such a solemn way.*

No one disputes the necessity of righteousness. And to plead for it with the fervor of a Savonarola does no more than start a solemn nodding of heads. Moreover, the pleader for "righteousness" is really talking about nothing at all. For righteousness is a word, a lifeless abstraction. It gets content only in the concrete instance. The preacher wins universal approval because he is not saying anything.

John Bowring wrote the hymn, "In the Cross of Christ I Glory." He was also a slave-trader. Bowring, one may suppose, heard many sermons on the brotherhood of man. If homiletical custom and good taste had not ruled out a statement to the effect that brotherhood means the abolition of slavery John Bowring might have walked out of the church; but the doctrine of brotherhood would, at least, have been given some practical content. What is the use of preaching on Jesus' concern for the underprivileged if we do not bring the matter down to date, telling our people that as modern followers of Jesus we must espouse the cause of labor in its fight for a living wage? Trying, on a recent Sunday, to make up my mind where to attend church, I was attracted by this sermon title, "What Is Justice?" That subject, I thought, ensured a vital discussion. The preacher had an attractive delivery, and for thirty minutes he talked fluently about justice. But of actual instances of injustice in the world about him—not a word! Mooney was in prison, the victim of terrible injustice. The Scottsboro boys were facing legal death, the victims of a shameful failure of justice. Millions of people were living on the edge of want, victims of society's injustice. Prisons were filled with men who learned crime before they could tell their right from their left hands, victims of our failure to achieve a just and decent social order.

The preacher stayed safely away from the specific—and left his people where they were when they entered the church, believing, as they always had believed, in justice.

Why do preachers confine themselves to the general and the abstract? Are they afraid? But they preach eloquently on courage. Are they not really concerned for men and women? But they are always telling us to love our fellowmen. Have they been betrayed into thinking that because certain words and phrases sound well they must mean something? But they are students of a Preacher who left no doubt as to the practical meaning of his principles. Probably all of these reasons operate together to give us futile sermonizing.

Closely connected with this defect is the absence of a certain tough and gritty quality in many sermons. Expository preachers and those who make much of the text seem especially addicted to a kind of roses-and-lavender speech—very beautiful, very "inspiring," but so different from the homely, rugged speech of Jesus. This kind of preaching is not difficult to manage once you get the hang of it. You swing back and forth on the text, pointing out the momentous significance of the exact sequence of the words, calling attention to this and that, engaging in a delicate and detailed analysis of spiritual imponderables. You find yourself quite carried away by it. You carry the less realistic minds in the congregation with you. It is all so "spiritual"—and so unreal! It is a spiritual boat-ride-on-a-moonlit-night. It is intellectual fluff. To insert in such a sermon a straight-out reference to an industrial strike or a lynching party or sex or fascism or wage rates would produce a disagreeable shock. This kind of preaching is immensely popular because it provides an escape from real life. It is to the congregation what drink was to the workingman—"the shortest route out of Birmingham."

I do not wish to suggest that the sermon must always deal with our tangible environment or that its medium of expression should invariably be indubitable prose. On the contrary, sermons ought often to lift us out of time, putting a song in our hearts. The addresses of Lincoln, particularly the Second Inaugural and Gettysburg addresses, are illustrations of speech that is exalted without being unreal. Here one finds loftiness, sublimity, spirituality, in sentences which could almost be set to music. But, withal, there is in them a quality which reminds us of some lines from Edwin Markham's poem, "Lincoln, the Man of the People,"

> *The color of the ground was in him, the red earth;*
> *The smack and tang of elemental things.*

And that poem is itself an example of lofty speech based upon, not in disregard of, the actual materials of life.

There is another indictment which can be brought against much preaching. I do not know how better to state it than to say that it sounds as if the preacher had never read anything except magazines and books written for preachers. It moves in a little world. It has neither height nor depth. It does not ascend into heaven nor descend into hell, nor does it go to the uttermost parts of the earth. It is a thin trickle of "thoughts" gleaned, apparently, from a note-book-in-hand reading of ethical and theological homilies. It seems to assume that we are all hungry for the most commonplace information and for the tritest advice on how to be good. It is the sermonic equivalent of the verses of Edgar Guest.

As a cure for such preaching, one would like to suggest a course of reading. The course would include many books of fiction, drama, and poetry. It would include all the novels of Dostoyevsky, the dramas of Eugene O'Neill, the poems of Whitman, Sandburg, and Edna Millay, John Masefield's, "The Everlasting Mercy." Shakespeare, of course, and the tragedies of classic Greece, and, as guide-books to other books, Lynn Harold Hough's "Vital Control" for critical and humanistic literature, and Halford Luccock's "Contemporary American Literature and Religion" for the highly revealing, if largely transient, books of the day. Such reading might help to save preaching from the moral triteness and the spiritual provincialism which make much of it so deadly dull. The service of ordination ought to include a vow to read constantly in poetry, fiction, and drama.

I will mention two further legitimate criticisms of contemporary preaching. Much of it is an insult to the intellectual capacity of the congregation. It gives the mind "nothing to chew on." Preachers who are fond of saying, "People like something simple," would do well to ask whether Browning was not nearer right when he said that he did not propose to make his poetry a substitute for an after-dinner cigar. The truth is, our sermons do not cost us enough hard mental labor. They come too easily. They do not grapple in mortal combat with the human problem. The sleepiest person who wanders late into the service can instantly grasp the whole import of what is being said and unerringly predict what is going to be said next. Gamaliel Bradford probably had the prevalence of this kind of preaching in mind when he wrote, "If the Protestant church is killed, it will be the sermon that has killed it." To a child who had made some first stumbling efforts to write poetry Frances Ridley Havergal sent advice which all who preach would do well to memorize:

> *'Tis not in stringing rhymes together——*
> *With your heart's blood you must write it,*
> *Though your cheek grows pale, none knowing,*
> *So the song becomes worth singing.*

To conclude with a word on the structure of the sermon, the training of preachers has not often, apparently, included instruction in the high art of sticking to the subject. Many a sermon is filled with good thoughts which are related to the subject only in the sense that everything in the cosmos is related to everything else. The ability to exclude every sentence and every word which does not carry the mind of the hearer one step nearer a clearly envisaged goal is one of the first marks of a disciplined mind. Dr. John Henry Jowett used to say that a sermon is not ready for the pulpit until its object can be stated in one short sentence. Having the object so clearly before him, the preacher should not find it hard to detect the illustrations which do not illustrate and the thoughts which have no relevance. But as one listens to most sermons he is persuaded that if the preacher had a definite object he had great difficulty in remembering it for thirty minutes. And as the hearer fidgets in his pew he thinks he would not care so much whether or not the preacher sticks to the Gospel, if only he would stick to the subject. It is perhaps this loose and vagrant character of sermons which, more than any other defect, helps to put the congregation to sleep and justified the lexicographer who, in a standard dictionary, defined the word "narcotic" thus: "Narcotic—figuratively, causing sleep or dullness, as a book or sermon." What a joy it is to listen to a preacher who knows where he is going, avoids all detours, and makes his sentences march straight on toward the goal!

I have tried to write on the subject assigned me. This has involved a critical note which, I hope, has not sounded like disparagement. I must join with a multitude of others in saying that some of the most stirring and beneficial hours of our lives have been spent in listening to sermons. Nevertheless, in answer to the question, "What is the matter with preaching?" these things, I believe, may be said: It talks too much about "religion," losing sight of the object in the subject. It lacks humility, compassion, and the breath of humanity. It deals too much with high-sounding but meaningless abstractions. It is too "soft," lacking the color and tang of actual life. It is often shallow and stuffy, as if the preacher lived exclusively in a world of churches and Sunday schools. It is intellectually weak. It often gets nowhere because it is allowed to run anywhere.

DOES THE WORLD STILL NEED THE PREACHER?

MORGAN PHELPS NOYES

CHAPTER XV

DOES THE WORLD STILL NEED THE PREACHER?

MR. T. S. ELIOT, referring to a generalization on the attitude of youth to ideals issued by the Lambeth Conference, has observed that the one thing you cannot do about modern youth is to generalize about them. "The youth of to-day are not 'as a whole' more or less anything than the youth of previous generations." No doubt that is equally true of younger churchmen, and even of those who, like the present writer, patently do not qualify for the adjective. But if there is any one thing which can be assumed about men who have entered the Christian ministry since the Great War, it is that they have not done so without serious searchings of heart. Their misgivings have been nowhere more acute than at the point where they have considered the validity of preaching. The reasons for this are manifold.

The head and front of this difficulty has probably centered in the fact that they themselves have endured a good deal of preaching which has seemed to them futile. I have a somewhat abashed recollection that as an undergraduate I once told a visiting university preacher that in all my experience (which at the time I considered extensive), I had heard only three preachers who seemed to me to have anything helpful to say. I hope that I assured him that he was one of the three, as he actually was, but my memory is not so clear on that point as it is on the other, for at the time I was nursing a sense of injury over having been compelled to endure a long series of sermons which did not seem to cut into my problems or to help me with my difficulties. I realize now that I had no right to expect any sermon to blow away all the mists that hang over this mysteriously fascinating universe. I can see in retrospect that some of the sermons which I labelled "futile" did something for me which was far more helpful than any neat and compact answers to all my riddles could possibly have been. They stimulated my own thought and study; they helped me to face my questions with an honest and realistic attitude; they encouraged the formation of the loyalties which make life possible; they opened up prospects which were worth exploring. But I imagine that my feeling of the futility of preaching was not uncommon, and that most men of my generation who have themselves become preachers have faced that bogie before they have done so.

This prejudice against preaching is something more than a personal reaction on the part of any individual. It is so widespread as almost to give the word *preach* an invidious connotation. In ordinary human intercourse, "don't preach" is generally accepted as axiomatic for those who would persuade others to adopt some particular line of conduct. In artistic circles, critics have only to say that a play or a poem *preaches,* and it stands convicted of being bad art. By some unfortunate combination of circumstances a word which ought to describe a noble exercise of intellectual and spiritual gifts has come in the general mind to suggest an assumption of moral superiority, authoritative pronouncements based on meager information, talking in a vacuum unrelated to life, or a one-sided argument to which there is no opportunity for response. All this is no doubt a reflection upon the quality of the preaching with which the average person is familiar, and in no sense a definition of what preaching at its best can and ought to be. Nevertheless the fact remains that the impression is so common as to put the office of preacher under something of a shadow.

This is accentuated by the fact that the modern mind puts a premium on action and looks with considerable suspicion upon talk. The current criticism of the church is that it has been eloquent in speech about righting the wrongs of the world, but short on accomplishment. There is widespread desire to-day to redress the balance. The intelligent layman is asking for something to do beyond listening. A great denomination has just formed a new agency which it has significantly christened a "Council for Social Action." Of course this insistence on the primary importance of doing rather than saying is at least as old as the New Testament, although the New Testament consistently recognizes human speech as one of the great forces, inspiring to fine action or disrupting the best in human life, according to its use. The creative power of sincere speech is often forgotten to-day, and a good many men are somewhat sensitive when they are accused of devoting a generous share of their time to the preparation and delivery of "mere talk."

Even if these considerations do not weigh heavily with him, any man who has entered upon the responsibilities of maturity during the past decade or two has seriously wondered whether it is still necessary to add the voice of the pulpit to the multitude of voices that are competing for public attention to-day. There was a time when the pulpit was the only place in the community where personal and social problems were discussed from the ethical and religious point of view. That is true no longer. The average community has numerous clubs and lecture courses where problems of personality adjustment, economics, international relations, child guidance, family welfare and civic betterment are discussed by experts, frequently on the highest plane of spiritual insight. Some communities are overburdened with such opportunities, and the conscientious citizens rush from one address to another at a speed which is fatal to reflection, and results only in intellectual or spiritual indigestion. Add to these agencies the radio, with its outpourings on every conceivable subject, the magazine (and it is a rare journal nowadays which does not include religion as one of the topics of major public interest), the school, which in every progressive community has taken over many of the functions hitherto regarded as within the field of the church, and the library, which has made popular literature on religious and social subjects easily available, and it is apparent that the pulpit has no monopoly on the discussion of the subjects with which it deals. The question naturally arises, is there any distinctive function for the preacher? Should he conclude that he belonged in an earlier era, but has been outmoded like the bicycle and the buggy?

The preacher does have a distinctive function. In spite of the fact that there are a multitude of inspirational agencies in modern life, none of them even attempt to be what the Christian minister's sermon is at its best. The sermon is unique, primarily because of its setting, which is the Christian church. The minister who preaches the sermon is not an itinerant lecturer, a free-lance journalist, or a disembodied voice floating over the air. He is the pastor of a church. He is preaching to people with whom he stands in a unique relationship. His message, if it is worth delivering, comes out of his own study and thought, but his own study and thought have as their background his contacts with a particular group of people. Their situation, their needs, their aspirations, the contributions which they have made to the minister's thought and life, all determine the nature and quality of the message. There is a communal aspect to a good sermon which sets it apart from other public speech. And the fact that it is a Christian church which is the setting of the Christian minister's sermon has a controlling significance. The minister's aim is not primarily to express his private opinions on various and sundry matters of common interest. His primary aim is to interpret life in the light of Christ, and to enlist life for the Christian cause. Moreover the Christian minister speaks from a platform of convictions peculiarly his own. He is not merely a spectator watching the world go by from the standpoint of disinterested curiosity. He is a convinced representative of the Christian faith, and he views life against the background of that faith in a living God. Any preacher who thinks of himself as competing with other voices for public attention has misconceived the distinctive nature of his calling. He has no competitor, for no one else is even trying to do what he is attempting, when in a Christian church of which he is the pastor he preaches in terms of his own day the gospel which he believes is the timeless truth.

When all is said that can be said about the apparent futility of preaching, the fact remains that although of course it has not always been on the right side, the pulpit of the Christian Church has been an incalculable force in molding thought and in directing life. The Christian preacher has on the whole an unenviable record in the long controversy between religion and science, and the churchmen of our time who are so earnestly endeavoring to effect an adjustment between religious and scientific thought are at best making belated amends for mistakes not confined altogether to earlier generations. Preachers of the gospel have often found it difficult to see clearly the ethical issues in that No-man's Land between property rights and human rights, and even so stalwart an independent as Martin Luther committed a grievous blunder in that area. It has frequently proved hard for Christian ministers to see clearly the implications of their universal gospel in times when nationalistic feelings have been inflamed, and time and again to their own humiliation they have found themselves ranged behind Cæsar rather than Christ. All that must be frankly admitted, and it will be a sad day if the church ever removes the Prayer of General Confession from its order of worship. To think only of these things is, however, to see a grotesquely distracted picture of the influence of the Christian church. Professor Whitehead has recently pointed out that while skeptical humanitarianism through the voice of Voltaire and others had a mighty part in the abolition of slavery as a recognized institution in civilized society, the great force at work in the anti-slavery movement was the religious influence released through the preaching of John Wesley and the Methodists. There is considerable food for thought in his contention that while the Wesleyans were deliberately seeking to prepare men for heaven rather than to transform contemporary civilization, the ideas which they made powerful tended to dignify human life and to make slavery unacceptable to the Christian conscience. John Wesley's influence was not an isolated phenomenon, although a conspicuous one. Chrysostom and Augustine, Francis of Assisi and Savonarola, Moody and Spurgeon, Beecher and Brooks, Rauschenbusch and Strong, these are all something more than the names of great men. They represent creative, transforming influences which have changed human life for the better through the ministry of preaching. Add to them the host of forgotten men who have never figured in the despatches, but have served as kindling and constructive spiritual forces in the communities in which they have preached, and you have one of the determining factors of which the history of civilization must always take account. John Henry Newman put so high an estimate upon the church's part in the preservation of civilization that he asserted "Not a man in Europe now, who talks bravely against the church, but owes it to the church, that he can talk at all."

The world needs a church, and will always have a church. Men are too much a part of each other to be able consistently to pursue their ideals or to affirm their faith only in the first person singular. Some sort of a spiritual fellowship is as essential as the family or state or any other form of social organization. It has been repeatedly pointed out that if all existing churches were destroyed, the human race would at once set about creating new ones. Periodically the suggestion is brought forward that perhaps the church had better confine itself to the conduct of public worship and dispense with the preaching function. The obvious reply is that to do so would be to turn the church over to the priests and to abolish the prophets. The church needs both types of leadership, and the ideal minister combines the best characteristics of both. The priest is needed to serve in a representative capacity in worship, and to speak for the church in the momentous hours of death, marriage, baptism and consecration, when the average man wants to hear not the personal opinions of any individual, however gifted or holy, but the voice of humanity's historic faith in the spiritual significance of life. But the priest needs to be supplemented by the prophet. Left to himself the priest becomes merely traditional, formal, verbal. He needs the prophet who can speak out of contemporary experience, and who can interpret the historic faith as a present reality. It is always the prophet, not the priest, who sees the points at which present wrong vitiates historic religion and says to the wrong-doer "Thou art the man." It is the prophet who keeps alive the spirit of self-criticism within the church, and so prevents decay. The prophet is never a comfortable person to have about. Ecclesiastical organizations are always a bit puzzled as to what to do with him. The petty priest, who has repeated words until they have lost all contact with reality, is always eager to disenfranchise the prophet, and he can generally find among his words a formula for the process. But any church which closes the mouths of its prophets by that act cuts itself off from ethical power. It may not be amiss to remember that while the pre-Revolutionary Russian church had developed a service of ritualistic worship which was profoundly moving and exquisitely lovely, it had pretty well abandoned preaching, and by so doing lost much of its moral influence. The priest serves at the altar. The place of the prophet is the pulpit. If we are going to have churches at all, by all means let them be open for untrammelled and conscientious preaching, as well as for the ministry of worship.

Every now and then there is a demand from the pews that

the pulpit confine itself more strictly to its fundamental purpose of preaching Christ. That is a perfectly legitimate
demand and one to which the pulpit needs to give serious
consideration. It is always an indication of failure on the
part of the preacher when his people get the impression that
he is not preaching Christ. But sometimes the man in the
pew does not fully realize the implications of his request.
He sometimes supposes that to preach Christ means to preach
contentment with things as they are, loyalty to the conventional usages of his social group, and the assurance that his
meager investments in morality will draw compound interest
in the future life. A fresh reading of the New Testament
would reveal to him a gospel which demands much more
than that of its adherents. Gamaliel Bradford was nearer
the truth when he wrote, "I do not dare to read the New
Testament for fear of its awakening a storm of anxiety and
self-reproach and doubt and dread of having taken the wrong
path, of having been traitor to the plain and simple God."
The only gospel worth preaching is Christ, but when Christ's
gospel is preached in its fullness it does not produce placid
satisfaction with things as they are, whether in personal, economic or political life. It challenges the self-interest on
which so much of our modern life is based. It points out the
denials of the brotherly spirit which are inherent in much
of the existing social structure. It appeals for recruits in the
creation of a better order of things in every sphere of human
endeavor. The early Christian apostles were accused of turning the world upside down, and there is no denying that the
gospel of Christ is upsetting when it is preached in its vigor
and simplicity. But it upsets only those aspects of personal
and social life which are built on the flimsy foundations of

selfish motives, and it upsets in order to put beneath life the durable substructure of the motives and faith of Jesus. The Christian message has been referred to as "the gospel which challenges and impels." At its best it does both. It challenges everything in human life which is inhuman and therefore fighting against God. It releases spiritual energy for the tasks of moral reconstruction, and therefore brings men into fellowship with God. At the bottom of every social and economic question facing mankind to-day is the prior question as to whether or not life has any spiritual significance. Are men to be exploited as machines, or respected as the sons of God? Is humanity caught in a trap of its own devising, or is there a purpose for the race in the mind of a God able to carry through His intentions? Is life at its best a curious flicker of the flesh into awareness of itself, or was Jesus right in asserting that life in its simplest terms is man's awareness of God? All man's highest hopes are bound up with the faith that life has a spiritual meaning, spiritual possibilities, and a spiritual background in God. Let any man be convinced of the truth of this faith of Jesus, and by the same token he is convinced that this is a gospel worth preaching in a time like ours.

THE CHURCH AND THE PERSECUTED

EVERETT ROSS CLINCHY

CHAPTER XVI

THE CHURCH AND THE PERSECUTED

YOUNGER churchmen, looking at the history of human relations involving Christian churches and other culture groups in America, have observed with grave concern the primitive tribal attitudes which have prevailed. The law of the jungle, *live and annihilate that which is different,* has characterized in a large measure the behavior of Christians toward other cultures, reproducing the patterns that have determined the mutual relations of cultural groups in Europe. Toward Judaism on the continent, for example, Christians have a record of outrages worthy of Dillinger gunmen. Again, the Roman Catholic Inquisition and widespread persecutions of Protestants in Europe were echoed later in America when Protestants rose against the Irish in the "Know-Nothing" movement in the 1850's, organized the anti-Catholic "A. P. A." in the so-called Gay Nineties, and rolled up two and a half million members for the Ku-Klux Klan in the twentieth century.

The inevitable question which arises in the minds of thoughtful Christian youth today is "How did we get that way?"

To answer that question is a longer and more complicated undertaking than the limits of this chapter permit. Anthropological, sociological, psychological, historical and economic factors are involved. One element in the situation, however, can be discussed and that concerns the degree to which democracy among culture-groups is possible. At first thought it may seem that in the American political democracy the fact of the existence of a community of cultures has already been accepted, for has not the tribal practice of *live, and annihilate* been displaced quite generally by the rule of *live, and let live?* An ever-increasing number of younger churchmen are unsatisfied with the condescending toleration of the latter attitude, infinitely more desirable than the former though it may be. Men and women of all ages are insisting not merely on the recognition, but on a cordial appreciation of group differences. They ask for associated living upon the plane of mutual respect. They hope for a conscious community-mindedness among groups. In short, the higher concept which they have in mind for inter-cultural relations, is *live, and help live*.

But before going further into theory, analysis of a concrete illustration may be profitable. Take, for instance, the Christians and the Jews. First of all, what are the plain facts? The origin of cultural differences between these two groups traces back to the Hellenizing influences of Stephen and Paul, under whose leadership the sect within Judaism known as the followers of Jesus (an Irsaelite who had remained a synagogue Jew as long as he lived) abrogated Jewish law and custom. The new culture was born in persecution and martyrdom, for Stephen, a Gentile proselyte, was stoned by certain Jewish bigots when he asserted that Jesus of Nazareth had freed that denomination from the Mosaic law. Paul, when he united with the radical movement, became its greatest instrument in so adapting the new cult as to make it acceptable to the non-Jewish world. As this new religion conquered the western world, it was, in a measure, conquered by it, as all conquerors are changed by their conquests, and Greek and Roman influences increased the differences between Christianity and Judaism. A new set of sanctities, folkways, loyalties and symbols came to differentiate Christians from Jews: to the Jews, as time went on, Christians became frightfully unlike and strange; to the Christians, Jews appeared as outsiders with outlandish beliefs and ways of behaving. In the development which followed, an even wider "social distance," as the sociologists put it, cut a chasm between Christians and Jews. The discussion in this paragraph has omitted supernatural considerations which Christians hold valid. The point is that Jewish-Christian relations were initiated in an atmosphere of coercion and violence on the part of prevailing Jewish masses. Later, Christians reacted similarly toward Jews.

The Middle Ages found the Christians numerically dominant. Feeling their power, Christians turned persecutors and attempted in every way possible to bind the future of the Jews. The following incidents of four bloody centuries beginning with the eleventh, indicate the nature of the course pursued. The story is told completely in "A History of the Jews" by Dr. A. L. Sachar.

In the eleventh century it became an annual custom in the week between Palm Sunday and Easter Monday, when the priests described the sufferings of Jesus, to pelt the Jews with mud and stones whenever they appeared.

The count of the city of Toulouse had the legal right to slap the face of the Jewish leader on Good Friday.

In 1078, Hildebrand, then Pope Gregory VII, issued a law forbidding Christian Kingdoms to employ Jews in any public capacity.

In three months time the First Crusade butchered twelve thousand Jews.

The economic motive led competitive traders to encourage destruction of Jews. The entire Jewish community in Carenton, France, was wiped out, and after five hundred Jews in York, England, had been put to death the mob went to the church repository and destroyed the records of indebtedness to all Jews.

Life was not the same in Europe after the holocausts of the Crusades. Normal, civilized life among the Jews disintegrated, and the caricature of what Jews might be, was created—the pariah with bent back, hunted look, and obsequious manner, bitter yet fearful.

The glorious thirteenth century brought Dante, Aquinas, St. Francis, great cathedrals and prosperous commerce, to Christians, and to Jews the yellow badge of shame, segregation in ghettos, complete loss of self-respect, and degeneration of mind and spirit.

It was the Lateran Council in 1215 which decreed that all Jews were to wear a distinctive garment or badge to set them apart from other men, a yellow circle to be worn on back or breast, or a hideous pointed cap on the head. This mark of shame brought insult, stones and curses, and, completely ostracized, the Jews were driven to slink like cats in alley-ways. Jews ceased to dress with care or to walk with head erect. They lost the ability to speak with ease, as they bowed and scraped their way past Christian tormentors.

Twenty-four cartloads of Talmudic literature were burned in the streets of Paris by order of church and state dignitaries in 1242.

The thirteenth century accusation that Jews had desecrated the sacramental wafer ignited an inflamed hysteria, and every Jew in one hundred and forty communities was burned or butchered to death.

The outrageous accusation that Jews killed Christian children for sacrificial blood rites resulted in pagan torturing of Jews, and maliciously discredited Jews from the Middle Ages even into the nineteenth century.

With the dawn of the fourteenth century, sixteen thousand Jews were uprooted and exiled by England.

Indicted as the cause of the plague of the Black Death, Strassburg mobs dragged 1,800 Jews to the cemetery and burned them alive; afterwards their possessions were divided among Christians. Two hundred and ten Jewish neighborhoods were wrecked.

In the fifteenth century the church ordered Christians not to eat with Jews, never to employ them as physicians nor admit Jews to any public trust. The ghetto rule was reinforced, assigning Jews to proscribed quarters.

Martin Luther exclaimed in the sixteenth century, "If the Jews refuse to be converted, we ought not to suffer them or bear with them longer." In the same period Frankfort am Main confined four thousand Jews in a narrow ghetto with severely restricted rules.

Every thoughtful Christian who reads records like these may well gasp just a bit as he realizes that as recently as the 1920's the chronic plague of trouble between Christians and Jews broke out on American soil in the Ku-Klux Klan. The Nazis turned back the clock in the 1930's. One can understand, therefore, why the Jews feel jumpy and jittery today: when Hitler says that Jews shall live as outlanders, and never as citizens of the state, Jews know what that means! The ignominious experiences in the Middle Ages scarred the Jewish memory with the nightmare spectacle of an outcast people. When a government issues Nordic cards to non-Jews for identification purposes, as Germany began to do in 1934, Jews know what that means! They were broken in spirit by the yellow badge of shame for hundreds of years. When a Nazi propaganda ministry directs school teachers to indoctrinate little children with hatred of their Jewish playmates,

Jews know what that means! Every living mother and father in Jewish homes in every land today shrinks with dread from the possibility of having to explain to their innocent children why Christian children scorn them, and exclude them, and abuse them because they are Jews. One of the severest indictments which can be brought against the church is its complacency today in the face of the unparalleled persecution of the Jews in Germany and its repercussions in the United States. For by leaving to the Jews themselves the responsibility for voicing the indignant protest that the situation demands, they contribute indirectly an increase in anti-Semitism at home. The vehemence of the Jews, though both natural and justified, may aggravate the disease of anti-Semitism, arrested but never wholly cured here.

In the opinion of younger churchmen the time has come for the churches and synagogues to focus their attention and their consciences upon this question of the relation of Jew and Christian. Christianity and Judaism are two human cultures, the boundaries of which separate their constituencies into two types of civilization, more or less distinct. Each group is too much influenced by past experiences marked by bitterness, and each is chained by prejudices against the other, both the bitter experiences and the prejudices being products largely or eras that the world has passed by. What, then can be done in this situation?

The first and immediate consideration is for the Christian church to immunize its members against the phobia of anti-Semitism. This is a task of huge proportion for preachers and religious educators. Medieval exclusions of Jews and wornout opinions about Jews can be sloughed off, and adults and children can be conditioned with more just and more appreciative attitudes by the church school and the pulpit. It is worth doing for its own sake; un-Christlike behavior toward Jews has too long marred Christian history. Moreover, by concentrating on this immediate intercultural problem the A B C's of intergroup relations may be learned, preparing people to deal intelligently with the more complicated difficulties of relations between nations, between Negroes and whites, and between the Occident and the Orient. If the problem of relations between Jews and Catholics, so insistent and so close at hand, cannot be solved in terms of a Christian way of life, what hope is there that our Christian culture is equal to the solution of the wider problems of race and national relations which confront us in the modern world? If you cannot love the Jew whom you have seen, how can you love the Japanese whom you have not seen?

In the second place, Christians can begin to bring up a generation which thinks in terms of cultural pluralism. Until now, both Christians and Jews have consciously or unconsciously conceived of civilization too much in a totalitarian fashion, as, "Christian" on the one hand, "Jewish" on the other. The ordinary assumption in the past has been that the ultimate solution of the difficulties in human relations in this area was a kind of cultural monism, one group dominating all, by fair means or foul. The present outlook calls for a society of diverse culture groups dwelling side by side in civic parity. It is not a question of watering down religious convictions: in a society which accepts cultural pluralism religious distinctions can be respected and maintained. Cultural pluralism implies the kind of society of which John Dewey speaks when he says that in a true democracy individuals will give freely to others the peculiar value, essence, quality and contribution of the group to which they belong, and receive freely the corresponding treasures of every other group, without violence to the complete uniqueness of any group.

That this challenge to the church is widely expressed is evidenced by the Christian Youth Council's 1934 report to its parent body, the International Council of Religious Education. These youth recognized that the American citizenry is composed of many contrasting culture groups: British, Teutonic, Scandinavian, Mediterranean Latins, Jewish, Negro, Latin American, American Indian, and Oriental, for examples. Especially in such periods of economic and political insecurity as the world is now experiencing, they said, tensions and misunderstandings among these divisions are likely to be felt. Here is a portion of their statement:

In order to appreciate our responsibility toward developing inter-cultural understanding, we must first understand the fundamental nature of a group. Our society is made up of a number of groups whose will-to-live and to perpetuate themselves is quite as basic as the individual's desire for self-preservation. This group expression may be so exaggerated that in a group, as in an individual, it may be irritatingly selfish and over-assertive, or may be so diminished that in a group, just as in an individual (and with the same disastrous effects) it loses its self-respect and distinctive identity.

Every group inspires in its young a firm belief in the superiority of the culture group. We must realize that other culture groups feel the same loyalty to their own solutions to the questions of life problems that we feel to ours. The problem before Christian youth is to build a world order in which each racial and religious group can develop and express its own distinctive elements in such a way that the culture of the whole society will be enriched.

We must reverence their right to their reverences, and respect their dignities and values, for only thereby can a rich and varied society, so possible in this continent because of the diverse racial elements, be achieved.

It is our responsibility as Christian youth to undertake all the activities we can which will broaden the lines of communication and cooperation between culture groups.

When Professor Torrey translated, on the basis of the Aramaic language which Jesus used, the sentence, "Be ye therefore perfect even as your heavenly Father is perfect," new insight for human relations was given: "Be therefore all-including," Torrey phrased it, "even as your heavenly Father includes all." That is the plea of younger churchmen: that the church be all-including in distributing justice, and as it has a record of a thousand years of inhumanity toward the Jew, let Christians begin a thousand years of decent treatment of the Jew; that the church be all-including in its application of religious idealism, and mobilize together with the synagogue to secure human rights for Negroes, a new economic order, world peace, and other mutual social ideals. Younger churchmen insist upon the principle of including-all not as an act of toleration, merely, but as a matter of inherent American rights required for all. Christianity invokes the including-all practice; democracy sustains it. Moreover, there is no growth of greatness in any man's spirit apart from the including-all principle, and the one who denies it is more damned than he who is denied.

THE CHURCH MUST WORSHIP

C. LAWSON WILLARD, JR.

CHAPTER XVII

THE CHURCH MUST WORSHIP

MANY younger churchmen feel that the Protestant Evangelical churches in America today are in a perilous condition. They are losing sight of the "chief end of man." Historic Christianity, Eastern, Roman and Protestant, tells us clearly and unmistakably that man's greatest function is to worship God. The Master himself taught, "Thou shalt love the Lord thy God with all thy heart, and with all thy soul and with all thy mind. This is the first and great commandment." But the majority of Protestants do not believe this. Although they number millions, few attend regularly the services of worship. Empty pews are the constant characteristic of our Sunday services. "How can we bring our people to church?" is the question on the lips of every interested clergyman and layman. The result is perilous to the welfare of this great branch of the Christian church. Not only has it lost the art of worship; it is losing the desire to worship!

And, more tragic than that, is the feeling of many who do attend church regularly that they are told again and again what they ought to do but are not shown how to do it. They hear the Social Gospel proclaimed earnestly and enthusiastically; they listen patiently to the most advanced ideas of religious pedagogy and theology; they are told that modern science is Christianity's strongest ally; but they are still groping for the power and strength to put this knowledge into practice. They are not finding in their worship the spiritual dynamic and compelling drive to live the individual and corporate Christ-like life that is held up before them. The very effectiveness of our great preachers is our greatest handicap; their eloquent and vivid sermons picture for us the Kingdom; we see it and realize what we might be, but we search in vain for the power to make it a reality. Consequently, we lose hope in the Kingdom. Our helplessness enervates our desire, and our religion becomes like our weather—something we talk of but do nothing about.

Many young churchmen are deeply concerned with this condition of their church. They realize more and more the impotency of Protestantism. They eagerly watch the efforts of certain leading pastors to recover the lost art of worship for their congregations. Our church is slowly and painfully awakening to this need. That is why young churchmen are hopeful.

The causes of this loss of interest and, therefore, ability to worship, are many. We are unconscious of most of them because they are part of our social and intellectual environment and not distinctly labeled "religious." Chief of these, perhaps, is the fact that Protestantism is still on the Reformation "rebound." Although that event occurred over four hundred years ago, we are still deeply antagonistic to anything that savors of the Pre-Reformation Church. This is particularly true of forms of worship. We are so eager to escape from the lion of "Romanish" practices that we are unaware of the bear of vacuous worship into whose arms we have run. At its best the Reformation was nothing more than the cutting away from certain superstitions and sterile practices;

we still have ahead of us the task to achieve the goal, to pursue which, our forefathers fought to be free. Yet in the field of worship we seem satisfied to rest on laurels won four hundred years ago, quite unmindful of the real task for which that battle freed us.

Another cause of our indifference is the subtle influence of our cherished individualism. For four centuries we have prided ourselves on our laissez-faire economics, our political freedom and our almost anarchic conception of democracy. Our religious practices could not escape this environment. Such piety as was developed was mystic and individualistic. It bound the individual soul but not the community or nation, to say nothing of the denomination (sic!), to God. This left no need for corporate worship. The goal of the Christian religion was to save "my" soul, not "our" soul. Literally we said "Our Father, which art in heaven," but practically we acted "My Father, which art in heaven."

Science has also contributed its part to our devotional enervation. Until recently we thought that loyalty to the laboratory required desertion from the church. The God of science displaced the God of the church. We did not recognize the limitations of science. Instead of displacing Christianity it is actually enlarging it. Now we are beginning to see that the power science has given us is another demand upon the necessity of spiritual power to control this giant so that it will serve us and not harm us. We realize more and more that the technique of the laboratory is not necessarily the technique of the church. One can be scientific in the twentieth century sense of the word, and still worship God in hymns and prayers and pæans of praise written in the first century. The timidity which we feel in the light of science need no longer prevent us from reaching out to worship God. This is not a plea for unscientific worship; rather, it is a fervent plea for worship which will be more than scientific; a worship which will lead us not only into the further knowledge of Law, but onward and upward into the experience of Spiritual Truth.

The combined effect of these three aspects of our modern environment has crystallized our attitude toward worship so that we instinctively regard all devotional practices which antedate the Reformation, laissez-faire capitalism and modern science as outworn and useless, and almost anything that is later. Preaching has replaced adoration; activity has replaced silence; barrenness has replaced beauty, as new and, therefore, effective. The present impotency of Protestantism eloquently bespeaks the result of this attitude.

Thus, the immediate task before the evangelical churches in America today is to recover the art of worship. Without corporate worship there can be no corporate strength. Psychologically and spiritually the latter must proceed from the former.

Obviously there is no one solution to this problem. Human backgrounds, temperaments and needs differ widely. In the past devout men and women have worshipped effectively in different ways, and there is no reason to believe there will be any change. However, there are certain conditions and basic elements of effective corporate worship which we have lost sight of today. Until these are recovered we cannot hope to release the dormant strength of Protestantism.

The conditions of successful worship appear to be:

1. A clear idea of the God whom we worship. Theology is not a popular subject with us. Too long have we tried to

get along without paying much attention to it. In our modernity we look down upon certain doctrines of yesterday as childish and primitive, but we have not yet formulated new ones to take their places. Our theology must be brought up to date if we are to worship intelligently. We must formulate a clear idea of God, His Nature, Properties, and purpose. When we behold Him as Creator and Sustainer of the universe and all that therein is; when we see Him as the God of justice and righteousness; when we perceive His Love as revealed in Jesus and His Guiding Hand in the Holy Spirit; when we realize that He is in us and in our world, working with us, suffering with us, sharing with us, building His Kingdom amongst us—then, we cannot help but worship Him!

2. The necessity of humility. The greatest obstacle to worship is pride. It is greater than indifference because it is openly hostile. Not until we humble ourselves before the Majestic Power and Perfect Love of the Christ-like God can He exalt us. Unfortunately, we have carried over into our attitude toward God our idea of democracy. Among the children of God there is a sense of equality and rightly so; but, can there in any sense be an equality between creatures and their Creator, except where the Creator has granted it? Equality connotes a degree of independence, but how are we independent of God upon whom we lean for everything? When we realize our complete dependence upon God, then, we approach Him humbly and by that attitude toward Him enable Him to work with us and through us.

3. A keen sense of the social nature of Christianity. Historic Protestantism has been chiefly concerned with the individual and his salvation. The influence of laissez-faire

capitalism has its effect. Our forefathers demanded their right to exploit nature (and also their fellow men) without interference and without regulation. Adam Smith's "Wealth of Nations" was hailed as the only way man could carry on his business; the Kingdom of God as taught by Jesus was forgotten. Smith was "practical," Jesus was a "theorist." Man's economic system controlled his religious system, and Protestant individualism was the result. The only purpose of the church was to save a man's soul.

However, now that laissez-faire capitalism has hopelessly broken down, we see the inadequacy of its Christian counterpart. Christian individualism never was successful, but in the rush of exploiting nature we did not realize its failure. Now we are slowly perceiving that only a social gospel will save society. In turning back to our New Testament we are rediscovering the Kingdom of God as the central focus of the Gospel. We are finding there the answer to the cry of today for salvation. We know now that there is no such thing as individual salvation apart from social salvation. The Fatherhood of God demands the Brotherhood of Man.

The result of this rediscovery is that our worship must be reset to accommodate it. Christian worship should impress upon us again and again the fact that we are "our brother's keeper," that we serve God only in so far as we serve our fellow men; that economic, political and social systems which exploit and oppress man must be fought as new incarnations of the Devil.

4. Successful worship is achieved only by the painful path of discipline. It does not require much discipline to think and talk about the Kingdom, but it does require a great deal to build up the spiritual power necessary to create the King-

dom among the children of men. This is, perhaps, the greatest problem among Protestants. As in all social movements, we must sacrifice our personal freedom for the sake of the group. We must learn that any liturgy and even any creed will contain one or two items which will not meet the approval of each member of the congregation. Rather than attempt to draw up such liturgies and creeds as will meet with exact and universal approval, we must use those that set forth clearly and vividly the main elements of our faith. Otherwise, relatively unimportant details will ruin the attempt to develop our corporate power.

Furthermore, we clergy and laity alike must resolve to take our part in the congregation, to worship regularly and enthusiastically Sunday after Sunday, to make whatever changes we desire by the democratic method, which is the basis of Protestantism, and to train ourselves and, by our example, our brethren to believe that only by worshipping together can we hope to work together. We must nail the flag of the Kingdom to our masthead and sail the ship of congregational worship through storm and calm until we land on the shore where corporate power is to be found. Deserters will only further disorganize the skeleton crew and increase the labor of the faithful. As discipline is the backbone of any crew, so is it the backbone of successful corporate worship.

When at least these four conditions of worship are met, we shall be ready to proceed without liturgy or order of service. What that will be depends not only on our ideas of the God whom we worship but also on what we believe He requires of us.

That brings us to the question, "What is worship?" The verdict of Christian experience is that worship is entering into the presence of God. It is more than thinking and talking about God, it is feeling Him near at hand; it is to behold Him "high and lifted up and His Glory fills the temple." In the presence of such Majesty and Sovereignty and Love we can do nothing but adore Him. Adoration is the heart of worship. It is the crown of aspiring love. It is the spontaneous pouring out of ourselves in awe, and praise, and thanksgiving, and love before Him. It is the complete lifting up of our hearts and souls and minds before His Eternal Throne.

Unfortunately, Protestants do not like the word "adoration." It smacks of superstition, of idol worship, as something unworthy of a rational being. But the experience of the saints of all branches of the Christian church—Eastern, Roman, Protestant, Quaker—tells us that only through adoration can we enter completely into the Presence of God. We can learn much about the worship of God from our Roman brethren. We should be humble enough to recognize that their corporate power and their church attendance is due to their emphasis upon adoration. We are excusing ourselves more than accurately interpreting them when we think it is primarily due to fear. There are too many learned and intelligent members of the Roman Church for us to hold they all are motivated primarily by fear.

If the inclusive idea of worship is adoration, then, the elements that naturally follow are:

1. *Confession of our sins.* In the presence of the Christlike God we are immediately struck, as Isaiah was centuries ago, by our unworthiness. "Woe is me! for I am undone; because I am a man of unclean lips, and I dwell in the midst of a people of unclean lips; for mine eyes have seen the King, the Lord of hosts."

"Sin" is another unsavory word to us. We regard it as a mechansm to instill fear in the hearts of people; as an undue emphasis upon the negative side of our life; as acts directly against the demands of a priestly cult. To use the word in such a limited sense is to misuse it. Sin literally means "missing the mark." It includes not only "the things we have done which we ought not to have done," but also "the things we have not done which we ought to have done." It means not only personal inadequacies but social inadequacies. In that full sense none of us are outside its scope. Anyone who does not feel a deep sense of humility in the presence of the Christlike God either does not know what the Christlike God is or is too proud to recognize His Greatness. We will confess our personal and social shortcomings in order that God can forgive us.

2. *Absolution.* After we have confessed our sins, the minister will proclaim the forgiving nature of God. He will remind us that when we repent—and not until then—God will forgive us our sins and cleanse us from all unrighteousness. If we really and truly believed this and realized that corporate sin is forgiven in corporate worship, nothing could keep us away from church!

3. *Praise.* We are now really to proceed with our acknowledgment of God's greatness. It is here that we use the prophetic poetry of the ages. We enter into fellowship with the faithful of all time in adding our praise to theirs. Their hymns become our hymns; their spirit becomes our spirit. Through praise the distinctly Christian element of Joy enters into our service.

4. *Instruction.* In order to assure the development of our knowledge of God and His Purpose for us, we need to learn more about Him. This is done by readings from the Bible

and other inspired books of the church; by responsive psalms and canticles; and by sermons. This is the formal educational part of our service. We honor God by learning more about Him.

5. *Intercession*. We do not approach the Christlike God as lone and separate individuals. We are bound together by our common Brotherhood. We will pray for that Brotherhood, for the coming of the Kingdom, for all the needs of a Kingdom-conscious people, for "all sorts and conditions of men."

6. *Petition*. We will also pray for ourselves. Our particular needs will be presented to Him who is able to make us worthy members of His Kingdom.

7. *Thanksgiving*. Gratitude is not only the expression of our thanks to God for "all His benefits," but it is the only way through which we can grow in our appreciation of His Love. Therefore, it is a necessary part of our worship. It reminds us of the true nature of His blessings, and deepens our desire to receive them and use them.

8. *Re-dedication*. This is the climax of our worship. In return for God's gift to us of Himself, the only appropriate offering we can make is that of ourselves. We rededicate ourselves, humbly and sincerely, as willing vehicles to transport His Redeeming Love to the world. We pledge ourselves as a group to serve him faithfully; to try our best to build his Kingdom with His power.

9. *Silence*. The Quakers can teach us a great deal of the power of corporate silence. It affords an opportunity for God to speak to us through the welling up in our minds of our consciousness of Him. We "wait upon the Lord" in quietness and we are strengthened by the stillness of His Spirit.

We have brought our service up to this point through the assistance of liturgies; now we are wrapped in the "living silence" of His presence. He has transcended all barriers and enters into us as deeply and fully as we allow Him. The benediction is pronounced quietly and simply, and the service closes.

Whatever liturgy we may use should include an active response from the congregation in every part. There can be no participation without sharing. The minister is not the only one taking part in the service; it is the minister and the congregation together that is the essence of corporate worship.

Many younger churchmen believe that when services of worship are based upon these conditions and include these elements we shall arrive at that spiritual stage where the corporate power to serve God effectively will be bestowed upon us. The Gospel will not only be proclaimed and taught, but built into our social fabric; we will not only be children of this world, but children of God's Eternal Kingdom; we will not only be the children of men but the children of the Christ-like God, worshipping Him and serving Him effectively.

THE INTERNATIONAL PROTESTANT CHURCH

HENRY SMITH LEIPER

CHAPTER XVIII

THE INTERNATIONAL PROTESTANT CHURCH

THE International Protestant Church does not exist. But that is not to say that the life of non-Roman Christianity is incapable of finding ecumenical expression. I want to deal with the question not from the point of view of theory: but from the standpoint of practical contemporary experience, viewed rather personally. I am writing this in London, England, where I am attending the annual sessions of the Federal Council and the National Free Church Council of England. The reason for my being here is not personal but official. It is as a fraternal representative of the Federal Council of the Churches of Christ in America that I am invited to attend and address these delegates of the non-conformist churches in England. This noon I lunched with Dr. Rushbrooke who is the Secretary of the Baptist World Alliance—and a few short weeks ago in Berlin, Germany, I had the pleasure of attending a meeting of that body which has touch with practically the whole world. This afternoon I had tea with Dr. J. D. Jones, president of the Congregational International Council, and we were discussing memories of the last meeting of that body at his church in Bournemouth. A few weeks ago I happened to have tea in Edinburgh with the present president of the Presbyterian World Alliance; and still more recently in Switzerland I was with one of the distinguished past presidents of that organization.

If I may continue for a moment in this same manner—I would add some other references to experiences of recent weeks which indicate the existence of a growing manifold of world-wide international organizations built up by the Anglican, Protestant, and Orthodox Churches. In July there met in Scotland the Central Bureau for Inter-Church Aid of the Evangelical Churches of Europe. In that connection we were dealing with the problems of the weaker churches, particularly in Central and Southern Europe. And there came under review the record of almost a dozen years of continuous activity in this work of brotherly helpfulness, done without distinction of denomination and with the underlying conviction that a common responsibility lies upon all to strengthen and encourage the weaker churches as they face the waves of atheism, extreme nationalism, and secularism which roll in upon them from all sides. The fact that the great newspapers of Scotland and England dealt generously with the reports from this annual meeting of the Bureau indicated the public conviction that it deals not with narrow national Church life but with the broader and deeper life of an invisible but real international Church which knows no bounds save human need and no ultimate loyalty save that to the universal Christ.

Following Edinburgh came Oxford. There I touched again two more expressions of this modern urge for ecumenical Christianity. One was the meeting of the World Alliance of Y. M. C. A.'s. The other was the final meeting of the annual "houseparty" of the Group Movement. In both of these gatherings in quite different ways, one found the evidence that an increasingly large number of churchmen of all kinds are thinking and acting internationally. Particularly in the first of these two meetings there was a distinct world-consciousness. In the halls of Balliol College and in the ancient church of St. Mary the Virgin we faced together the challenges of the modern world to Christian youth of all churches. John R. Mott in the latter circle and Frank Buchman in the former were in themselves and by reason of their activities evidences of the sweep and reach of contemporary church life. Whatever else one might say about the movements associated with each of these personalities, one would have to admit that they are in no sense confined to any denomination or group of denominations, certainly not to any one nation.

At Oxford these two wholly different Christian groups were dealing with the message and the method of Christian world work. And the kind of thinking that comes out of such consultations is in itself a living witness to something real in the life of ecumenical Christianity.

From Oxford I went to Copenhagen and came into touch with the Conference of Religious Liberals. Meeting in an old Unitarian Church these delegates from most of the modern world were handling the same problems from the point of view congenial to those who are still proud to be known as liberal and progressive. The members of this particular group with whom I had the longest conversations were Bishop Gregorio Aglipay and Bishop Isabelo de los Reyes of Manila, who represented the remarkable development of a liberal Catholic Church in the Islands. Nothing very narrow or nationalistic about that expression of contemporary churchmanship!

But Denmark was host to two other quite different organizations this summer. From beautiful Copenhagen—where I had the pleasure of addressing a huge audience of Danes in company with a British Bishop, the Orthodox Archbishop of Bulgaria, the Bishop of Novi-Sad, Jugoslavia, the President of the French Protestant Church Federation, and a superintendent of the German Evangelical Church—I went to the little Island of Fanö in the North Sea for the joint sessions of the Universal Christian Council and the World Alliance for International Friendship through the Churches. One who knows the work of these bodies in the many lands where they are increasingly strong can at once recognize something which has every aspect of true ecumenicity. (If you don't like that word, and I confess I do not, please think up another which means the same and is as short!)

During the ten very full days more than a hundred delegates from the whole of the Western World and the Orient dealt with the emergent problems of Church and State— struggling to find common ways by which non-Roman churches may assert effectively the supremacy of loyalty to Christ and His Church in the face of pressure which has come to most dangerous expression in Hitlerite Germany. The struggle against State worship, against economic imperialism, autocracy, nationalism, and war was acute in the minds of all: and the values of common thinking from widely different backgrounds and church connections was apparent as we listened to Russians, Germans, Danes, Scots, Englishmen, Americans, and Orientals. No one who listened to those discussions could come away thinking that the modern Church is without promise in the face of even desperate challenges from other institutions claiming the allegiance of mankind. In particular it was illuminating to watch the efforts of this representative group to be of aid in the present German church struggle. A commanding utterance, issued in friendship and only after long discussion with the Germans themselves, voiced the universal concern of Christians over the prostitution of the Church which is taking place under Hitler and his associates. Ways were found to recognize and encourage the brave opposition pastors and their congregations. What Rome is to the Roman Catholics struggling for the preservation of the identity and freedom of their Church, the Universal Christian Council is to the Evangelical Church of Germany. One could be very thankful that they did not have to turn in their extremity to denominational bodies. Curiously and unfortunately, no American Lutheran was present: but there were American Episcopalians, Presbyterians, Congregationalists, and Methodists, who understood German and were deeply desirous of helping their German brethren as fellow-heirs to the same liberty in Christ, the same unchanging truth, the same household of faith.

The fact that every newspaper in Europe wanted full reports of what went on at Fanö may be interpreted by the cynic as simply the result of morbid interest in a fight among churchmen. But it was not a fight! There were deep differences, and some things happened which would not be regarded as altogether friendly by the officials of the German Evangelical Church. Yet in it all there was present an atmosphere of comprehension, as well as comprehensiveness; of charity as well as conviction; of helpfulness as well as criticism. Ecumenical Christianity at its best was seen to be constructive, characterized by a common sense of sin, a common desire for unity, and a common realization of dependence upon the unique and indispensable leadership of Jesus.

The World Alliance in its deliberations dealt with the munitions traffic, with the threats to peace seen in many of the modern trends which the Church could meet if it would act unitedly, and with plans for increased activity among youth. A joint youth conference, under the combined auspices of the Alliance and the Universal Christian Council, brought together an able and fearless group of young men and women from all over Europe, including Germany, and one saw in their attitude toward war something of the possibilities of such common action. Particularly interesting, perhaps, was the fact that one of the aggressive leaders of that group is a young man who came first as a communist to get information on which to base a more effective fight against Christianity. Like Paul, he who came to persecute was so impressed by what he found that he was converted to Christ's way of meeting human need. Abandoning his economic determinism, his atheism, his trust in force, he cast his lot with the ecumenical movement as the most promising agency for combating the evils of modern life.

The presence at both Fanö meetings of an official of the International Labor Office was but another sign of the manner in which the world influence and developing international work of such bodies is regarded by those who are passionately committed to the task of improving working conditions and removing the existing threats to peace— between classes and nations alike.

If I may be pardoned for adding yet further to this catalogue of meetings, I may note two more. The first of these was a meeting of the Continuation Committee of the Lausanne Conference on Faith and Order. Although the expenses of no delegates were paid by the Committee and only forty had been expected, when we assembled in Hertenstein, Switzerland, there were double that number on hand. Here is another approach to the problem of a divided Church. To those who view it in the abstract it may or may not seem to hold out promise of concrete results. But to those of us who have been in touch with it constantly since that memorable meeting in Lausanne in 1927 it is seen to be developing in ways that may yet yield valuable and lasting fruit. To the theoretical and somewhat academic commissions dealing with abstract theological questions the Committee added a new one on the empirical, or practical, approach to unity and gave it a mandate to prepare for the next session of the world conference in 1937 a study of the ways in which unity has been achieved and of the factors which must be dealt with on the practical side before a more united Church can come to be.

The second Hertenstein conference (first, as a matter of fact, in point of time) was that of a small informal consultative group which has been gathering for several years under the chairmanship of Dr. William Temple, Archbishop of York, to discuss closer relationships and a harmonized program for the five best known Christian world movements. These are the International Missionary Council, the World Student Christian Federation, the Lausanne Conference, the World Alliance of Friendship, and the Universal Christian Council for Life and Work. We continued there a process which has been going on with increasing promise, making possible more effective service to the world interests of the churches. Out of this has come the elimination of overlapping, the exchange of workers, the consolidation of some offices, common employment of certain officials, and the co-operative planning of all future world gatherings representing the non-Roman churches. This may not sound very remarkable but, believe it or not, it is something new under the sun!

It will be obvious to the reader who has followed to this point that I for one cannot feel that International Protestantism is non-existent! It is a very definite reality; although to tell the truth it falls far short of what we all hope for. But those who talk glibly about what it should be are too often blissfully unaware of the difficulties to be overcome. We must never underrate the formidable nature of that task. Here we have Christian churches of hundreds of kinds in over sixty nations. The Bible is available to them in over nine hundred dialects. Evidently any effective world organization of them all must be prepared to deal with almost insurmountable language difficulties. The handicaps of distance and expense in getting representatives together is self-evident. Then come psychological differences. One has to come into close personal contact with them to realize their true force. But even more important is the problem of reaching the mass of church people in our manifold churches throughout the world with any practical means or methods for building up the sense of unity. Theoretically this exists among Roman Catholics. From personal experience I must admit a doubt as to how far it really does exist. What has happened recently in Mexico, Spain, and Italy gives point to this observation. To be sure the clergy of the Roman Church has an ecumenical consciousness. The system of the Papacy and the Thomistic emphasis in education insure it. We have nothing comparable—and probably desire nothing exactly comparable!

A further difficulty grows out of the tendency to over-simplification in the minds of most enthusiasts for world unity. This is an aspect of the psychological problem already noted. Americans are prone to think of the problem as much less complex than it really is. Many Europeans go to the other extreme. Both groups envisage solutions which are congenial to their own historical past and contemporary preferences. The appalling ignorance which exists in all parts of the Christian Church with respect to other parts is a major difficulty. And since people in general will not take the trouble to know the facts concerning even their own churches it is evident that effective knowledge of others is practically unattainable for the masses. An aspect of this ignorance which strikes one particularly in America is the constantly recurring tendency always to want to start some new world movement to express a particular interest in one approach or one emphasis dear to the initiator.

Again, one sees with sorrow the tendency to confuse means and ends. Organization always tempts its devotees to confusion of this nature. Even among the officials of the greatest modern Christian movements one finds this almost fatal weakness. It is the more regrettable when one stops to think that all the contemporary movements in the non-Roman Christian world are based on the same constituency! Their real future lies not in rivalry but in cooperation and coordination. But to hear their leaders talk one would sometimes think that they suppose the future to lie wholly with one such organization as against the rest. The common assumption in the average American church that home and foreign missions are two quite different undertakings is an example of what is meant here. The pastor who has overcome that difficulty by presenting the total work of the Church as an integrated whole will know how to proceed in making the same integrating presentation of the ecumenical task of the churches in all its fulness.

I do not wish to dwell on difficulties. We do need to be certain that we recognize them and are prepared to meet them intelligently. Whatever tends to build up a world-consciousness of unity is important for those committed to it. And what means now lie at hand! Only in recent times have international conferences become frequent and relatively numerous. The presence in Geneva, where the headquarters of the major Christian world movements are located, of almost sixty international bodies is significant. The up-building of the International Missionary Council following the 1910 conference in Edinburgh is most encouraging. To anyone who has watched it from the early stages to its present development there is no need for ultimate pessimism about the possibilities along similar lines in other fields of church activity. Now that the International Missionary Council has formally accepted—in its Executive Committee meeting at Salisbury, England, this summer—the responsibility for building up the Oriental section of the Universal Christian Council, a process of more effective integration may be said to have begun.

As I have already suggested, the existence of organizations is to many minds almost a positive evil. No one who deals with them can fail to see their dangers and weaknesses. But at the same time their indispensable character must be recognized. World unity must be a great ideal, a great passion, a major objective of the Christian who understands the implications of his Lord's Life and Work. But it must find symbolic and visible expression. It cannot live solely in the realm of ideas, although it must first live there before it can live in the flesh. The International Protestant—I should prefer to say Non-Roman—Church of the future will not be like anything we can now imagine. But if it is to be at all it will come into existence as the resultant of a long and complex process. It will represent all of the present activity of the churches and more.

Let us see what the processes are that may be said to move in the direction of a truly harmonious, interrelated, if not organically unified, world Christianity. I have referred incidentally to many of them in the foregoing paragraphs. I wish now to consider them in a more systematic fashion.

First, I think we must put the development on an international scale of denominational bodies. Practically every great denomination now has its world organization. Increasingly those who lead in these organizations are coming into touch with each other. The Episcopalians have their Lambeth Conference. When it met the last time in London it was my good fortune to be in the city and to attend numerous functions where its delegates were in consultation with representatives of other churches. The Methodists have an Ecumenical Conference which grows in significance and increasingly draws in the active participation of Eastern Christians as well as those from the Western world. I have already had occasion to speak of the Presbyterian, Baptist, and Congregational world organizations. I have watched them all at work and see in their life many factors of similar order. They all tend to break down nationalism: and that is something for which to thank God in our time. They all tend to cultivate the feeling that the younger churches have a contribution to make to the totality of Christian experience. And that is a countervailing tendency to the patronizing process so apt to become a part of the foreign missionary enterprise. They educate their respective lay groups as well as their clergy in things that extend beyond any sectionalism or racialism. They stress more and more the practical tasks of Christianity and less and less the petty distinction which characterize denominations. Most of the criticism I hear of such organizations comes from people who have had very little contact with them; who are unconsciously lacking in the necessary perspective for adequate appraisal, and who have nothing better to suggest!

Second, I would like to list those great interdenominational bodies which have come into existence in response to certain felt needs in the whole of the Christian world. Some of them are dealing with the threat of war; some have to do with educational problems; others are facing theological and social issues. I have mentioned certain of them already. I would list also the World Sunday School Association; the International Council of Religious Education; the Christian Endeavor Society; the Near East Foundation; and other similar bodies. Whatever else one may say about them, they do weave back and forth across wide areas of geographical, racial, social, and national difference strands of personal understanding, mutual confidence, active good will and practical cooperation.

Third, we must take into account the growing number of national federations of churches which are gradually finding their way into more or less direct contact across national lines. In one sense, the Universal Christian Council is a federation of such federations. In Scandinavia, Switzerland,

Holland, Czecho-Slovakia, and North America, the link between it and denominational bodies has come to be federal councils of churches in the respective lands. There is no great transition needed from the mood natural to those interested in church federation on a local scale to attitudes out of which grow the will to cooperate on the same plan in a larger area—such as the nation or the world.

Fourth, I would mention the steadily growing body of Christian literature which is available in numerous languages and tends to create a sympathetic and intelligent understanding. Without the foundation which such a literature can lay and is laying there would be less chance than there is of developments of international organization that will really function. In many an international gathering I have found that progress was possible not only because the men from different lands were acquainted with the same underlying ideas in the Bible and Christian history but also because they had been reading the same books by modern prophets and were familiar with the same ideals of practical Christianity. You find it somewhat surprising, and very exhilarating, to sit down in the palace of some bishop of the Eastern Orthodox Church in the Balkans and there to discover that he has been reading Oldham or Fosdick or Niebuhr! That kind of thing is happening more and more frequently. The expansion of the process holds promising possibilities for the future.

In individual nations one sees the necessary foundations for an effective international Christian life being slowly laid. Let me point out what has been happening in England, Switzerland, Sweden—and the United States.

In this country—I am writing in England—about half of

the people who count themselves actively Christian in the non-Roman sense are in the Anglican Communion. The other half are in the Free Churches—Presbyterian, Methodist, Baptist, and Congregational. The Anglicans have been very active participants in the Lausanne and Stockholm movements (Faith and Order, Life and Work). The Free Church groups have been somewhat less active in these movements but very well represented in the World Alliance for International Friendship, to which the Anglicans have likewise given sympathetic attention. There are various Protestant bodies interested in the welfare of Continental Protestantism and these have been for the most part interdenominational. They have been active participants in building up the Central Bureau of Inter-Church Aid and through it have been brought into relatively close touch with Lutheranism and the Reformed Churches in Northern Europe. Now we find a strong movement to bring the World Alliance and the Life and Work groups in England into one body: and the process which seems likely to be completed in a year will strengthen both of these international bodies. The Federal Council and the Free Church Council are national interdenominational bodies which are increasingly conscious of the need for international relations with non-Roman churches. This they find chiefly through the bodies already mentioned. No unity of outward form is apt to appear in the immediate future. But a sense of common concern, a desire for understanding, and a technique for cooperation are all quite definitely in the making.

The Swiss churches have a well-knit Federal Council much like the organization of the same name in the United States. Through this they are related organically to the Central

Bureau of Inter-Church Aid and likewise to the World Conference on Faith and Order and the Universal Christian Council for Life and Work. Blessed in being free from major denominational differences, with an amazing adaptability and the natural command of four languages, the Swiss church leaders constitute a factor of importance in the international life of contemporary Protestantism. They already possess a sense of what they call "ecumenicity" and can be counted on to put forward any well-conceived movement for a greater degree of effective world-organization in matters of common Christian concern.

In Sweden the great majority of the Christian people are in the National Lutheran Church. Under the leadership of the late Archbishop Nathan Söderblom they came to feel strongly the need for relations of a practical nature with the churches of other lands. They joined in the various movements which were in existence and then set about to create a body in their own country which would facilitate active cooperation, in a harmonious way, with all of them. This they did by merging all the Swedish "sections" of the various movements into one body—a sort of Ecumenical Commission—which enjoys the support of the National Church and of the Free Churches as well. Archbishop Eidem, who is the successor to Dr. Söderblom, has shown deep interest in this continuing and expanding work. It seems to many observers that Sweden has perhaps gone further in the right direction than any other land. It has certainly been able to bring to the average congregation of church people the consciousness of their relations with the churches of other lands —not in a denominational but in a broadly interdenominational sense.

In America the process has been inevitably complex. No one would have sat down to plan it as it now exists. But history is not planned. It grows. Sometimes the resulting growth needs pruning, sometimes grafting, sometimes plowing under. As I see it, the picture is somewhat as follows. Until the beginning of the twentieth century there was very little contact between the American churches and those of other lands—save the new churches founded as a result of foreign missionary endeavor. Relations with them and with the mission bodies in other sending countries began to be developed through the formation of the Foreign Mission Conference of North America which has grown until it numbers about ninety denominational agencies in its membership. This body forms one link in the chain of twenty-eight Conferences and Councils making up the International Missionary Council with offices in New York, London, and Geneva. (From a theoretical point of view it is curiously out of balance, since in the Western lands its constituent bodies are groups of missionary societies, not churches, while in the mission lands its relationships are knit up with the National Christian Councils that have grown up as a result of its own activities. These Councils are virtually Federal Councils of Churches, although part of their membership is made up of missions organized on a regional or national basis and representing the Western Churches either denominationally or interdenominationally.)

Next in order after the I. M. C. international link—the Foreign Missions Conference of North America—we find the denominational bodies organized on a regional or national scale and linked with their respective denominational bodies in the international field. These carry on activities, but their functioning is intermittent and comes to visible expression internationally only about once a decade.

The history of the third group of international links—those organizations made up of interest groups held together by their common concern for certain activities and emphasis in the Christian life—is too varied to be described in a short paragraph. But they are by no means unimportant. They do weave strands of contact and understanding. They send delegates to far places and receive visits from representatives of churches or church groups in other lands. They are conscious of their international relationships and seek from time to time to express them in concrete form. But there is no present connection between them. They exemplify real American "rugged individualism" at its best and at its worst. They refuse to be catalogued or classified. But they exist and will go on existing as an evidence that the spirit of Christians is incurably international and missionary in the sense of not being content to remain forever sectional or national in its expression. In this category one would include the American Bible Society, the Salvation Army, the Oxford Groups, the Christian Endeavor Society, the American Section of the World Alliance for International Friendship, the Christian Temperance Union, the American Tract Society, and numerous similar bodies.

Lastly I would mention that link which, in theory at least, has the most promise of bringing into existence a working unity of non-Roman churches as such. It is an outgrowth of forces working both nationally and internationally. On the one hand, it expresses the desire for Christian unity and co-operation of the federation movement. It is embodied in the Department for Relations with Churches Abroad of the Federal Council of the Churches. On the other hand, simultaneously it represents the American Section of the Universal Christian Council which came into being at Stockholm in 1925. That has been wisely made identical in administration with the Department of the Federal Council just mentioned. It is through this means that the Churches banded together in the Council—and any others wishing to take part in the movement—are brought into organic touch with the churches in Europe and other lands. For the most part this is a coordinating body—not one which seeks to build up its own work on a large scale. It is necessarily opportunist rather than academic or theoretical in its activity. It seeks to create, and does create, personal acquaintance among Christian leaders by bringing them into regular contact. It promotes exchanges among the ministers of different lands. It shares in the International Christian Press Service at Geneva which was organized by the Universal Christian Council in conjunction with the other ecumenical bodies working at Geneva. It desires to relate the work of the various commissions and committees of the respective denominations concerned with the practical application of Christian teaching to social problems, with international understanding, and with peace. Its means of doing so is through bringing the responsible leaders of these various activities into personal relationship and cooperation in the American Section of the Universal Christian Council and in the Council itself wherever possible. It is recognized by the churches in other lands as the most comprehensive and effective link for them with the combined life of the churches in America.

What shall we say in conclusion? The reader who has come thus far with me will, unless already familiar with the complexity of Christian world organization—be feeling a bit dizzy and puzzled. It all does sound very complicated. But I would urge him not to be discouraged. A wheel-barrow is very simple. But it does not commend itself to the modern man as a vehicle to be compared with the automobile or the steamship. But automobiles and steamships are bewilderingly complex in structure. They seem simple because their manifold functions are coordinated and controlled. If you have been thinking of ultimate Christian international life as if it were to come through the creation of "one big union" you have been dreaming! The plans for future organization have to take into account existing "locals." And they are numerous, varied, hard to relate, sometimes disconcertingly individualistic. But they represent reality. They are living and they will go on living. Any Christian statesmanship which would seek to disregard them, to scrap them, or to duplicate them in the process of building something better is shortsighted and in the end doomed to failure. The trains have to be kept running while the new bridge is being built! And what is more, in this instance the new bridge has to be built in large measure out of the materials in the old!

To the reader who despairs of seeing anything effective come out of all the efforts of the churches to build adequate international organizations, I would say, in closing this all too brief and fragmentary sketch of the present status of that process, consider the modern suspension bridge as a sort of parable. The George Washington Bridge over the Hudson is near my home. When it was in process of construction I used to see it frequently. When the great towers—each six hundred and thirty-five feet high—were completed, the first strand of wire was spun across from shore to shore. It was quite invisible from below. If you had been asked to believe that those first invisible strands represented what was actually to be a structure strong enough to support the weight of thousands of cars, trucks, busses, and pedestrians two hundred feet above the river and on a span of three-quarters of a mile in the clear, you might have refused to regard them as practical means toward uniting the mighty traffic of New York and New Jersey. But when they were multiplied over and over through patient months of slow building activities they grew at last into clusters of strands which, when brought into coordinated relationship with their fellows, were quite visible and wholly reassuring in appearance as well as performance! They are not even now "one"; they are federated. Each strand has its own individuality, its own separate existence. Each goes all the way from one shore to the other. But they are doing a united work and doing it effectively because of the organization into which they were fashioned by intelligent planning and wonderful engineering cooperation.

I think I see a similar possibility for the strands which are even now being spun across the living oceans from Christian church to Christian church. Taken separately they are all but invisible. Alone they would not support a very great load. But if through patient and discerning work we can bring them into line, relate them each to each, and organize their individual weakness into collective strength, we shall have produced a bridge which shall be a highway for our God as He moves among the nations of mankind. For He waits to strengthen and to bless those who, each in his own way, have come to know and trust His fatherly goodness as revealed in Jesus who prayed that we might all be one.

BUILDING A NEW WORLD

RALPH H. READ

CHAPTER XIX

BUILDING A NEW WORLD

LAST May Day I stood in Union Square in New York City and watched thousands of ragged Communists thrill to the inspired singing of their songs for a better world. In awed silence I witnessed the locked, upraised hands of Chinese, Japanese, Negro and American Communists as they vowed to stand together for the solidarity of the human race. I was able to sense the evangelistic fervor of the occasion and to feel the cosmic thrust of the Communist faith.

It had in it something not unlike early First Century Christianity, and was more closely akin to it in spirit than might at first be supposed. The utterances most loudly cheered were those calling for the treatment of all men alike. Race hatred was openly denounced. Freedom for the colored man was on every lip and placard. World revolution that would bring to pass a new and warless world was heralded in flaming red and in interminable speech. Poor faces, haggard and starved countenances, but hopeful and radiant spirits were everywhere in great numbers. It so happened that these were not violent men bent upon human destruction. Under given circumstances they could become violent. But on this May Day they were peaceful and needy, demonstrating in behalf of the new world which they some day hoped to build.

In the midst of all this variety of color and abundance of faith my mind suddenly reverted to the Christian Church. Somehow, by way of contrast, the Church appeared drab and colorless, if not socially useless. I pictured its petty priests and preachers, myself among their number, as all too respectable, happy and comfortable. I thought of straggling church congregations, of listless singing and empty pews. I thought of endless church benefits and bridges, of members who dig dirt in their backyards on Sunday mornings, and of ecclesiastical conventions which oppose resolutions looking toward a new society based upon the spirit of love. I thought of high-salaried parsons, and of lovely cathedrals exquisitely appointed, of bake sales, church bazaars, and of the countless church schools whose children parrot the Bible verses which they have learned for their teachers. I was unable to forget the choir quarrels, the dissension in church vestries and committees that I had known. Ice-cream socials, attendance records, membership lists, and vaudeville stunts sometimes used to draw the crowds, crowded their way into my mind for a brief moment of attention. Elements of human grandeur in the one scene seemed to dwarf the lack of conviction in the other. I thought of all these things and wondered.

Leaders in the Christian Church must once again ask themselves whether the Christian religion is a cause for which men are really willing to live and die. It cannot be doubted that our religion once possessed such power over men. It ought to have today and in some instances does have. At any rate the future usefulness of the Church will await such a revival of quickening life.

The Church is rightly a conservator of historic values in

society which must not be lost. It dare not surrender the true and tested truths of the past. Some customs and conventions, however, will have to go before a new world may be built. Conventions hold us together while they possess social significance. Many conventions live on the relics of dead or dying convictions. Each new age must have new convictions of its own. Conventions and customs, as well as institutions which have lost their meaning because they no longer possess social usefulness, will have to go. In fact, after their purpose for existence is gone they will one day snap like dead wood, if strained to the breaking point. When such a moment comes, laws will not be strong enough to hold intact that which the people no longer either desire or need. Neither will the selfishness of man be able to preserve anti-social practices from destruction. All that has served its day must ultimately cease to be. The American people will support the time-honored and revered institutions of American life only until they discover that those institutions have been rendered meaningless by the practices and precepts of greedy men. In that day ancient cords will snap and changes take place.

Revolution of the heart and mind is the finest possible preparation for the new day. In the final analysis it is the only security against bloodshed and violence. The speed with which modern life is moving demands a like quickening of the mental impulses. Right thinking in this day and age implies spiritual travail and mental discipline of the highest order. Each new thought-transition in history is achieved by intellectual confusion as well as by pure reason. This confusion today is augmented by the pace of the contemporary scene. Unless a man is prompt to serious thought, it may be expected that he will not know what it is all about. Such a one will be a poor citizen in the new society of the kingdom of God.

The approach to the new world that is contemplated must take place along two roads which tend to merge into one another. The first is the road of personal religion, which is closely tied to the second road of social change, from which it can never be divorced. There is great need today that these two highways shall be made clearer to the Christian Church. In a measure, it is true that we do not suffer as much from inability to analyze our limitations as from the lack of a clear understanding of the goal. The critics of the Church have been more numerous than its positive leaders. It is to be hoped that this chapter will not be entirely devoid of positive suggestions.

The need in the world of personal religious faith is for someone who shall have the courage to work out a new technique for the furtherance of the spirit-life that shall combine the personal qualities of warmth and glow with the social passion for mercy and justice. Renewed Christian power awaits such a union of two factors in the religious life not easy to associate together in a single life. Traditionally speaking, it is often true that where the one factor is present the other is absent. The fostering of such personal and social character in religious people will require discipline. For discipline in one form or another is a prerequisite to all progress, spiritual or otherwise.

The modern church has tended to lose both the approach to, and an understanding of the meaning of personal discipline in the spirit-life. We suffer the ill effects of having made recreational and social centers alone out of religious institutions. The Church has moved forward in membership.

Promotional schemes have added to the lists of interested people, and have acquired from them their money. One's business has been improved by belonging to an influential and respectable church; for good people come to the services of the Church. By declaring the world to be no longer moral or immoral, and by believing that every man is eternal, we have automatically filled our churches with members whom we have declared to be good. A speaker recently devoted the whole of an evening to the task of convincing his listeners that they were Christians in worthy standing. We have made people religious by denying their irreligion. Hence one can be a member of the average church today and believe almost anything. The tolerance of liberal religion is, in part, to be seen in its lack of deep conviction. Men do not fight over what they little believe in.

The banal and hackneyed character of much of our religious life may be attributed, therefore, to its undisciplined nature. The kingdom of love, or any other kind of kingdom, does not come through such ready simplification. Life is an issue and it must be met as an issue. The spiritual seers of the human race who have contributed most to it have been men of great inward discipline. Prayers, thoughts, and moments have been carefully employed. Like his church steeple, the character of the puritan may have been too straight, but the absolute quality of his life's laws acted as a useful teacher in giving him strength. The use of close discipline by political groups which have not yet won their way to popularity is evidence of its necessity, and a symbol of the price which must be paid for progress. The Church has too often longed for the progress without desiring to pay the price.

The disciplinary aid of prayer meetings and of periods of protracted revival has largely gone. Orchestrated ball rooms and the music of jazz have filled in the gap; or is it filled? Can the soft music of the cinema organ or even the formal, dignified service of morning worship in the church provide the soul-food that was once furnished by the disciplinary fellowship of small groups in the Church's life? The confessional meeting may have produced its moments of mirth, but it likewise furnished an avenue of individual expression of the light within which has now been chiefly preëmpted by the minister alone. Faith which has no opportunity of asserting itself is sure to die. Only a miracle would make it live.

There have been modifications in practice of these conditions. However, the trend is present, as has been outlined. Denominational policies in the future must concern themselves with building inner disciplinary groups within the larger organization. To do this would only be to regain a church procedure which was once employed. It was a technique, despite its limitations, which produced results within the scope of its light. We ought now to use such an approach to the development of personal religion in order to realize what we now believe to be broader and more inclusive Christian ends.

Spiritual development by means of the inner group technique is not only an approach which the Church once employed with excellent results, but it is being used, as has been suggested, by radical organizations intent upon acquiring a large body of followers. Growth in any form of discipleship makes the sharing, disciplinary fellowship of an inner group an imperative need. The highest spiritual life possible for man, either on the personal or social side of his character, is seldom achieved without some such technique. In this respect one may well study the methods of cultivation used by Gandhi of India or by St. Francis during the Middle Ages. The approaches to this problem that have been worked out by great religious and political leaders can teach us much, if we wish to study them.

The enlarging of church rolls or the meeting of church budgets means nothing in relationship to this problem. In fact, the instrumentalities by which most of the causes of our churches are maintained do more to destroy the position of true religion than to save it. The Christian Church will not continue to grow without the aid of surrendered and disciplined disciples. It needs disciples in whom the Spirit of God lives as a consuming flame which cannot be quenched. John Wesley on the Moors in England is to be preferred to all contemporary expressions of religious life, for to Wesley religion was as a consuming flame.

There is renewed evidence that men are hungry for such spiritual life and discipline. They desire causes which may not be possessed cheaply. In a single day in New York one woman offered her life as an experiment for science, and four men offered themselves as suicides in a revivification test for the cause of science. We ask for dimes or an occasional presence at a weekly meeting and that is what we get. It would be easier to demand lives and get them.

The positive program of supplementing the social program of the Church with the inner groups described should form the soil in which activity in behalf of a new world may be rooted. The radical spirit springs most readily from souls possessed of divine discontent. This discontent first begins with the self and then proceeds outward into society. He who has seen the dawning light of a new day in his own heart will, with proper educational influence, come to desire a new day in his world. The condemnation due the Christian Church, solemnly ascribed, is not alone that its social gospel has not been adequate, but also that it has at the same time been unable to do that which the majority of its members will so vehemently insist it is the chief business of the church to do.

It is the business of the Church to do these things and not to leave the other things undone. Effective social action upon the part of the Church requires individual consciences which are spiritually sensitive. Informal disciplinary groups within the Church, whose avowed object is to deepen the personal devotion of the human spirit, should perform such a function. They will do it by their methods of education, by their sharing, and by the support which they furnish one another in fellowship. All great cleansing movements in the history of religion tend to give credence to this assumption. The disciples of Jesus belonged to such a group. Probably no group ever possessed greater leavening power in society or was more effective.

This chapter can scarcely suggest all the methods which may be used in developing such a spiritual program for the personal life. The most suitable technique will have later to be devised. Each denominational need will vary somewhat. But who is there that can doubt that the renewal of the religious life of our churches awaits the creation of such a program of inner group life.

If such life is not planned for under intelligent leadership it tends to spring up of itself in less desirable forms to probe and perplex the hearts of intelligent Christian people. If present movements in the Church are too narrowly circum-spect in their approach to the problem, it behooves the church to answer by initiating a better program in their place. The catalogued criticisms of Barth, Buchman or Shoe-maker must be expressed through improved substitutes or lose their weight.

Finally, it is clear that a revival of personal religion is futile unless it is integrated with virile social religion of a radical character. It is a travesty to suppose that the soul may be saved apart from the salvation of the social order in which its existence is carried on. Religion which shows no concern for a radically altered human society is at best a selfish expression; and ultimately will be unable even to save itself from extinction.

Liberal religion has rather deserved the attack that is being made upon it both from the right and the left. It is ethically and spiritually moribund. As the herald of a more scientific reading of theology it served a useful purpose, though it fell the victim of a false interpretation of history. As has been pointed out, its evolutionary optimism grew out of an ex-panding economic development which was thought to be endless. We now know that progress does not move evenly upward, but that it is likewise born of catastrophe. Tragedy is written deep into the nature of life.

This need not blind us to the lasting contributions which liberal religion has made in history. Its high esteem for human life and personality will continue to be felt. While its spirit of tolerance may be superseded by long years when it may seem as if tolerance were dead; nevertheless, tolerance like truth is a condition of progress, and must remain to do honor to the liberal faith. Other contributions will be passed on, but liberal religion as a system of belief is going. In fact, only the vestigial remnants of its former glory now abide.

The social gospel is the child of liberal religion. It too is leaving the stage with its liberal parent. In a broader sense it will remain. The spirit of liberalism and of the social gospel will continue to exist when their systems of faith have been forgotten. But the allegiance to all tenets in the creed which made systems of them will vanish. Prompted by true prophetic Christian spirit the social gospel became primarily a system of amelioration of human suffering rather than its abolition through a drastically revolutionized human state. The liberal interpretation of the function of Christianity in a liberal world was responsible for this.

A real ray of light broke in upon religious history when Walter Rauschenbusch suffered ecclesiastical displeasure by denouncing the soul-destroying forces of a ruthless economic order. Had this light not been dimmed by the liberal reading of economic history the system of the social gospel might have become a more powerful force in American religious life. As it is, even its own champions become discouraged. Social religion demands a new orientation of a radical character. This orientation must think in terms of a new world in the place of a world made more endurable through philanthropy and generous impulse alone. It will have to conceive a new political state little similar to the state now in existence, and it will have to organize for political action in order to bring that state to pass.

The battle will no longer be waged by preachers endeavoring to modify or check the acquisitive instinct of their wealthy parishioners. It will not be conducted in terms of missionary programs of social betterment supported by the financial aid of those who have made the recipients too poor to help themselves. Under the right kind of economic order home missionary work, as it is now being carried on, would not be necessary. There would be Christian sharing but little patronization of backward people, made backward and underprivileged by injustice and by a poor distribution of national income. The task of social religion tomorrow will not spend itself in an occasional basket for the poor or even in well-worded resolutions suggesting some evil in the present order. Religion must struggle to create a new kind of state or forfeit its right to existence.

The Church must concern itself with Socialism's dream of a new world wherein the people own and plan those resources and instruments of production upon which they are dependent, and where goods are produced for use and not for selfish gain. Capital and land must be used by the people for man's salvation and not for his destruction. The new gospel of social religion will be kindled by the old spirit, but it will be possessed by a new hope required by a society which can no longer maintain itself without both justice and intelligent planning. It must come to the defense of the weaker groups in society who are now suffering defeat and exploitation. Their needs demand a release from those who now have power to bring about their physical and spiritual destruction. The Church must help to carry their burden. The power these groups seek is just, for without it they cannot achieve freedom. The church must recognize this fact. Social religion will not fight for the rule of any one class. The true Socialism which must motivate the social religion of tomorrow demands a classless world in which there will be neither Jew nor Gentile, bond nor slave, black nor white, but where all men shall be brothers and children of one universal God. The brotherhood and solidarity of the human race will be its goal. Socialism in its broadest and highest sense will be the human instrument for bringing this world into being.

By Socialism it is well to realize that we do not mean any particular group of the followers of Karl Marx. Neither do we mean that the doctrines of Marx must be adhered to in any absolute sense. Marx gave the world the kind of realistic appraisal and dissection of modern industrial civilization that the Christian Church, by virtue of its professions, should have made possble. If Marx was antagonistic to traditional religion, it was not without reason. He was reacting against what paraded under the name religion in his day. He then perceived some things which we now admit. But to say this does not mean that we must follow Marx in any slavish sense.

By Socialism we mean a general set of principles which will have to be adhered to if a modern industrial society is to be planned scientifically for the social and spiritual well-being of all. By Socialism we mean a society wherein land and capital, and all resources and instruments of production upon which the people are dependent, shall be owned and operated by the people for the sake of their highest good; and a society wherein goods shall be produced for use and not greed rather than a society where these things are exploited for the benefit of the few. Such a goal is simple and does not require a complicated system of theology to be followed. Here again, not even the label matters. The only kind of workable state possible for the future of American life will be Socialistic or Collectivistic in this sense. The reasons for the collapse of Capitalism should have already made this clear. It is a peculiar form of blindness which is unable to see that this is so.

A few men did not create the surplus wealth of the economic machine. This wealth does not therefore belong to the few. It is society's and should be used by society. In fact, if society does not have it, it cannot even keep operating the machinery which its men of genius have created. There is only so much wealth in a given nation. Concentrate the bulk of that wealth in the hands of a privileged few and you destroy the buying power of the many. Without their buying power all industrial operation must cease.

The living standards of a nation are determined by its productive capacity. When lack of buying power through poor distribution of wealth shuts down machinery and creates unemployment, productive capacity (that is living standards) is being destroyed. Unemployed men cannot pay good prices for marketable farm products; hence farms cannot afford to market what they raise, and we have living standards and productive capacity further destroyed and lowered. Thus are we compelled to witness the sad spectacle of corn being burned by farmers for fuel, fruit rotting under trees, potatoes being left to rot in the ground; all because the farmer cannot get enough money for his crops to make possible the marketing of what he has produced. Railroads cannot get their rates and cotton lies idle in stations or wharves. In a futile effort to solve this problem the government further destroys the same food which its own agricultural colleges have taught the people to raise. And thus are the people made poor!

The fault does not belong to God. He gave us the soil, and

has made possible sufficient and enormous production. The fault lies only in man's inability to plan carefully what has been created.

When the world was living in a simple agrarian civilization it was quite possible for life to move along under a minimum of social planning. It did not matter so much if each person did as he pleased because others were not so much affected as today. But once a modern industrial society develops to a certain stage you have much the same analogy as in a factory. A factory, if it is not to go on the rocks of bankruptcy, must be scientifically planned and centrally controlled. Its owners would not imagine for a minute that they could allow each employee to do as he pleased. The complexity of modern traffic makes necessary well-devised traffic laws, if it is not to take some a day to move across a city by car, barring accident, while the lucky do it in an hour. The greatest individual freedom under complexity comes by way of plan. All industrial societies must learn to plan or perish!

If you ask for the conditions under which industrial planning may prove possible, you are forced to the conviction that the people must own or completely control that which they are endeavoring to plan. If I were to plan your business which I did not own, and you did not desire my planning, you would be able to thwart me. Scientific planning without ownership, or its equivalent, is an impossibility. Thus today do American attempts at control without ownership break down. Under new deals and other forms of control it is too easily possible for the regulators to regulate the regulators. The dominant economic group tends to be the dominant political group.

These statements may appear at first to be bold and unjustified. It would be possible, if space permitted, to demonstrate with facts how ineffectual it is to hope for a solution of technological unemployment, or even for a better distribution of the nation's wealth, under the private ownership of American industry. Hours and days of labor would have to be shortened far below the ability or inclination of private ownership to shorten them. Competition is too great and the financial burden too heavy. But what it is not possible to do under private ownership and control can be done through socialized ownership. In fact it is now being done in those places where it is being tried.

To follow these socialized principles ought not to frighten Christian people. To do so merely means the extension of a principle already at work in American life. We already have a socialized school system, postal system, and municipally owned and publically used highways. No longer do we pay private operators to carry our mail, and seldom do we pay to drive our cars on the highway. If this degree of socialization has been necessary, how much more necessary is it for us to socialize those processes upon which we are dependent for our physical and spiritual existence. We had better prepare ourselves for some such change, for all future states will have to be collectivistic to carry on. Our pet fears and arguments will not change this fact.

The Church ought to be able to read the signs of the times. Continued support of present-day amelioristic measures in the place of a united program for complete social change will further render religion helpless and futile. Already we are being compelled to witness a diminution in the resources available for the religious, cultural, and spiritual side of life. This depreciation will continue in any future attempt at saving Capitalism, for by its very nature Capitalism cannot be saved without doling the margins, which would otherwise go for religion and education, to the hungry and the poor, in order that they may not revolt.

Capitalism's foreign markets are gone. Its expanding days are over. As selfishness at home strikes precipitously against selfishness abroad, it retreats into its own shell, out of which it can never hope to climb. For its shell becomes its grave. There it must be interred. Marx was right when he claimed that when the conditions of production, instead of being aids to production, became fetters upon it, then the period of revolution begins. This period of revolution becomes also the death rattle of the profit-taking way of life. Man's physical and spiritual life must famish in the midst of plenty because he has been unable to organize his society along socialized lines.

Doctors and druggists have some tendency to welcome sickness as a means of prosperity. Undertakers live on death, and grave diggers live by the more of their fellow men they can bury. Strange order of life that would seek to survive by the creation of an artificial starvation of body and soul. But evil creates death and to follow evil is to die. Religionists should perceive the handwriting on the wall. They must move forward with open minds but with certain definite principles in view. These principles will look forward to a new world and will be of a socialized character.

To realize these objectives will require some kind of united front upon the part of all radical, religious, and political groups, for the desired changes can scarcely take place without definite political action. Possibly it will require the organization of new religious movements in the Church. No minister ought to put his professional career ahead of the contribution which he hopes to make in behalf of the new world. For some it will mean martyrdom, or at best, social ostracism and persecution. For all of us it will mean a new and more exalted conception of the Church in society. We will have to believe in the Church. We will have to believe in men. As Phillip James Bailey has said, "Men might be better if we better deemed of them. The worst way to improve the world is to condemn it." James Russell Lowell expressed the same truth when he said, "The surest plan to make a man is to think him so." The critical outlook portrayed in this chapter and in the first chapter is justified only as a point of departure in building a new world. Except we know our diseases we cannot heal them. Beyond this we must have the faith to believe that humanity has the power to heal itself. Without such faith our radical understanding may easily lead us into cynicism and a policy of inaction.

In America we will have to take more into consideration the innate idealism of our people. The Marxian materialist tends to underestimate the religious character of the American people, and to imagine that this quality in our life may either be ignored or abolished. If rightly comprehended, our native American idealism can become one of the most powerful factors available in the reconstruction of our society. I have hope that religious radicalism may yet become the salvation of American economic life.

At present this will mean placing our faith in a minority group. There may yet be a saving remnant who, seeing the light, will dare to follow it into prison and death. The future of this remnant will not be easy. We must banish the thought of ease from our minds. But let those who have seen the light follow it, for there is no other way. It is the way of life, and it is the way the Master walked before us. Jesus also dreamed of a better world and suffered for it. We will remember and rejoice.

BIBLIOGRAPHIES

BIBLIOGRAPHIES

RALPH H. READ was born in Denver, Colorado, October 28, 1903. His early education was in Franklin Academy, Bethany Academy, Bethany College, and Grinnell College, Grinnell, Iowa, with a B.A. degree from Grinnell in 1925. He received his B.D. from Union Theological Seminary, New York City, in 1928, after three years of study in that institution. Since that time he has been the minister of the Hollis Avenue Congregational Church, Bellaire, Long Island. The editor's activities have included work as president of the Conference of Younger Churchmen, Metropolitan New York and vicinity. (Rev. John Elliott is the present president of this organization, having been recently elected to that office.) Mr. Read is chairman of the Social Service Committee of the New York City Congregational Church Association, member of the Executive Committee of the National Conference of Jews and Christians, and has an active interest in the Minister's Union of America, the Socialist Party, and the Fellowship of Socialist Christians. He is a member of the program and religious education committees of the New York City Congregational Church Association and of the Executive Committee of the Manhattan Brotherhood of Congregational Ministers, a member of the faculty of the Blairstown Young People's Conference of the Congregational Church in New York. He has contributed articles to denominational and religious journals.

JOHN COLEMAN BENNETT was born in 1902 in Kingston, Ontario, Canada, and lived the first sixteen years of his life in Morristown, N. J. In 1920 he graduated from Phillips Exeter Academy, and in 1924 received a B.A. from Williams College. Mr. Bennett studied at Oxford University, England (Mansfield

College), where he was given the degrees of B.A., M.A. in 1926. He also secured a B.D. (Magna Cum Laude) from Union Theological Seminary, 1927, and an S.T.M. (Summa Cum Laude) from the same institution in 1929. Mr. Bennett was formerly president of the Conference of Younger Churchmen, chairman of the Executive Committee of the Fellowship of Socialist Christians and a contributing editor of *The World Tomorrow*. He is a contributor to *The Christian Century, The Intercollegian, The Student World,* and *The Presbyterian Tribune,* a member of the National Executive Committee of the Student Division of the Y. M. C. A., and of the Social Service Committee of the Synod of New York. He was formerly assistant and instructor in the Department of Systematic Theology, Union Theological Seminary, New York. At the present time, Mr. Bennett is assistant professor of Christian Theology in Auburn Theological Seminary, Auburn, New York. His record speaks for itself. He is one of the keenest, and most thoughtful, and scholarly of the younger leaders in the Christian church. Consequently his insight and understanding are much in demand.

CAMERON PARKER HALL was born in Pelham, New York, in 1895. He graduated from Williams College in 1921; studied for the ministry in Edinburgh, Oxford, and in the Union Theological Seminary. He served as assistant minister in the Broome Street Tabernacle, New York City. In 1926 he became the minister of Christ Church on the West Side of New York City, where he is today. He is chairman of the committee on Social Service of the Synod of New York of the Presbyterian Church, U. S. A., and has served on other influential committees too numerous to mention. Mr. Hall writes for various religious journals, including the new *Presbyterian Tribune.* He is a former president of the Conference of Younger Churchmen, member of the Executive Committee of the Ministers Union of America and of the Socialist Party and the Fellowship of Socialist Christians. Compelled by a strong radical vision, deeply Christian in character, and of an humble spirit, Mr. Hall has achieved for himself a well-earned position of fine leadership in his church. Many religious groups look to him for help and guidance. He represents the best in the younger leadership of the Christian Church.

FREDERICK KUHNS was born in Dayton, Ohio, March 19, 1903, and received there his early education. He has since felt the influence of three seminaries: the Divinity School of the University of Chicago, the Lutheran Theological Seminary, Gettysburg, Pennsylvania, and the Union Theological Seminary, New York City, where he completed his theological work. Mr. Kuhns has also done graduate work at the University of Chicago. While studying in New York, he gave one year of service to the Holy Trinity Lutheran Church as student assistant to the minister. In 1930 he became the associate minister of the Plymouth Congregational Church of Shaker Heights, Cleveland. Since 1933 he has been the minister of the Congregational Church in Rochester, New York. As minister of South Congregational, Rochester, he has served as a member of the Executive Committee of the Rochester Federation of Churches. He has contributed articles to *The Christian Century* and other religious journals. A younger churchman, possessing a radiant spirit, and rare Christian mind, Mr. Kuhns is well qualified to write in this book. He is a scholar, an illuminating and intelligent preacher, and is well loved by his people.

BEDROS KEVORK APELIAN was born in Kessab, Syria, an Armenian town on the Mediterranean coast, October 10, 1886. After graduating from Central Turkey College, Aintab (now Aleppo College), he came to America to study education and theology. Here he studied in Iowa State Teacher's College, three years in Oberlin College Graduate School of Theology, and two years as a graduate student in Union Theological Seminary and in Columbia University. At the beginning of the war, Mr. Apelian entered the ministry at the Wyckoff Heights Presbyterian Church, from which he resigned to serve with the Near East Relief. In 1921 he returned to the pastorate at the First Presbyterian Church of Bensonhurst, Brooklyn, in which field he is now serving. Mr. Apelian edits a very fine church paper, and does other writing as well. He is on the executive committee of the Conference of Younger Churchmen, a member of the Minister's Union of America, member of the Executive Committee of the Youth Department of the New York Federation of Churches, and on the faculty of the Teacher's Training Institute of the Greater New York Federation of Churches. His political interests include a membership and keen interest in the Socialist Party and in the Fellowship of Socialist Christians. Mr. Apelian has a radical and penetrating mind which is constantly seeking new ways of expression for the Christian spirit, and he is known and loved for his fearlessness and for his generous, enthusiastic Christian spirit.

EDMUND B. CHAFFEE was born in Roset Center, Michigan, in 1887. He graduated from the University of Michigan, class of 1909. In 1913 he graduated from the Law School of the same university with the degree of J.D. (Doctor of Jurisprudence) and was admitted to the Bar. All this, however, was but preliminary preparation for the work of the Christian ministry. He graduated from the Union Theological Seminary in 1916. After serving as captain in the American Red Cross in Palestine, he was called to be the minister of the Labor Temple in New York City, where he is today. Recently Mr. Chaffee has assumed the editorship of the New Presbyterian magazine called *The Presbyterian Tribune.* His recent book, selected by the Religious Book Club as the best religious book of the month, entitled, "The Protestant Churches and the Industrial Crisis," has been widely read. Among other organizations and committees, too numerous to mention, in which Mr. Chaffee has had a part, he is the founder of the Minister's Union of America and a charter member of the Conference of Younger Churchmen. A clear, courageous thinker, writer and preacher, with a steadily increasing influence in the life of the church, Mr. Chaffee is easily one of its outstanding leaders. He has made an especially deep impression upon all younger clergymen who have had the privilege of being closely associated with him.

H. LINCOLN MACKENZIE was born at Cardigan, Prince Edward Island, Canada, July 19, 1893, and received his elementary and high school training in the public schools of Boston, Massachusetts. He was in business for four years before entering Bangor Theological Seminary, from which institution he graduated in 1918. He later entered Brown University. In 1922 Mr. Mackenzie received his B.D. and Ph.B degrees from Bangor Seminary and Brown University respectively. He also studied at Oxford University during 1925-1926. Since 1927 Mr. Mackenzie has been the minister of the Community Church (Interdenominational) of Great Neck, Long Island. He is frequently a contributor and writer for *The Community Churchman* and other religious and secular journals. He belongs to the Phi Gamma Delta fraternity, is president of the Nassau County Ministers Association, vice president of the Religious Education Association and of the Board of Child Welfare of the same county. Mr. Mackenzie possesses an informative and lucid mind which endeavors to probe the heart of every problem, whether it be religious, political or social in its nature. Combined with this is a deep philosophical insight. He is a member of the Conference of Younger Churchmen, and as a leader of the Community Church Movement, he is well capable of discussing the perplexing question of church unity.

STANLEY U. NORTH was born in Pleasantville, New Jersey, February 10, 1892, and received there his high school and university training. He is a graduate of the Union Theological Seminary, and holds an M.A. from Columbia University. At the present time he lives in Briarcliff Manor, New York, where he is the minister of the Congregational Church. Apart from his preaching and pastoral work in New York churches, since his graduation Mr. North has been doing outstanding work with young people. He was dean for five years of the Blair Congregational Young People's Summer Conference, Metropolitan New York and vicinity. He has served as the chairman of the State Congregational Religious Education Committee, is now chairman of the Religious Education Committee of the New York

City Association, and is the state moderator of the New York Congregational Conference of Churches. He writes occasionally for denominational papers, is a member of the Conference of Younger Churchmen, the Listeners Club, and Beta Theta Pi fraternity. In his own words, Mr. North belongs to the war generation that was thoroughly disillusioned and cured. He says, "At what a cost!" The words express the quality of his spirit— honest, radical and fearless, he has been an inspiration and guide to all the younger ministers who have served under his fine leadership and who have felt the power of his personality and social vision.

DAVID MUNROE CORY was born in New York City, February 10, 1903. He received his education chiefly in the New York City schools from which he took General Honors. He also has a B.A. degree from Columbia University, 1923. From Union Theological Seminary, New York City, he received his S.T.M. in 1926 and a Th.D. in 1931. He has had three years of resident social work in the slums of Edinburgh, and is a graduate of New College, Edinburgh, 1926. Since finishing his education, Mr. Cory has been the minister of the Cuyler Presbyterian Church in Brooklyn, where he is today. He has been a candidate for public office six times on the ticket of the Socialist Party in America, is Secretary of the Standing Committee on Social Service of the Presbyterian Church, and President of the Ministers' Union of America. He is the author of "Faustus Socinus," Boston, 1932, a member of the American Society of Church History, member of the Socialist Party of America and of the Conference of Younger Churchmen. Mr. Cory is one of the most courageous of the younger ministers in the church, having taken an active part in labor struggles, championing the cause of the exploited and oppressed. In October, 1931, he was severely injured by thugs when assisting to organize employees in the Brooklyn Edison Company. A radical of deep conviction, and a scholar, Mr. Cory is well qualified to write on modern religious and social issues.

FRANK OLMSTEAD was born at Honeaye, New York, September 9, 1890. He received his B.A. degree from the University of Michigan, 1917, with casual work since at Penn State, Colorado School of Mines, New York University, and Union Theological Seminary. For two years Mr. Olmstead was with the Y. M. C. A. in Russia, being in Moscow during the Bolshevik Revolution. Since that time he has been constantly engaged in Student Y. M. C. A. work and is now a secretary of the Intercollegiate Branch of the Y. M. C. A. in New York City. He is the chairman of the Strategy Committee and co-chairman of the Student Enrollment Committee of the War Resister's League. In the summer of 1934 he was a delegate to the War Resister's International Conference in England. He is a member of the Executive Committee of the National Religion and Labor Foundation and was the grand marshal of the Anti-War Parade which, last May, in New York, assembled ten thousand marchers. Mr. Olmstead is the author of the pamphlet, "Interpretation of the College Peace Poll," and an occasional contributor to the *Intercollegian* and the *Green International*. As a member of the Conference of Younger Churchmen, and as a friend and Christian of the finest character, Mr. Olmstead has always demonstrated in his rich spirit those principles to which he gives so much of his sincere devotion. His tireless and unceasing efforts in behalf of world peace are everywhere well known, as are the depths and strength of his spiritual insight.

JOHN HARLAN ELLIOTT was born in Toledo, Ohio, in 1905. He received his B.A. degree from the University of Michigan in 1926, and graduated from the Union Theological Seminary with the degree of B.D. in 1930. Until recently Mr. Elliott has been the assistant minister of the Central Presbyterian Church, New York City. He has since been called to the pastorate of the First Presbyterian Church of Easton, Pennsylvania, where he is serving at the present time. He was recently elected to the presidency of the Conference of Younger Churchmen to succeed Ralph H. Read, term expired. Formerly the secretary and treasurer of the Conference, Mr. Elliott was an invaluable aid to the editor of this book in carrying on the work of that organization. Because of the quality of the religious background from which he comes, and because of his genuine and extended interest in the international situation, Mr. Elliott is well qualified to write upon the subject of the church and world peace. He brings a quiet and sincere Christian spirit into all that he does.

RUSSELL J. CLINCHY was born in New York City in 1893. After being educated in East Orange, New Jersey, High School, Columbia University, Drew Theological Seminary, and after having taken a year of postgraduate work at Yale Divinity School, he became the associate minister of the Church of the Sea and Land, a Presbyterian social settlement Church on the lower East Side in New York City. From 1920-1922 he served with the American Friends' Service Committee (the Quaker reconstruction work) in Philadelphia in an executive capacity, especially in writing the description of the work which the Quakers were doing to restore the devastated areas of Europe. He then became the minister of the First Congregational Church, Cornwall, Connecticut, remaining there until 1925, when he went to Detroit as associate minister of the First Congregational Church of that city, where he was associated with Dr. Gaius Glenn Atkins. In 1927 he became the associate minister of the Broadway Tabernacle Church, New York City, with Dr. Charles E. Jefferson. In 1931 he was called to the pastorate of the Mount Pleasant Congregational Church, Washington, D. C. Mr. Clinchy has been especially interested in student and young people's work, having been a leader at the Y. M. C. A. Student Conference at Northfield and Lake Geneva; registrar of the Connecticut Congregational Young People's Conference; and dean of the Michigan Congregational Young People's Conference. In 1930 Mr. Clinchy was one of the ten interchange preachers between America and Great Britain, under the Federal Council and Church Peace Union, and preached in Scotland and England. He was also a delegate to the International Council in Bournemouth, England.

Mr. Clinchy is a frequent contributor to outstanding denominational and religious journals, including *The Christian Century*. He is also a Washington correspondent for *Advance* (Congregationalist). Mr. Clinchy was the founder and a charter member of the Conference of Younger Churchmen. The quiet force of his leadership and personality, together with the spirit and keenness of his social discernment, were invaluable factors influencing that organization in its early existence. Motivated by a rich Quaker temperament and fine social vision, Mr. Clinchy has won for himself an enviable position of splendid leadership in the church. As in the case of his brother, Russell is known for his mature wisdom and true spirit of friendship.

JOHN I. DANIEL was born in Plainfield, New Jersey, in 1903. He graduated from Lafayette College with the degree of B.S. in 1925. From 1925-1927 he was engaged in business in New York, where he was on the editorial staff of *Automobile Topics* and English editor for a group of Italian-American publications. After receiving his B.D. from Union Theological Seminary in 1930 he was called to be the minister of the First Congregational Church in Sharon, Connecticut, where he resides today. He is also acting as chaplain of The Indian Mountain School, Lakeville, Connecticut. Mr. Daniel is a contributor to religious journals and is an interested member of the Conference of Younger Churchmen. He has always shown himself highly interested in personal and social problems and, in effectively integrating these two fields, is of a deep mind and fine spirit.

HERMAN F. REISSIG was born February 13, 1899, at Farmington, N. Y. He is a graduate of Wagner Memorial Lutheran College and of Mt. Airy Lutheran Theological Seminary. After one year in the Lutheran ministry he entered the Congregational Church, serving the West End Congregational Church in Bridgeport, Connecticut, from 1925-1930. Since 1930 Mr. Reissig has been minister of the Kings Highway Congregational Church, Brooklyn, New York. He is a frequent contributor to *The Christian Century* and *The Christian Century Pulpit,* wrote for *The World Tomorrow* before that magazine discontinued publication, and has written for other papers. In 1932 he was awarded first place in a nation-wide sermon contest conducted by the Macmillan Company. Mr. Reissig is a member of the Executive Committee of the Conference of Younger Churchmen, and of the Brooklyn Committee of International Justice and Goodwill, and other organizations including the Brooklyn and Manhattan Brotherhoods of Congregational Ministers. Mr. Reissig thinks deeply with a radical and analytical mind of unusual strength. In addition to his great social vision and spiritual insight he is also a very fine preacher and is in large demand as such. No one is more capable of writing upon the subject with which he deals in this book.

MORGAN PHELPS NOYES was born in Warren, Pennsylvania, March 29, 1891. He graduated from Phillips Exeter Academy in 1910 and from Yale University in 1914. In 1922 he received his M.A. from Columbia University and he is also a graduate of the Union Theological Seminary, where he now teaches classes in the department of Homiletics. His various pastorates in the church have been as follows: assistant minister, Madison Avenue Presbyterian Church, New York City; minister, Presbyterian Church, Dobbs Ferry, New York; minister, First Presbyterian Church, Brooklyn, New York. He is at the present time the minister of the Central Presbyterian Church in Montclair, New Jersey. Mr. Noyes is the editor and compiler of "Prayers for Service" (Scribners, 1934) and he is also a member of the Conference of Younger Churchmen. As a forceful and superb preacher, and as one of the most gifted and versatile of the younger clergymen in America, the life counsel and services of Mr. Noyes are always much sought for and his preaching is always heard with eagerness.

EVERETT ROSS CLINCHY was born in New York City, December 16, 1896. He received the degree of B.S. at Lafayette College, Easton, Pennsylvania, in 1920. He was engaged in graduate study at Union Theological Seminary, 1920-1921; at Yale graduate school, 1922-1923; Drew University Graduate School,

1932-1934. He received an M.A. from Columbia University, 1921, and the degree of Doctor of Philosophy from Drew University in 1934, where he is now a teaching fellow. He was ordained as a Presbyterian minister in 1924 and was pastor of the Presbyterian Church at Fairmont, New Jersey, 1921-1923, and of the Church of Christ at Wesleyan University, Middletown, Connecticut, 1923-1928. From 1928 to 1933, he was a member of the secretarial staff of the Churches of Christ in America. Since 1928 he has been director of the National Conference of Jews and Christians. He originated "seminar" conferences for the study of Catholic-Protestant-Jewish relations. He was the leader of a team, consisting of a Catholic priest, a Jewish rabbi and himself, which visited thirty-eight states in the fall of 1933 in the interest of justice, unity and understanding among the three major religious groups of the country. He was second lieutenant, Field Artillery, U.S.A., during the World War. He is a member of the American Sociological Society. Mr. Clinchy is a frequent contributor to *The Christian Century* and other journals. The John Day Company has published a pamphlet by him called "The Strange Case of Herr Hitler" (1933) and a book entitled, "All in the Name of God" (1934). Mr. Clinchy has served as secretary of the Conference of Younger Churchmen and is an interested member of that organization. He has a genius for friendship, and through his personality and leadership is doing much to bring the members of different religious groups and faiths closer together.

LAWSON C. WILLARD, JR. was born in Philadelphia in 1898. He graduated from Pawling School in 1916, after which he served for three years in the navy. He received his B.A. from Stephens College in 1925, and his B.D. from Union Theological Seminary in 1928. He has also done graduate work in Columbia University. For two years Mr. Willard was chairman of the Department of Social Service of the Diocese of Long Island. Since his graduation from Union Theological Seminary he has been the rector of the St. James Episcopal Church of Elmhurst, Long Island. He is a member of the Conference of Younger

Churchmen, the Fellowship of Socialist Christians and other influential groups. Mr. Willard has always taken a deep interest in social problems and seen the need of a new society, but he knows that the lasting quality of the character of that society is dependent upon the spiritual character of its people. This realization has given Mr. Willard a strong interest in worship, concerning which he speaks with understanding, insight and conviction.

HENRY SMITH LEIPER was born in Belmar, New Jersey, September 17, 1891. A graduate of Blair Academy, Mr. Leiper received his B.A. from Amherst in 1913; graduated from Union Theological Seminary, 1917, and received an M.A. from Columbia, 1917. He studied Chinese at North China Union Language School, Peking, 1919, and received a D.D. from Amherst, 1934. Ordained to the ministry in 1915, Mr. Leiper became a traveling secretary of the Student Volunteer Movement, 1913-1914. In 1918 he served with the Army Y. M. C. A. in Siberia, was missionary A. B. C. F. M., Tientsin, China, 1918-1922; member of the governing board of the China International Famine Commission, 1919-1920; Chinese International Friendship delegate to Japan, 1921. Mr. Leiper has also held several national missionary secretaryships in the Congregational denomination and was the associate editor of *The Congregationalist,* 1927-1930. Since 1930 he has been executive secretary, American Section, Universal Christian Council for Life and Work, also same Commission on Relations with Churches Abroad, Federal Council of Churches of Christ in America, and secretary, China Famine Relief, U. S. A. He is a member of the American Academy of Political Science, the Amherst Club, Quill Club, and Clergy (Board of Governors). Mr. Leiper is the author of "Blind Spots," "Experiments in Cure of Race Prejudice," and the writer of numerous magazine articles. He lectures on the Orient, race relations and European relations. Mr. Leiper lives in Leonia, New Jersey, and has one office in New York City and another in Geneva, Switzerland. He is likewise an interested member of the Conference of Younger Churchmen.

As Foreign Secretary of the Federal Council of the Churches

of Christ in America, Mr. Leiper has touched life at many points and in many parts of the world. His background of world travel and his comprehensive information make him a fascinating speaker. He represents, to those who know him, the best in the world movement for Christian unity. Having recently returned from a trip to Europe, he is well capable of discussing intelligently the many puzzling aspects of the European situation. His major work is in the world movement for Christian unity, which the Universal Christian Council represents. It includes work among all Christian churches, save Rome, and has its principle offices in Geneva.

REFERENCE BOOKS

ABRAMS, RAY, Preachers Present Arms. Round Table, 1933.

BARTH, KARL, The Word of God and the Word of Man. Pilgrim, 1928.

BENNETT, CHARLES A., A Philosophical Study of Mysticism. Yale, 1923.

CHAFFEE, EDMUND, The Protestant Churches and the Industrial Crisis. Macmillan, 1933.

CLINCHY, EVERETT R., All in the Name of God. John Day, 1934.

HENDERSON, FRED, The Case for Socialism. Socialist Party, 1934.

HENRI, ERNST, Hitler Over Europe. Dent, 1934.

HERMES, GERTRUD, Die Geistige Gestalt des Marxistischen Arbeiters.

HINDUS, MAURICE, Humanity Uprooted. Smith, 1930.

JOSEPHSON, MATTHEW, Robber Barons. Harcourt, 1934.

JUNG, C. G., Modern Man in Search of a Soul. Harcourt, 1933.

HOUGH, LYNN HAROLD, Vital Control. Abingdon, 1934.

KINGSLEY, CHARLES, Water Babies. Macmillan.

LUCCOCK, HALFORD E., Contemporary American Literature and Religion. Willett, 1934.

LUNN, ARNOLD, John Wesley. Longmans, 1929.

MACDONALD, J. RAMSAY, The Socialist Movement. Holt, 1911.

MACKAY, JOHN A., The Other Spanish Christ. Macmillan, 1933.

MARR, HEINZ, Das Religiöser Deutschlander Gegenwart.

MARTIN, HUGH, Christian Social Reformers of the Nineteenth Century. Doran, 1927.

MARX, KARL, Capital, Volume I. International Publishers.

MOON, PARKER, Imperialism and World Politics. Macmillan, 1926.

NIEBUHR, REINHOLD, Does Civilization Need Religion? Macmillan, 1927.

335

——, Moral Man and Immoral Society. Scribner, 1932.

——, Reflections on the End of an Era. Scribner, 1934.

OVERSTREET, H. A., A Guide to Civilized Loafing. Norton, 1934.

PAGE, KIRBY, Individualism and Socialism. Farrar, 1933.

——, National Defense. Farrar, 1931.

PIECHOWSKI, PAUL, Proletärische Glaube.

Re-Thinking Missions: A Layman's Inquiry After One Hundred Years. Harper, 1933.

SACHAR, A. L., A History of the Jews. Knopf, 1932.

SACK, A. J., The Birth of the Russian Democracy. Russian Information Bureau, New York, 1920.

SPENGLER, OSWALD, Decline of the West. Knopf, 1926.

STOCKER, A., Christlichsoziale Reden und Aufsätze.

TAWNEY, R. H., Religion and the Rise of Capitalism. Murray, 1929.

TILLICH, PAUL, Religiöse Verwirklichung.

VAUTEL, CLEMENT, Mon Curé chez les Pauvres.

——, Mon Curé chez les Riches.

WARD, HARRY F., In Place of Profit. Scribner, 1933.

——, Our Economic Morality. Macmillan, 1929.

——, Which Way Religion? Macmillan, 1931.

ZWEIG, ARNOLD, Erasmus of Rotterdam. Viking, 1934.

INDEX